Large-scale 3D Data Integration

Challenges and Opportunities

Large-scale 3D Data Integration

Challenges and Opportunities

Edited by
Sisi Zlatanova and David Prosperi

CRC Press
Taylor & Francis Group
Boca Raton London New York

CRC Press is an imprint of the
Taylor & Francis Group, an **informa** business

A TAYLOR & FRANCIS BOOK

First published 2006 by Taylor & Francis

Published 2019 by CRC Press
Taylor & Francis Group
6000 Broken Sound Parkway NW, Suite 300
Boca Raton, FL 33487-2742

First issued in paperback 2019

No claim to original U.S. Government works

ISBN 13: 978-0-367-45400-5 (pbk)
ISBN 13: 978-0-8493-9898-8 (hbk)

Library of Congress Card Number 2005043748

Library of Congress Cataloging-in-Publication Data

Large-scale 3D data integration / edited by Sisi Zlatanova and David Prosperi.
    p. cm.
  Includes bibliographical references and index.
  ISBN 0-8493-9898-3
  1. Computer-aided design. 2. Geographic information systems. 3. Three-dimensional display systems. I. Zlatanova, Siyka. II. Prosperi, David.

TA174.L37 2005
006.6'93--dc22

2005043748

Visit the Taylor & Francis Web site at
http://www.taylorandfrancis.com

and the CRC Press Web site at
http://www.crcpress.com

About the Editors

Dr. Sisi Zlatanova is an assistant professor at the GIS Technology section, Delft University of Technology, The Netherlands. She graduated as a surveyor from the University of Architecture, Civil Engineering and Geodesy (UACG), Sofia, Bulgaria, in 1983 and obtained her Ph.D. in 3D GIS for urban modelling at the Graz University of Technology, Graz, Austria, in 2000. She worked as a software programmer at the Central Cadastre in Sofia, Bulgaria, from 1984 to 1989, as an assistant-professor at UACG, Sofia, Bulgaria, from 1989 to 1995, and as a researcher at the International Institute for Geo-Information Science and Earth Observation (ITC), Enschede, The Netherlands, from 1995 to 1999. Her research focus is on the third dimension: 3D object reconstruction, 3D data structures and geo-databases, 3D spatial relationships (topology) and 3D visualization (VR and AR). She is an international editor for *Geo-Science Journal*, reviewer for *PE&RS*, *JGIS*, and *JC&G*, and author and editor of lecture notes. She is a Chair of ISPRS Working Group IV/8 *Spatial data integration for emergency services*. She has been granted a number of fellowships and prizes. In the last several years she is actively involved in international and national activities, groups, and projects related to integration of 3D spatial information and providing spatial services for real-time applications.

Dr. David Prosperi is Professor of Urban and Regional Planning at Florida Atlantic University, United States. Trained as a quantitative economic geographer at Indiana University, since 1980 he has taught in urban and regional planning programs at the University of Illinois, the University of Cincinnati, and since 1989 at FAU. He has specialized in quantitative and computer applications in urban and regional planning ranging from regional economic structures to micro-urban form. The author of over 200 publications and/or conference papers, several of which have received prizes, former editor of two international journals (the *Journal of Planning Education and Research* and *Computers, Environment and Urban Systems*), his current research interests include the dynamics and role of creative economies, the use of the Internet on planning processes and products, with applications ranging from citizen participation to emergency management, and emerging new urban forms. He remains active as an editorial board members and/or reviewer for several journals in planning and computer applications including the *Journal of Architectural Planning and Research*, the *Journal of the American Planning Association*, as well as several computer-related organizations including the Urban Data Management Symposium, Digital Communities, and Computers in Urban Planning and Management.

Contributors

Thomas Bittner
Department of Philosphy
Department of Geography
New York State Center of Excellence in
  Bioinformatics and Life Sciences
University at Buffalo
Buffalo, NY

Heiko Blechschmied
Department of Graphic Information
  Systems
Fraunhofer Institute for Computer
  Graphics
Darmstadt, Germany

Martin Breunig
Research Centre for Geoinformatics
  and Remote Sensing
University of Osnabrück
Vechta, Germany

Volker Coors
Department of Geomatics, Computer
  Science and Mathematics
University of Applied Sciences
Stuggart, Germany

Maureen Donnelly
Department of Philosophy
New York State Center of Excellence in
  Bioinformatics and Life Sciences
University at Buffalo
Buffalo, NY

Markus Etz
Department of Graphic Information
  Systems
Fraunhofer Institute for Computer
  Graphics
Darmstadt, Germany

Erik Jansen
Computer Graphics, Faculty of
  Electrical Engineering, Mathematics
  and Computer Science
Delft University of Technology
Delft, The Netherlands

Roberto Lattuada
Customs Solutions
TTPCom Ltd
Melbourne, Royston, UK

Hui Lin
Joint Laboratory for GeoInformation
  Science
The Chinese University of Hong Kong
Hong Kong

David Prosperi
Department of Urban and Regional
  Planning
Florida Atlantic University
Fort Lauderdale, FL

Carl Reed
Chief Technology Officer
Open Geospatial Consortium
Ft. Collins, CO

Jantien Stoter
Department of Geo-Information
  Processing,
International Institute for Geo-
  Information Science and Earth
  Observation (ITC)
Enschede, The Netherlands

C. Vincent Tao
Faculty of Science and Applied Science
York University
Toronto, Canada

Rodney J. Thompson
Department of Natural Resources,
  Mines, and Energy
University of Queensland
Queensland, Australia

Peter van Oosterom
GIS Technology, OTB, Faculty of
  Policy, Management and Technology
Delft University of Technology
Delft, The Netherlands

Stephan Winter
Department for Geomatics
The University of Melbourne
Melbourne, Australia

Qing Zhu
State Key Lab of Information
  Engineering in Surveying Mapping
  and Remote Sensing
Wuhan University
Wuhan, China

Sisi Zlatanova
GIS-Technology, OTB, Faculty of
  Policy, Management and Technology
Delft University of Technology
Delft, The Netherlands

Contents

PART IV Alternatives

Chapter 8

Rodney J. Thompson

Chapter 9

Hui Lin and Qing Zhu

Introduction

Sisi Zlatanova and David Prosperi

Large-scale 3D models are the cutting edge of computer technology for understanding and planning our urban environments and infrastructures. These models have emerged from two modelling structures — systems for architecture, engineering, and construction (AEC) and geographic information systems (GIS). The problems and challenges facing today's modelers, developed for different purposes, focus almost exclusively on data integration — the ability to use data originally developed in one modeling system in the other and vice versa.

This need for data transportability is not new, as evidenced by several authors in this volume. What is new is the desire to go beyond various conversion programs into an environment where data is truly integrated, where the modeling framework is more universal, and where data standards cut across software programs and vendor-specific platforms. This book captures the excitement of researchers, organizations, and vendors in this quest.

The border between data structures used within GIS and AEC continues to diminish. As these two principal forms of modeling continue to merge, as the result of increased interest in large-scale 3D models, the need for data structures capable of supporting both types of modeling efforts, as well as new types of modeling efforts that combine the best features of both simple efforts, is manifest.

In its original concept, computer aided design (CAD) software was designed to deal with large-scale (complex), but small in size (in terms of area), models. Its fundamental feature was providing tools for design. There was no need to maintain attributes and geographic coordinate systems. GIS software, almost in direct contrast, was designed to manage small-scale (simple) models but very often covering large geographic areas. Its fundamental feature was the maintenance of attributes and a variety of different geographic coordinate systems. The first were used to create new objects (buildings, roads, landscapes); the second were used to represent existing phenomena and analyze it. CAD software provided extended 3D tools; GIS was mostly 2D.

As CAD has developed into AEC solutions and GIS has developed into 3D solutions, there is a renewed interest in large-scale geo-information among the diverse set of AEC and GIS end users. AEC designers are frequently challenged with requests to provide the means to link small-scale models to construction representations. The aim of AEC engineers is no longer designing in a local environment. The local environments are now part of a wider world, where project(ed) coordinates are needed. Since the same information is reused and updated, a system is needed to maintain the integrity and consistency of geodata. GIS users are using tools available in AEC to reconstruct and edit large-scale, realistic 3D models. Since the same information is reused and updated, a system is needed to maintain the integrity and consistency of geodata. These developments have given impulse to database management systems (DBMS) to emerge as integrated systems managing administrative and spatial data. CAD and AEC/GIS use in large-scale 3D models extends the spatial data types offered by DBMS.

But many fundamental issues still need to be addressed. Most of these issues can be captured by the need for better integration. Two stand out: data integration issues and modeling integration issues. On the data side, the major questions include how and where to maintain topology, how and where to maintain attribute information, how and where to maintain geographic coordinate systems, and what kind of functionality would be offered where. Similar questions exist on the modeling side. 3D GIS modelers are struggling to incorporate several AEC tools — such as the notion of primitives (such as 3D parametric primitives, splines, etc.) to design and visualize objects — that are currently not supported in most GIS software.

Within this research and application environment, the need for an Open GIS compliant environment, capable of sharing data across platforms, programs, and policy areas, is obvious. How can Open GIS primitives be used in combination with AEC functionalities (textures, shading, etc.) to represent a model close to reality? While 2D GIS have quite advanced tools to edit and update geometry, 3D GIS users are only provided with visualization and navigation environments. AEC designers may become major providers of large-scale 3D geodata with the ability to edit and update in 3D.

These and related questions were explored at a Geospatial Research Seminar held in Orlando, Florida, in May 2003, supported by the software vendor Bentley Systems. This book arose from the papers and discussions at that seminar. Many of the papers were rewritten as a result of collaboration and review by the seminar participants and other selected reviewers.

The book is organized into four parts. Part I, titled Nature of the Problem, presents a historical overview of the issues involved integrating GIS and AEC, and points to the issues that still need to be addressed. Simply put, these issues are data integration and semantics, ontology, and standardization. Part II, titled Data Handling and Modeling, consequently focuses on the data issue from a number of viewpoints: data collection, database structures and representation, database management, and visualization. Part III, titled Interoperability, covers the areas of semantics, ontology, and standardization, from a theoretical perspective (using semiotic theory to define the primitives and relationships in the use of language), and details some of the best examples of this approach in developing real-world applications. The book concludes in Part IV, titled Alternatives, with contributions that focus on recent advances in virtual geographic environments as well as alternative modeling schemes for the potential AEC/GIS interface.

Part I consists of a single chapter. In highly accessible language, Peter van Oosterom, Jantien Stoter, and Erik Jansen review the question of integrating data between CAD and GIS, provide examples from plan development, visualization, data collection, and location-based services, and discuss existing (theoretically and practically inferior) existing conversion capabilities. These parts of the chapter are extremely well illustrated and provide a firm foundation of well-known similarities and differences (e.g., CAD systems are design-based, AEC and GIS are more linked to data collection — survey, remote sensing, photogrammetry — and analysis; CAD systems maintain minimal or no attribute information on geometric objects, while AEC/GIS have theoretically unlimited means; AEC systems have 2D/3D geometry with topology, while GIS has 2D/2.5D geometry with 2D topology, etc.; AEC/CAD software clearly provides elaborate tools for editing and visualization of 3D data, while GIS software offers more extended tools for analysis of 2D data).

Moving to the future, the authors suggest, based on their earlier assessment of common applications, that a framework needs to be developed that can incorporate both real-world and designed objects. They suggest a view based on two principles: formal semantics and integrated data management. These themes are picked up throughout the book, forming the essential components of Parts II and III.

The second part of the book consists of four chapters focusing on data acquisition, data representation and data structures, database structures and operations, and the issue of transmitting and receiving geodatabase information on mobile devices.

In Chapter 2, C. Vincent Tao provides descriptions and analyses of the three major approaches to data acquisition — image-based, point cloud–based, and hybrid. Each of these approaches are illustrated and compared using the criteria (advantages and disadvantages) of resolution, accuracy, turnaround time, and cost. Emphasis throughout this discussion is on how improvements in technology for data collection (aerial and close range photogrammetry, airborne or ground-based laser scanning, surveying and GPS) and in the automation of 3D object reconstruction is revolutionizing the field. While significant time and nonautomation costs remain, and the nature of a good system for 3D management and the difficulty of modeling 3D within GIS remain issues, the message here is that the technology for collecting accurate, high resolution 3D data progresses over time. Detailed large-scale real-world 3D models will be available in large amounts soon, waiting for good tools for editing, management, and analysis.

Roberto Lattuada, after a brief but compelling metaphor on the need to integrate AEC and GIS, provides an extensive literature review of data representations and corresponding structures used for both AEC systems and 3D GIS. Included are discussions about object types, spatial representations, and surface and volume modeling. The author then takes the reader through the problems associated with converting or extending 2D systems into true 3D systems. Attempting to integrate AEC and GIS "problems," he offers the Extended Simplex Model (ESM) as a solution and concludes the chapter with a critical, but forward looking, evaluation of the model.

Chapter 4 focuses on the management of data. Martin Breunig and Sisi Zlatanova describe how database management systems (DMBS) are currently used to manage spatial data, including a cogent discussion of needed improvements. They argue for a wider utilization of geo-database management systems, discuss the historical "top-down" and "bottom-up" approach, and argue cogently for the latter. 3D geo-DMBS is discussed in terms of geometry, topology, 3D spatial access methods (predicates, functions, and operations), and extensions for spatial query language. The last two sections provide several examples of 3D representations in object-oriented DBMS and object-relational DBMS, as well as two case studies — one for man-made objects and the other for natural environments, to illustrate the possibilities of geo-DBMS in maintaining 3D spatial data.

In the last chapter of Part II, Heiko Blechschmied, Volker Coors, and Markus Etz, explore the state of the art in using mobile devices to query and retrieve geo-database information "on the fly." The authors review the status of augmenting reality for location-based services through such existing mobile systems as ACRHEOGUIDE, GIEST, TellMaris, and LoVEUS. Design features, such as the inclusion of multi-media databases, representation, connecting multimedia and GIS information, and the handling of visualizations, are discussed in terms of the LoVEUS model. The chapter provides extensive exploration into system architecture requirements and various ways to generate and transmit 3D information to mobile devices. The chapter concludes with several operational examples from ongoing research projects.

The third part of the book focuses on one of the major challenges facing data integration in large-scale 3D or, in fact, any modeling efforts. This is the problem of interoperability, perhaps more appropriately described in terms of problems of language and standards. This section has two papers. The first is a theoretical discussion of the issues; the second describes organizational and industry perspectives.

Thomas Bittner, Maureen Donnelly, and Stephan Winter place the problems and challenges of data integration on language. Semantic difficulties arise when different modeling approaches term the same domain differently. After briefly describing both syntax and semantic heterogeneity, the authors present a discussion of various ontologies (terminology systems) including: logic based ontologies, nonlogic-based ontologies, meta-standards vs. reference ontologies, logic-based reasoning, and interoperability. They then discuss potential uses of standards and reference ontologies for spatial information systems and conclude with a discussion of reference, domain, and top-level ontologies. The message is that ontologies have to be developed for AEC and GIS integration.

While Bittner, Donnelly, and Winter present the theoretical argument, the next paper in this part represents the best of the thinking in practice. The contribution is by Carl Reed, executive director of the specification program of the Open Geospatial Consortium Inc. (OGC). The OGC is a global, voluntary, and consensus-seeking standards organization that envisions seamless geographic information across networks, applications, and platforms. Reed describes a number of OGC initiatives — mostly associated with the Abstract Specification Model — that have resulted in numerous adopted standards recognized by the ISO. After describing more fully the Abstract Specification Model, the author directs his attention specifically to the AEC/GIS integration issue by focusing on the ability of the Web to facilitate integration, and then by providing an extended discussion of how the Land XML model used by civil engineers and transportation planners is being developed into an interoperable Land GML model.

The final section of the book consists of two chapters that represent important, cutting edge research, not discussed above, in areas related to the AEC/GIS integration problem.

Rod Thompson presents an alternative model for topological management in spatial databases. Based on identifying conceptual gaps within an extensive literature review, Thompson introduces the concept of the *regular polytope*. The remainder of the chapter examines the potential usefulness of the concept and identifies possible future lines of research.

In the final chapter, Hui Lin and Qing Zhu present an overview of *virtual geographic environments* (VGE). Here, the authors review general theoretical issues, based mostly on the work of behavioral geographers, involved in designing and using such a system including detailed discussions of, for example, how people process spatial data, the attributes of multidimensional representation, and modes of interacting with VGE systems including speech, hand, sketch, and geocollaboration.

In conclusion, large-scale 3D models are clearly the present and future in the design of tools to assist policy makers (who need better information to make choices), designers and engineers (working in the entire range of both the natural and built environments), and individuals (who make daily decisions regarding their own personal welfare). The chapters in this book address all three types of constituents for 3D modeling efforts. Problems and challenges in the integration of modeling perspectives and data will never go away, but the contributions in this book take a major step in both ameliorating some of the current problems and showing the ways to better models and modeling strategies.

Part I

Nature of the Problem

1 Bridging the Worlds of CAD and GIS

Peter van Oosterom, Jantien Stoter,
and Erik Jansen

CONTENTS

1.1 INTRODUCTION

Computer aided design (CAD) and geographic information systems (GIS) are being used more and more in the development of plans and products (bridges, tunnels, railroads, etc.) as well as for visualization, surveying, and location-based services. As a result, the worlds of CAD and GIS are becoming increasingly intertwined — but not without problems. Several real-world examples point to incompatibility in data formats and levels of abstraction. The need for an integrated CAD and GIS functionality has arisen from the fact that both systems are used throughout the life cycles of the same set of objects. The interoperability problem between CAD and GIS can only be solved by examining it at the right level of abstraction and by studying the different semantics used in both worlds. This chapter presents an outline for an integrated CAD–GIS framework on the basis of two concepts: formal (shared) semantics and integrated data management.

Information systems that involve geometry are used for many different purposes. One could classify CAD as one such family of systems; this, in turn, is often related to another family of systems, "computer aided manufacturing" (CAM). The products that are designed and manufactured consist of moveable objects (tables, cars, airplanes, engines, coffee machines, electronic circuits) and unmoveable objects (plants, buildings, houses, railways, roads, bridges, tunnels, utility networks). CAD systems for unmoveable objects are applied in AEC fields (architecture, engineering, and construction). In this chapter, the term "CAD" is used generically. In other words, it covers all kinds of computer-aided design, manufacturing, engineering, etc., and is not limited to a certain class of objects nor is it limited to a certain aspect (that is, CAD is considered more than geometric modeling).

Unmoveable objects (or fixed objects) are also well known from another family of information systems, GIS. GIS is applied in urban planning, land use, and cadastral data handling, among other fields. CAD and GIS share one major characteristic — both deal with geometry — but they differ in many aspects (size, storage, analysis, semantics, attributes, etc.). The primary aim of this chapter is to explain the need to integrate GIS and CAD. We shall also present the various factors that need to be considered when embarking on this process.

Let us first go back to the fundamental question, why would one like to bridge the gap between the two systems? Though CAD and GIS have been developed and used in different areas and organizations, a growing tendency has emerged in trying to integrate them and use them together in projects. This can be easily explained by the fact that CAD and GIS systems provide information on and deliver representations of the same real-world (man-made) objects in each phase of the life cycle. There are several areas of application (or different phases of the same application) that illustrate the need for an integrated approach (which will be discussed in more detail in the cases in Section 1.2):

- *Plan development:* The design of large infrastructures (roads, railways, bridges, tunnels, etc.) needs both CAD and GIS information — CAD techniques are applied for the design engineering, and construction, while GIS data are essential for the initial planning and layout. In the design phase, the geographic description of the region is often transferred from a GIS to a CAD system. Once the design has been completed in CAD, it is reimported into GIS. So an interesting cycle of information conversions takes place between GIS and CAD. It is not unusual for these conversions to be carried out "by hand," as the differences in the underlying data representations in CAD and GIS cannot be resolved automatically (see Section 1.2.1).

- *Visualization:* Plan presentation and data interaction often require different "views" of the data: a 2D "plan view" for the initial context analysis, a 2.5D "model view" to create and evaluate the different design concepts, and a 3D "world view" to realistically visualize the subsequent design (Verbree et al., 1999). While the 2D plan view is more or less a traditional GIS interface (based on geographic data), and the 3D world view is more or less a traditional CAD interface, the 2.5D model view asks for an interesting combination of the two (see also Section 1.2.2, Figure 1.4).

- *Data collection:* In recent decades, data collection techniques have progressed from manual measurement (resulting in vector-oriented data) to remote sensing (interpretation of 2D raster image data) and photogrammetry (interpretation of 3D data). Some advanced photogrammetric techniques assume knowledge about objects, such as buildings, bridges, and other landmarks, in a CAD-like format (see Figure 1.6). That is, the objects to be reconstructed should be seen as specific instances of classes from a generic library of designs (blueprints). The difficulties of surveying certain types of objects, such as the ever-increasing number of subsurface constructions, in traditional ways (remote sensing, photogrammetry) are fueling an interest in CAD models in 3D GIS modeling (see also Section 1.2.3).

- *Location-based services:* These services also employ a combination of CAD and GIS techniques for positioning, deriving viewing directions, and supplying the user with relevant "sight" information. It will take a lot of GIS and CAD integration before a sentence such as "on your right hand you now see a 12-story building" is generated automatically by the computer (see also Section 1.2.4).

1.1.1 PROBLEMS WHEN BRIDGING THE GAP BETWEEN CAD AND GIS

As indicated above, there are several applications that require input and analysis from both worlds (as will be illustrated in more detail in the following section). So why are these worlds so difficult to bridge? Essentially, because CAD and GIS traditionally focus on different domains and purposes:

- CAD is often used to represent the man-made world, while GIS is also used to capture the natural environment. The underlying mathematical description (and data structure in the subsequent implementation) is there-fore quite different. Whereas CAD represents single complex objects in 3D with a high degree of accuracy (including free-form surfaces, etc.), GIS aims to capture large numbers of objects in a common embedding based on an efficient 2D vector (mainly edges and polygons) and raster formats.

- The timescale is quite different. As CAD generally works on a "project" basis, life cycle maintenance is a fairly recent issue. GIS, on the other hand, is geared to a very long period of data collection and maintenance (almost an endless life cycle). Second, whereas CAD often stores data in a file format and performs complex operations on geometric data in "core," GIS analyses data, which is more often maintained consistently and permanently in large databases.

- As a result of all this, CAD systems generally assume a (2D or 3D) orthogonal world, while GIS systems deal with data sources based on many different coordinate systems, which are used to model the spherical (ellipsoid or geoide) world. However, CAD and GIS meet each other during use at larger scales, where local (orthogonal) coordinate systems are dominant.

Appendix A contains a longer list of perceived differences (including those above) and shows how they have evolved over time, as reported in the literature. In general, we can say that, although CAD and GIS information relate to the same real-world objects, the data are quite different and take into account different aspects. To complicate things further, all these different pieces of information are created and maintained by totally different sectors (e.g., industry vs. urban planning) with different tools, optimized for specific tasks. It would, therefore, be no mean feat to merge the two modeling families into one shared representation, which is able to support the entire life cycle.

In the late 1980s and early 1990s many chapters were published on GIS vs. CAD and on how they could be effectively combined (Cowen, 1988; Hobbs and Chan, 1990; Logan and Bryant, 1987; Newell and Sancha, 1990; Shepherd, 1990). However, those chapters tended to focus mainly on how to use CAD systems for certain GIS tasks, ranging from geographic data entry to automated map production (including some cartographic aspects). Using CAD or GIS tasks was motivated by the fact that, two decades ago, CAD systems were more generally available than GIS systems. Moreover, there was no obvious desire for true integration of the different CAD and GIS data models and functionalities. About 10 years ago, inspired by application domains, such as urban and landscape architecture and planning, attention turned to the integration of CAD and GIS functionality (Hoinkes and Lange, 1995; Movafagh, 1995; Schutzberg, 1995; Smith et al., 1998; Sun et al., 2002; Kolbe and Plümer, 2004). But the solutions were often ad hoc (capturing and transferring simple 3D models between the different systems), or they required customized software. Often these chapters ended with the remark that applications would work more effectively if off-the-shelf CAD/GIS functionality could be integrated, but they seldom offered a clue as to how this could be achieved, and they did not specify the fundamental problems behind the integration difficulties.

More recent sources seem to be more of a commercial or development nature (e.g., Maguire, 2003), which emphasize providing data-exchange mechanisms through shared files, translators, or inter-application program interfaces (APIs), but pay very little consideration to fundamental issues, such as integrated geometric data structures (3D and topological support, e.g., see Lee and Lee, 2001, for an overview), harmonized semantics of the concepts, and integrated data management (in contrast to independent and inconsistent information islands with loose data conversions and transfers).

1.1.2 OVERVIEW

In the following sections we will explore ways of addressing the differences between GIS and CAD. We will begin by looking at some examples and cases to illustrate the integration problems (Section 1.2). In Section 1.3 we will describe some well-known conversions *within* GIS and *within* CAD to provide some insight into the conversions that are needed *between* GIS and CAD in order to bridge the gap between the two systems. We will then move on to semantic modeling, a topic that is of interest for both CAD and GIS. Moveable and unmoveable (that is, fixed) objects both have geometry. They also have all kinds of other attributes (e.g., name, function, type of material), explicit relationships (e.g., topology and application-dependent associations), and constraints (within an object and between objects: no overlap, minimum distance between objects, maximum size). Together, the geometrical and thematic aspects provide the semantics for the objects being designed. GIS already has a long history of thematic information related to functional items (houses, roads, etc.), while in CAD, there is a growing interest in product data management, including life cycle and project and process information. A major issue in both CAD and GIS is the maintenance of consistency in geometric and functional data during (complex) modeling or edit operations. Data exchange at a higher semantic level can help to prevent what current data exchange formats do, i.e., destroy most of the topological and semantic meaning and inevitably lead to data loss and re-entry. Section 1.3 concludes with a short discussion of the life cycle concept, which could play a central role in the integration of GIS and CAD.

Section 1.4 presents an outline for an integrated framework along two lines — formal semantics and integrated data management. The development of formalized semantics is crucial to achieving the true integration of CAD and GIS. First, the semantics (of geometry and other information) within a domain need to be formalized, i.e., a domain ontology has to be developed. Next, these domain ontologies have to be matched against each other. This could be realized through an integrated (and refined) ontology covering the CAD and GIS concepts in one framework. Integrated data management is needed to support multiview access and data interrogation while maintaining the overall consistency. In Section 1.5 we draw conclusions and summarize the requirements for the conceptual and technical framework that is needed to bridge the gap between GIS and CAD. Different aspects of this will then be covered in subsequent chapters.

1.2 CASE STUDIES INTEGRATING CAD AND GIS

In this section we present a number of case studies relating to the application areas mentioned in the introduction; these include plan development, (3D) visualization, (3D) data collection, and location-based services. Some of the cases will illustrate open issues (problems) with respect to the integration of CAD and GIS, while other cases may also show initial parts of the solution (often by making agreements and adapting the dataflow for the anticipated integration of CAD and GIS). After studying these cases, we will conclude with an analysis and summary of the problems we encountered when trying to bridge the gap between CAD and GIS.

1.2.1 PLAN DEVELOPMENT

1.2.1.1 Example 1: Hubertus Tunnel

The first example in the planning process is taken from 3D cadastre research (i.e., actual property registration). Property registration, including the geographic and thematic information, is often implemented with a GIS, usually with an underlying geo-DBMS for data management. Information in 3D on physical objects is required when registering the property of constructions above and below the surface. The question is, how can this 3D description be obtained?

In general, 3D object construction is a complicated process (even with advanced sensors and reconstruction software). It is also relatively time-consuming, as part of it still needs to be performed manually. In addition, underground constructions, such as tunnels and pipelines, cannot be obtained with laser scanning and (nonterrestrial) photogrammetric techniques, since the objects are not visible from above. The next step is, therefore, to take a closer look at the CAD models. Figure 1.1 shows a typical example illustrating the problem that it may not be easy to obtain a 3D description from 2D drawings.

As 3D data on many (new or future) objects are available to designers — mainly as CAD models — they could be used to model 3D physical objects in the DBMS. But how should CAD designs be used? And what selections and generalizations are needed to obtain the required information for a GIS environment, such as the outer boundary of objects? As part of the 3D cadastre research, we visited a municipality (Rotterdam, the Netherlands), two departments of the Dutch Ministry of Transport and Public Works (Projectorganisatie HSL and Bouwdienst Rijkswaterstaat), and an engineering company (Holland Railconsult) in an effort to find usable CAD models. We found that, in the present design process, there are very few, if any, CAD models that are suitable for the GIS (3D cadastral) database and that (automatic) conversion is nearly impossible. This is largely because 3D physical objects are still designed in 2D (in CAD) with the aid of linear profiles and cross sections (see Figure 1.1). Contractors and builders are accustomed to 2D drawings; understanding 3D drawings would require special skills.

1.2.1.2 Example 2: Cycle Tunnel, Houten

In addition to the 2D drawings describing accurate designs of objects to be constructed, there are also plenty of examples of 3D CAD models, which are generated

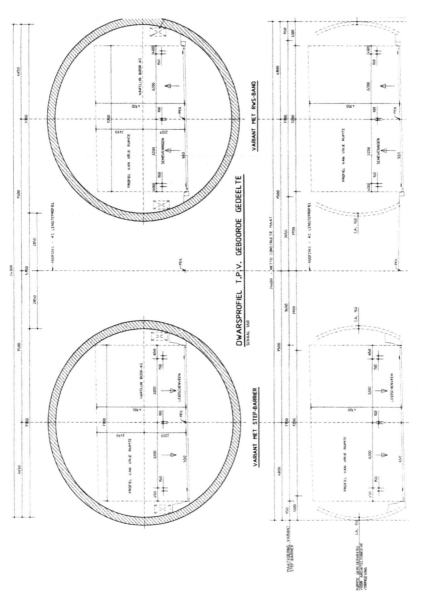

FIGURE 1.1 CAD model designed for the Hubertus Tunnel in The Hague. Courtesy of Bouwdienst, Rijkswaterstaat.

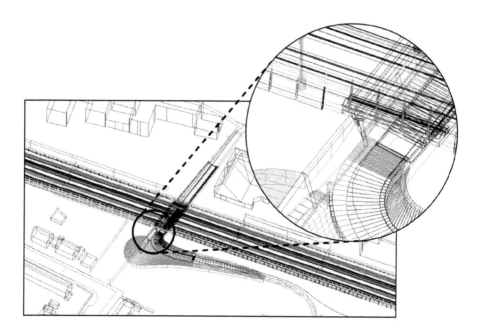

FIGURE 1.2 The CAD model designed for a cycle tunnel in Houten, the Netherlands. Courtesy of Holland Railconsult.

in the design process. However, these are mainly for visualization purposes (see Figure 1.2). Hoefsloot (2003) describes a case study on how 3D CAD models could be converted into a set of 3D geo-objects. This revealed that CAD models, which are designed primarily for visualization, are not (directly) deployable for 3D GIS (cadastre) purposes. Often, the classification and thematic attributes are missing, and the files can easily become unwieldy, as they are not primarily intended for interactive purposes but rather for the generation of animations. Furthermore, they contain too much detail: objects can hardly be recognized in the file-based models, let alone easily selected. Finally, 3D spatial data in CAD models are defined by complex geometries, most of which are described parametrically. At the moment, this data cannot be automatically converted into the primitives that are available in spatial DBMSs (point, lines, polygons, polyhedrons).

1.2.2 Visualization

1.2.2.1 Example 1: Bridge Amsterdam-Rijnkanaal near Utrecht

Rijkswaterstaat, part of the Dutch Ministry of Transport and Public Works, recently designed (and built) a bridge over the Amsterdam-Rijnkanaal near Utrecht in a 3D CAD system (see Figure 1.3). This new bridge is also included in the 3D topographic base map of Rijkswaterstaat (named "DTB-nat") via a flat polygon in 3D space. For visualization purposes, it was decided that the bridge would be drawn again in another environment, as this would involve less work (than reusing the existing CAD

FIGURE 1.3 Bridge Amsterdam-Rijnkanaal near Utrecht. Courtesy of RWS/AGI.

model or the topographic base map). The operators were experts in the different software packages (so the problem was "real" and had nothing to do with unfamiliarity with the software). This approach comes across as somewhat unsatisfactory, not only because it introduces redundant data (which may cause inconsistencies), but also because somehow, in the detailed design information is present to be used in a less detailed model, while this information remains unused in current practice.

1.2.2.2 Example 2: Karma System

The Karma system (Verbree et al., 1999) was devised to support plan development for large infrastructural objects (bridges, railway tracks, etc.) and to allow interaction with the model data in 3D virtual reality. Interfaces were written to link the Arcinfo-SDE database to virtual environments that were developed on the basis of the WorldToolKit (WTK) (Sense8, 2004). The WTK allows the same virtual reality program to run on PCs, virtual workbenches, and CAVEs. Three views were developed and introduced to support meaningful interaction on these different platforms: the 2D plan view for overview and orientation, the 2.5D model view for interaction and manipulation (preferably on a workbench), and the 3D world view for visualization (preferably in a CAVE) (see Figure 1.4). The actual integration of CAD and GIS is particularly relevant in the world view, where the abstract 3D representations of GIS objects (extruded 2D objects) from the plan and model view are replaced by CAD models. To implement this idea, CAD models were needed that could be related to the GIS references. However, it proved extremely difficult to relate the complex CAD data structure to the simplified GIS references in such a way that automatic scaling and orientation could be realized. The operation proved just as difficult the other way around (i.e., simplify the complex CAD model to a geometry

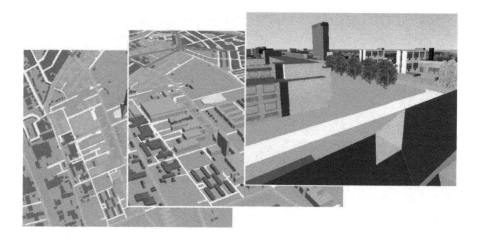

FIGURE 1.4 (See color insert after page 86). 2D plan view, 2.5D model view, and 3D world view in Karma.

that could be linked to the "ground plan" of the object in the GIS database). So, the Karma system did indeed succeed, up to a certain level, to integrate CAD and GIS objects and their functionality. However, as described above, this was not easily achieved, and it involved much nonautomated "hand work," taking too much time.

1.2.3 DATA COLLECTION

1.2.3.1 Example 1: 3D Cadastral Parcel

In some parts of the world (e.g., Queensland, Australia) 3D properties are already commonplace in cadastral registration. These properties can be surveyed (measured), but the geometrical description may also have originated in a CAD environment. This would be the case, for example, if the 3D property did not relate to a construction that can be surveyed (e.g., the outside boundary of a subsurface construction). The models delivered to the cadastral database in Survey Plans (Queensland Government, 2003) are relatively easy to incorporate in a GIS; see Figure 1.5. Here, the gap between CAD and GIS need not be all that great, as long as the model and procedures are correct and clear from the beginning. This also implies that a shared set of concepts (between CAD and GIS) has been used in the communication. The case shows a part of the solution when bridging CAD and GIS: when the concepts are well defined in advance, communication between the different systems is achievable.

1.2.3.2 Example 2: Point Clouds

Other examples, closer to surveying, originate from the use of multibeam sonar or airborne and terrestrial laser-scanned data sets resulting in "point clouds" from which objects can be reconstructed (see Figure 1.6 and Figure 1.7: house, power cable respectively). The task at hand is to derive from the point clouds well-structured CAD models (according to their design) of the surveyed object types to be included

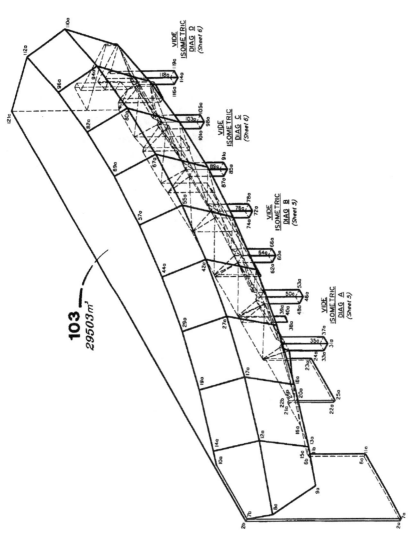

FIGURE 1.5 Survey plan for 3D parcel in Queensland, Australia.

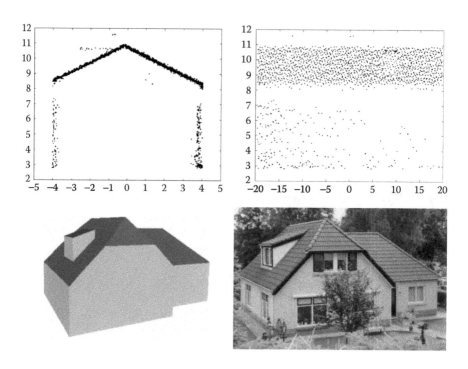

FIGURE 1.6 House object reconstruction from laser scanning 3D point clouds (from Vosselman and Dijkman, 2001).

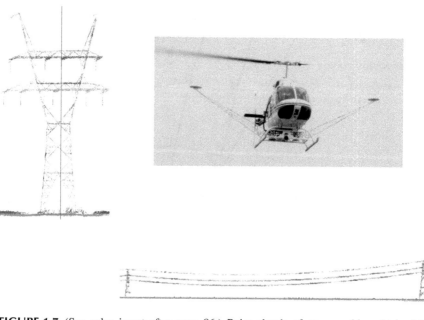

FIGURE 1.7 (See color insert after page 86.) Point clouds of power cables obtained by Fugro's Fli-map (Haasnoot, 2000).

in a 3D GIS environment. This is a nontrivial problem to be solved (automatically). Again, a mix of CAD and GIS functionality occurs (when capturing large scale 3D geo-information).

1.2.4 LOCATION-BASED SERVICES

1.2.4.1 Example 1: Augmented Reality

Location-based services (LBS) have many forms. One of the more advanced forms is Augmented Reality (AR), which requires a mix of GIS and CAD processing to visually insert "virtual" objects (designed in CAD) in good registration (by matching visible objects also available in a GIS database) with the real image of the environment. In the Ubicom system (Zlatanova, 2001), the user wears a see-through mobile augmented-reality display, which is fitted with a camera to record what is seen. A 3D database of the real-world environment is maintained at the server, and lines from the model in the database are matched with the edges in the camera image to derive the exact viewing direction and provide the virtual information at exactly the right spot (see Figure 1.8, top two figures). Different types of "virtual" objects can

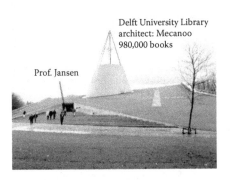

FIGURE 1.8 Ubicom example of outdoor augmented reality (top row: matching features from the 3D database with the real world image for correct positioning and orientation; lower left: adding textual information to objects in the real world image; lower right: adding designed objects to the real-world image).

be added to the real-world image: 1. Planned and designed objects not yet realized in the real world, 2. Real, but invisible objects could be displayed in the right perspective (e.g., subsurface objects), and 3. Textual information can be added in "clouds" attached to real-world objects describing certain properties. Again, these cases show the integrated use of CAD and GIS functionality.

1.2.4.2 Example 2: Disaster Management

Another example is the (geo-) ICT support for police, ambulances, and firefighters in emergencies or crisis situations; the emergency services might want to use both outdoor and indoor information in an integrated manner (via the interfaces of their mobile equipment). At present, interior building designs from CAD systems and geographic information (from GIS) have to be combined in one environment. Again, this case shows the need to offer integrated GIS and CAD functionality within one application or user environment.

1.2.5 ANALYZING THE OPEN ISSUES WHEN BRIDGING THE GAP BETWEEN GIS AND CAD

As several of the above examples illustrate, large-scale 3D geo-information is a subject of great interest for CAD and GIS users alike. This is also reflected in the GIS-extended CAD software packages of the market leaders such as Autodesk's AutoCAD/map, and Bentley's MicroStaton Geographics (Bentley, 2004). Recently, CAD designers have been confronted with more and more requests for geo-information (i.e., the geometry of identifiable objects with a fixed location with respect to the earth) to which other information can be linked. This data can serve many purposes, e.g., spatial analysis or the updating of existing geographic data sets with planned (designed) objects. Much progress has been made in 2D in the past few years; after all, cadastral parcels can now be designed in CAD systems (with some kind of geographic extension) and maintained in a DBMS. These local, designed environments are now part of the complete world for which coordinates are needed. As the same information is constantly being reused and updated, a system is needed whereby the integrity and consistency of the spatial, temporal, and thematic data is maintained.

However, data sharing between CAD and GIS appears to be difficult in practice. It is not unusual for two departments (one working with CAD and another with GIS software) in one organization, such as a province or state, to not communicate because they cannot exchange data. Everybody who has tried to import CAD data into GIS software has experienced this in one way or another, e.g., lack of object definitions in the CAD models, different scale representations, transformation of the local (CAD) coordinates into a reference system for both the horizontal and vertical coordinates, parametric shapes that cannot be converted into GIS objects, different levels of detail that require generalization, etc. Often, there is also a conceptual or semantic difference between the concepts in a design (CAD) environment and the concepts in the observed and measured geo-information (as in GIS). These conceptual frameworks (ontologies) have to be made explicit and compared and related to each other before things can improve.

In 3D, spanning a bridge between CAD and GIS is even more of a challenge. CAD software provides all kinds of primitives to create geometric (and their visual attributes) models close to reality; however these primitives are not supported in GIS. How can CAD primitives (e.g., parametric primitives) be used in an Open Geospatial- (or ISO TC211-) compliant environment or the other way round? How can Open Geospatial primitives be used in combination with CAD functionalities (textures, shading, etc.) to represent a model close to reality? In 3D, CAD designers may become major providers (holding the set of tools to edit and update) of large-scale geo-data for use in GIS once a fundamental bridge between CAD and GIS has been established. It should be noted, at this point, that up-to-date, large-scale geo-information is being used more and more as the source of derived medium- and small-scale geo-information after (dynamic or on-the-fly) generalization.

Not surprisingly, if we convert data from GIS to CAD and vice versa, enormous mismatches will arise in the elementary data representations and automatically lead to a loss of (implicitly encoded) semantic meaning or information. Maintaining the integrity and functional meaning of the data is, therefore, a crucial issue in "bridging" the two domains. Much research is needed to examine in detail the interoperability problem between GIS and CAD.

1.3 CONVERSIONS AND MULTIPLE REPRESENTATIONS

To get a "feeling" for conversions between CAD and GIS, it is worthwhile to take a look at some conversions within a domain. Important lessons can be learned up front from these examples, which can later be useful when widening the scope again (and covering both GIS and CAD representations). We will start with some conversions (including geometry and thematic information) from the GIS domain (Section 1.3.1) and then move on to the CAD domain (Section 1.3.2). The important role of semantics during the conversions and several aspects of semantics (attached to the geometric objects) are discussed in Section 1.3.3. Often, the different representations of the same object are due to the specific application environment. Instead of considering the different representations as different objects, it is better to consider them as the same object to which different views are associated (depending on the context). Section 1.3.4 will show that these views are closely related to the phase of its life cycle the object is in (design, construct, survey, maintain, etc.).

1.3.1 CONVERSIONS BETWEEN AND WITHIN GIS

Examples from the GIS domain include the following:

- From large-scale (detailed) to small-scale (overview): This process is called *generalization* (not to be confused with specialization and generalization within the object class hierarchy). It is essential to understand the meaning of the different objects and the purpose or task of the person using the representation or map.

- From digital landscape model (data structure or database) to digital cartographic model (display on screen, paper, etc.): This process is called *visualization*. Again, the semantics are important in order to choose the right graphic primitives or symbols (for the different object classes) and the right graphic parameters (color, width, texture) to represent the value of relevant attributes.

- A thorough understanding of semantics is required to achieve *schema integration* (creating models with "the best of both worlds" in one uniform environment) and *schema mapping* (converting models, objects, or descriptions from one world into the concepts used in the other world) on the basis of geographic data from heterogeneous sources covering the same region.

1.3.2 CONVERSIONS BETWEEN AND WITHIN CAD

Examples from the CAD domain include the following:

- *Levels of detail*: In order to maintain interactivity and real-time display, a complex CAD model often has to be simplified in the polygon count, but not at the expense of visual quality. In a flight simulator, the resolution of the terrain model is adaptively improved and simplified according to the position of the aircraft above the terrain. Here we strive for a continuum between the local detail and the overview. Another technique known as "occlusion culling" reduces the polygon count when rendering large urban environments from street level, where large parts of the town will not be visible anyhow. Using the facades of the street as "clipping planes," and merging these complicated facades into simplified "virtual occluders" will speed up the visualization process with orders of magnitude (Wonka and Schmalsteig, 1999.)

- *Meshing*: Although the same basic geometry is used for several functional analyses (e.g., calculations of strength and stiffness), the exact form can differ from application to application. For instance, finite element stress analysis needs volumetric meshing. Ideally, the mesh resolution should be adapted to the gradient of the local stress in order to avoid unnecessary computations in regions where nothing is happening and to achieve high accuracy in regions with large stress concentrations. A different mesh topology might figure in other finite-element simulations such as "mould flow," because here we want to concentrate on the thin and distant parts that the flow might have difficulty reaching.

- *Feature modeling and conversions* (Bidarra and Bronsvoort, 2000; Bronsvoort and Noort, 2004): The notion of "feature" has been defined to encode thematic information in combination with geometry. A feature is a shape element with some predefined functional meaning. For instance, a cylindrical hole might be defined as a through hole or a blind hole depending on the topology (open or closed at the bottom) and the manufacturing process. Again, the same part of the geometry might "feature" in different feature representations, depending on whether we want to use a piece of the geometry (e.g., a surface plane) as a reference for the surface smoothness properties, or as a reference plane in an assembly, or as a fixing plane in a machining operation.

1.3.3 FUNCTIONAL AND THEMATIC SEMANTIC ASPECTS

As we can see from these examples, model conversions are seldom based on pure geometric "translations." In most cases, some functional knowledge (*"semantics"*) about the geometry is also applied to interpret the functional meaning and to maintain consistency (e.g., the geometry is closed) and validity (it still performs its intended function). The different aspects of "semantics" can be encoded in the following ways:

- Parametrization: Some of the geometry variables are used as defining parameters that discern the product in different classes (discrete parameters) or in continuous shape ranges
- Procedural definition: Algorithmic or computational shape definition to define repetition or a certain randomness
- Topology: Relations between geometric elements to encode "connectiveness" and "uniqueness," i.e., elements do not overlap, and the boundary is complete and closed
- Constraints: As in the case of topology relations but with a general numeric or computational character to define certain geometric or topological properties

A powerful modeler with at least some "solving" capabilities is needed to maintain the functional relations. For instance, if a bridge is lowered, this may inhibit a pass-through function for trucks. Ideally, the system would check and maintain this type of functional constraint. It often takes a complicated process to specify the constraint and determine the degrees of freedom, which are left for adjustment. All of these observations indicate that simple conversions do not exist and, hence, that simple schemata based on "geometry alone" will not work.

1.3.4 MULTIVIEW MODELING

The semantic content of models can also be organized by arranging the data according to aspects of design and manufacturing or life cycle stages. There are several ways of classifying this life cycle. One approach is described below:

- Plan/design
- Engineer/construct/manufacture
- Survey/measure/register
- Maintain/analyze/operate

It should be noted that this life cycle is ongoing, because objects are added, deleted, and redesigned in new cycles (in the spatial context), which again follow the same phases. Different sectors are interested in different aspects of the same real-world objects and use different tools to create and work with the information (models) associated with them. Each sector or organization chooses the tools that are optimized for the task at hand. Also, the (data) model and the data storage (DBMS, files, formats) might be completely different.

The life cycle should be given a central place in the integration, as it comprises the different design, manufacturing, and analysis aspects. To address the life cycle concept in GIS and CAD at a fundamental level, the data should be explicitly stored only once at a basic level, and a "view specific data" structure should support and allow data analysis and manipulation from a variety of perspectives without disturbing the underlying consistency.

Generally speaking, conversion between different representations is not simple — not even within the GIS and CAD packages, let alone between them. The conversions cannot be fully automated within the current state-of-the-art GIS and CAD software and technology, and human intervention is still required to obtain acceptable results. Hence, both versions of a model (original and post-conversion) are often kept and stored explicitly. This could be called a multiple-representation solution. Care must be taken to maintain consistency during updates. However, with technological progress (and the trend toward more formal semantics), it should be possible to have fully automatic conversions (perhaps also by lowering the requirements for the different views). It should be possible in the future to have only one (integrated) source of the model and to compute (updatable) views.

1.4 FRAMEWORK FOR BRIDGING THE GAP BETWEEN GIS AND CAD

The open issues when integrating GIS and CAD representations and functionality (see Section 1.2.5), illustrated in the case studies (see Sections 1.2.1–1.2.4), can be addressed by applying the experience and knowledge gained from the conversions that are already available within GIS and CAD (see Section 1.3). These conversions use both semantics and geometry to arrive at different representations of the same real-world object. What is needed in order to bridge the gap between GIS and CAD is a framework that covers both the geometry and the semantics. This section will begin with a preliminary remark on model class and instance level and then consider the conditions for such a framework, namely: formal semantics (see Section 1.4.1) and integrated data management (see Section 1.4.2).

When we refer to modeling, we can distinguish between two levels:

- Model class level: Define a blueprint (structure) for the objects later on, describe their attributes (spatial and thematic), relationships, etc. Essentially, this is the object class model (derived from object-oriented approaches to modeling and design) with everything at object class level (including the class inheritance hierarchy and aggregation/composite relationships).

- Model instance level: Create an actual abstraction of (some part of) the (planned or designed) real world, i.e., create instances of the object classes defined above: specify actual geometries and thematic attributes, create relationships, and satisfy specified constraints.

Design tools are available to create models at class level. The Unified Modeling Language (OMG, 2002) is used to create models in all kinds of disciplines. Highly appropriate in this context are the class diagrams. These are not only used in the development of information systems, but also to capture (formal) semantics in specific domains (e.g., the semantic web and structured dictionaries).

1.4.1 FORMAL SEMANTICS

It can be concluded from the above discussion that an important key to bridging CAD and GIS is to capture the semantics in the different models. However, implicit knowledge or tidy pieces of natural text and tables are not sufficient for this purpose. A more formal approach is required, as developed in disciplines such as knowledge engineering, ontologies, and object-oriented modeling. On the basis of this formal semantic approach, it becomes possible to decide whether different domain models (or even models within one domain) are or can be harmonized. Meantime, more meaningful handling of spatial information (by machines) will become all the more important and make the formal approach even more necessary. In the last decade, significant technological progress was made in knowledge engineering (via the developments from UML, ontology, semantic web, OWL), which enables knowledge to be further formalized in a practical way.

At present, most spatial (both CAD and GIS) information is used more or less directly by humans; in the future large parts of the information will also be processed (first) by machines (before recommencing communication with humans). Whereas humans are capable of interpreting different concepts by using implicit context information (which domain is involved, who supplied or produced the information, etc.), this knowledge will have to be made explicitly available for a machine. A large part of the formal structural knowledge about the concepts (objects being modeled) is captured in the relationships that one object has with other types of objects (specialization/generalization, part/whole, association), characteristics (attributes), and operations (methods, functions) belonging to the object class. The principles of object-oriented modeling are also discernible in this knowledge-engineering approach.

To make the idea of machine handling of geo-information a little less abstract, one could think of automating the conversions as described in Section 1.3. Other examples are automatic interpretation of sensor information (e.g., aerial photography, remote-sensing, or laser-scanning data sets) or recognizing and classifying objects or executing several (spatial) analyses in the context of a "decision support system." What all these tasks have in common is that, without the "domain knowledge," a machine could never execute them in an adequate manner. Interestingly, the wish for formalization of knowledge also occurs in many other disciplines and domains. Attempts are being made to formalize knowledge within specific domains (e.g., ship construction and medical disciplines) or even to compile complete collections of common and general concepts (dictionaries). Most of the time, these attempts are launched for exactly the same reason (to make a machine do certain tasks in a meaningful manner). For example, efforts are underway in the context of the "semantic web" to provide more meaningful search operation by developing formal frameworks of concepts ("ontologies" and making them operational). The UML class diagrams are frequently used for this purpose (OMG, 2002). Additional methods and tools are also used to, for example, map equivalent concepts in (different) frameworks or "rewrite" information from one set of well-defined concepts to the terminology of another (a geo-information example would be translating from the GBKN (Large Scale Map of the Netherlands) to the TOP10NL (Top10 vector data set of the Netherlands)).

Though UML class diagrams more or less constitute the "default" approach when creating formal knowledge frameworks, the graphic diagram has limited semantic accuracy. A nongraphic language is provided within UML for the further modeling of semantics (knowledge frameworks) with the aid of the Object Constraint Language (OCL, see OMG, 2002; OMG, 2003). This can be used to specify the criteria for a valid model (constraints), such as invariants for classes and pre- and post-conditions for operations. The advantage of using UML is that, as in the case of UML class diagrams, generic tools are available to support OCL (i.e., not CAD- or GIS-specific). The context of an invariant is specified by the relevant class; e.g., "parcel" if the constraint were that "the area of a parcel is at least 5 m^2." It is also possible within a constraint to use the association between two classes (e.g., "parcel" must have at least one owner, which is an association with the class "person"). The following are two examples in UML syntax (keywords in **bold** print):

```
context Parcel inv minimalArea:
   self.area > 5
context Parcel inv hasOwner:
   self.Owner -> notEmpty()
```

Besides UML (and OCL) for the formal description of the semantics (knowledge) of the different object classes in information models, there are specific tools for handling ("reasoning with") formal concepts (semantics, ontology). Cases in point are OWL, the Web Ontology Language (W3C, 2004) or the new ODM (Ontology Definition Metamodel) development from the OMG, which resulted in a proposal submitted in January 2005 (DSTC et al., 2005). The potential use and application of OWL in forming a bridge between CAD and GIS needs to be further explored.

It is already difficult enough to agree on the concepts and their (formal) definitions within a domain, so it will be even harder to do so between quite different domains (as in the case of CAD and GIS integration). A number of domain standards are currently being developed in the Dutch geo-information community (IMRO/ spatial planning, IMWA/water, IMKICH/cultural history, GRIM/natural and agricultural environment, topography, cadastral/ownership, soil/subsurface, etc.). These crystallize out after lengthy discussions with many of the parties in a community.

The more recent domain models are described in UML class diagrams, which are a first step toward formal knowledge representation. Needless to say, it is also important to have these domain models in an international context and to harmonize the models from different countries (within one domain). Here, the discussions become even trickier (because laws, regulations, habits, and cultures vary in an international setting). One example of an attempt to create an international domain model is the FIG initiative to specify a "core cadastral model." It should be realized that multiple (natural) languages also feature heavily in the international concepts and that the labels of the concepts need to be translated into different languages (Lemmen et al., 2003).

It is becoming harder to agree on formal concepts, which should be shared between multiple disciplines of domains (already the case in the geo-information world, but even more so in the broader scope of CAD and GIS). Sometimes the same words (labels) are used for concepts with different meanings; other times the same concepts get different labels. This problem can only get worse in our network (information) society, but even so, attempts must still be made to harmonize the different domains. Probably the best approach is to start with a number of formal models in different domains (with a certain amount of "overlap") and to try to reach agreement (or at least try to develop mapping rules for the concepts of one domain to the ones of another domain and vice versa). One country that is relatively advanced in the geo-information domain is Australia, where a harmonized model between different (geo-information) domains has been developed: topography, cadastral, addresses, hydrography (ICSM, 2002).

The time has come to relate the concepts in the geo-information (GIS) world to the world of design, engineering, and construction (CAD/CAE/CAM). As we have seen in the case studies, huge differences (semantic and geometric) can exist even within one single organization (due to the use of different models and different software packages). Obviously, this is deeply disconcerting, given that in the real world, these systems relate to the same objects (roads, bridges, buildings, etc.) but in different "phases" of their life cycles (and from different perspectives).

1.4.1.1 Formal Geometry Semantics in the GIS Domain

In GIS, the geometry (and topology) is standardized by the Open Geospatial Consortium and ISO TC211, that is, also the geometry itself has a well-defined meaning and the different concepts are indicated by the names of the primitives or data types (the semantics). Since 1997, ISO and OGC have worked together on the basis of the large overlap in their area of work. One important concept in the OGC model is a spatial (or geographical) feature, which is an abstraction of a real-world phenomenon associated with a location relative to the earth (OGC, 2001). The conceptual model of the spatial feature is metrically and topologically described in Topic 1 of the OGC Abstract Specifications (called "feature geometry"). The aim of the Abstract Specifications is to create and document a conceptual model that is sufficient to create the Implementation Specifications. The geometry of spatial features is described by the basic class "GM_Object" (see Figure 1.9). At the moment, the implementation of the spatial feature in GIS is usually limited to simple features such as points, lines, and polygons.

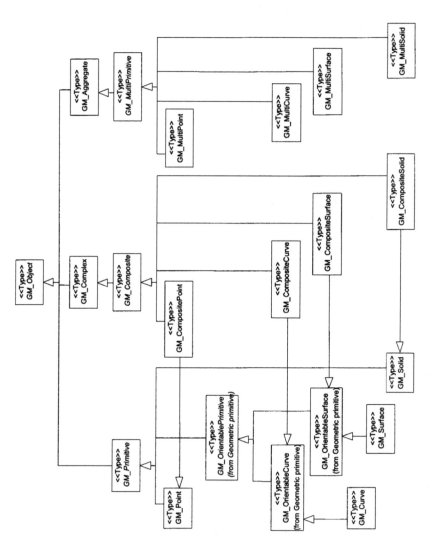

FIGURE 1.9 UML class diagram of geometry basic classes in GIS (from OGC, 2001).

1.4.1.2 Formal Geometry Semantics in the CAD Domain

Several file formats (DGN, DWG, X3D, SVG) have found their way into everyday practice as exchange formats in the CAD and graphics domain, each with their own advantages and disadvantages. The STEP project (STandard for the Exchange of Product model data) was initiated in 1984 by ISO TC184 Industrial Automation Systems and Integration, SC4 Subcommittee Industrial Data, to create a single international standard to describe product model data and provide a basis for sharing life cycle data. The STEP standard was approved as ISO International Standard ISO 10303. Pratt (2001) provides a short overview, and its current status is summarized in STEP (2004). Mason (2002) provides a useful overview of the life cycle aspects.

1.4.2 INTEGRATED DATA MANAGEMENT

After solving the semantic differences, the next step is to create an integrated model that can serve multiple purposes (from both a CAD and GIS background). Different views may be defined on this representation. The integrated model is managed in a way that maintains consistency (during updates or when model data is added to the data management system). So the same model is used as the foundation for planning, design, construction, management, analysis, presentation, etc. The integrated model implies that different applications can be used to perform these specialized tasks and also that different users can be working with the same model at the same time in different environments (or at different locations). As in the GIS world, where a gradual shift has taken place from file-based approaches to database management system (DBMS) approaches in situations where the use of (geo-) information has become more structural and where more than one person updates the data, a tendency toward a DBMS approach has emerged in the CAD world. For example, about two decades ago, when one of the authors was busy with his M.Sc. project (van Oosterom, 1985) at Fokker Aircraft Company, several different departments (predesign, aerodynamics, construction) needed access to the same CAD information on the new aircraft designs. Instead of a file-based approach, a DBMS was used, which served as a common baseline for all applications. Back then, specific interfaces to Oracle had to be developed for the different applications, but today some of these are available in standard products. Be that as it may, to date the CAD systems are still dominated by a file-based use, despite the fact that all modern CAD systems have connections to a DBMS. However, the 3D geometric primitives supported in a DBMS are rather limited, which is of course a serious drawback. A second explanation for the still dominant file-based use, is that the CAD systems are often used in design and construction contexts, which are project (or contract) based; see Appendix A. However, when full life cycle support matures and the information is (re)used throughout and between organizations (and not just by individuals), these needs will change.

Shared data management does away with conversions and all the accompanying problems (as illustrated in Section 1.2). Different applications will operate on (different views of) the same set of objects. So no data conversion is needed and inconsistencies are avoided, because there is only one source for a specific object. Good data management also offers other well-known advantages from DBMSs: multiple user support, transaction support, security and authorization, (spatial) data clustering and indexing, query optimization, distributed architectures, support for the concept of multiple views, maintenance of integrity constraints (especially referential integrity, but also other types), and integration with other relevant information systems within an organization. In a nutshell, "island" automation will be abandoned, as company-wide information management becomes a reality. Though most current DBMSs support spatial data types (Oracle, DB2, Informix, Ingres, PostgreSQL, and MySQL, to name just a few), these are not (yet) capable of supporting the higher geometry demands from CAD systems. That said, it should not be that difficult to extend the DBMS with more spatial data types. The authors of this chapter were involved in extending Oracle with a new spatial data type, the polyhedron (Arens et al., 2003). It should also be possible to implement other required types, but it should be stressed, at the same time, that a DBMS alone is not the answer to bridging the gap between CAD and GIS. The prerequisite is an integrated model, which is rich enough to support the semantics required or implied by the different domains.

The DBMS can be considered as an implementation platform for an integrated CAD–GIS model (with different views). However, when exchanging information (or using services from other sources), the structured exchange of information becomes an important issue. The UML (OCL) models are the foundation for both the storage data models (further described in the data definition languages (DDLs) of the DBMS) and the exchange data models. The latter have not been addressed in this chapter, but they are vitally important in our network society. The eXtensible Markup Language (XML) can be used for the models containing the class descriptions at class level (XML schema document "xsd") and for the data at object instance level ("normal" XML document with data "xml"). XML documents also include the geometric aspect of objects (e.g., LandXML, GML, X3D).

1.5 CONCLUSIONS

This chapter has explained the need to integrate GIS and CAD. Although such integration would offer great potential for the management of representations of real-world objects, it has been very difficult so far to use representations from GIS and CAD in one environment. The life cycle concept takes a central place in the integration: different representations or views of the same real-world object are needed throughout the life cycle of an object (plan, construct, survey, maintain).

It can already be concluded from conversions within one domain (GIS and CAD examples in Section 1.3) that geometric and semantic aspects both need to be taken into account. The same will be true for bridging the gap between GIS and CAD systems. However, as both the semantics and the geometry may be more different than within GIS or within CAD, the task is more challenging. At least two major developments are needed to close the gap between GIS and CAD (which many users want to see). The first is to perform a semantic analysis of the concepts of these "different" worlds and, if possible, develop a two-way translation between the two (or an integrated model with multiple views). Second, both GIS and CAD should base their data management on the same technology, i.e., as proposed in this chapter, a spatial DBMS, which is compliant with Open Geospatial (ISO) and CAD standards.

In this chapter we sketched the framework that is needed to bridge the gap between GIS and CAD. First, a formal description is required of the semantics used in both domains. The preliminary steps were set out in this chapter. The next step is to design one central formal semantic that is compliant with both GIS and CAD semantics. This formal semantic can be used in the factual integration of GIS and CAD, which should be implemented in an integrated data management structure based on the multiview model. This structure should be well defined in a DBMS environment. In effect, this will then close the gap between GIS and CAD in the future, and the user can select his favorite tool for a specific task, operating on a view of the shared model managed by the Spatial DBMS. Of course, this assumes that the GIS and CAD tools will all be adapted to the spatial DBMS with the different (semantic) views. Also, this approach should be used from scratch, which will then make the day-to-day practice of the cases mentioned in Section 1.2 much easier.

ACKNOWLEDGMENTS

We would like to thank Justin Simpson and Daniel Edwards for their inspiring discussion, which started in the spring of 2003, on the differences (and affinities) between CAD and GIS. Thanks also to Wim Bronsvoort and Sisi Zlatanova for their input in the early stages of the discussion. Finally, we would like to thank Bentley for organizing the "geospatial research seminar" (23 May 2004) and the participants in this seminar for the inspiring discussions related to the topics such as large-scale 3D geo-information and the integration of CAD and GIS.

REFERENCES

Arens, C., Stoter, J.E., and. van Oosterom, P.J.M., Modelling 3D spatial objects in a GeoDBMS using a 3D primitive, in *Proceedings AGILE 2003,* Lyon, France, April 2003.

Bentley, Bentley MicroStation GeoGraphics, http://www.bentley.com/, 2004.

Bidarra, R. and Bronsvoort, W.F., Semantic feature modelling, *Computer-Aided Design,* 32, 201–225, 2000.

Bronsvoort, W.F., and Noort, A., Multiple-view feature modeling for integral product development, *Computer-Aided Design,* 36 (10), 929–946, 2004.

Cowen, D.J., GIS versus CAD versus DBMS: what are the differences? *Photogrammetric Engineering and Remote Sensing,* 54 (11), 1551–1555, 1988.

DSTC, IBM, Sandpiper Software, Ontology Definition Metamodel, Revised submission to OMG/RFP ad/2003-03-40, http://www.omg.org/docs/ad/05-01-01.pdf, 10 January 2005.

Haasnoot, H., Het gebruik van het FLI-MAP system voor tracé kartering in verschillende industriën (in Dutch), KvAG themadag Laseraltimetrie in Nederland, Verder kijken dan het AHN..., 11 May 2000, http://www.geo.tudelft.nl/frs/laserscan/kvag/haasnoot.ppt.

Hobbs, F. and Chan, C., AutoCAD as a cartographic training tool: a case study, *Computer-Aided Design,* 22 (3), 151–159, 1990.

Hoefsloot, M., 3D Geo-Informatie uit bestaande CAD modellen (in Dutch), Case study report, TU Delft, section GIS technology, 2003.

Hoinkes, R. and Lange, E., 3D for free—toolkit expands visual dimensions in GIS, *GIS World,* 8 (7), 54–56, July 1995.

ICSM, 2002, Harmonised data manual — the harmonised data model, *Intergovernmental Committee on Surveying & Mapping* (ICSM), 2002.

Kolbe, T.H. and Plümer, L., Bridging the gap between GIS and CAAD — geometry, referencing, representations, standards and semantic modelling, *GIM International,* 12–15, July 2004.

Lemmen, C., van der Molen, P., van Oosterom, P., Ploeger, H., Quak, W., Stoter, J., and Zevenbergen, J., A modular standard for the Cadastral Domain, in proceedings of *Digital Earth Information Resources for Global Sustainability,* Brno, Czech Republic, September 21–25, 2003.

Lee, S.H. and Lee, K., Partial entity structure: a compact non-manifold boundary representation based on partial topological entities, in proceedings *Solid Modeling,* Ann Arbor, MI, 159–170, 2001.

Logan, T. and Bryant, N.A., Spatial data software integration: merging CAD/CAM/Mapping with GIS and image processing, *Photogrammetric Engineering and Remote Sensing,* 53 (10), 1391–1395, 1987.

Maguire, D.J., Improving CAD–GIS Interoperability, *ArcNews Online,* http://www.esri.com/news/arcnews/winter0203articles/improving-cad.html), January 2003.

Mason, H., STEP and the other SC4 standards — a backbone for industry, www.estec.esa.nl/conferences/aerospace-pde-2002/presentations/ SLIDES_APDE2002_mason.ppt

Movafagh, S.M., GIS/CAD convergence enhances mapping applications, *GIS World,* 8 (5), 44–47, 1995.

Newell, R.G. and Sancha, T.L., The difference between CAD and GIS, *Computer-Aided Design,* 22 (3), 131–135, 1990.

OGC, OpenGIS Consortium, The OpenGIS Abstract Specification, Topic 1: Feature Geometry (ISO 19107 Spatial Schema), Version 5, Herring, J.H., Ed., OpenGIS Project Document Number 01-101, Wayland, MA, 2001.

OMG, 2002, Object Management Group, Unified Modeling Language Specification (Action Semantics), UML 1.4 with action semantics, January 2002.

OMG, 2003, Object Management Group, Response to the UML 2.0 OCL RfP (Object Constraint Language), January 2003.

Pratt, M.J., Introduction to ISO 10303 — the STEP Standard for product data exchange, *Journal of Computing and Information Science in Engineering,* 1 (1), 102–103, 2001.

Queensland Government, Registrar of Titles — Directions for the Preparation of Plans, Department of Natural Resources and Mines, version 3.3, 1 May 2003.

Schutzberg, A., Bringing GIS to CAD — A Developer's Challenge, *GIS World,* 8 (5), 48–54, 1995.

Sense8, WorldToolKit® Release 10, http://www.sense8.com/products/wtk.html, 2004.

Shepherd, I.D.H., Mapping with desktop CAD: a critical review, *Computer-Aided Design,* 22 (3), 136/150, 1990.

Smith, A., Dodge, M., and Doyle, S., *Visual Communication in Urban Planning and Urban Design,* Centre for Advanced Spatial Analysis, University College London, CASA chapter 2, June 1998.

STEP-on-a-page, www.mel.nist.gov/sc5/soap/soapgrf030407.pdf, 2004.

Sun, M., Chen, J., and Ma, A., Construction of Complex City Landscape with the support of CAD Model, ISPRS Comm. V, WG V/6, *International Archives of Photogrammetry, Remote Sensing and Spatial Information Science* (ISSN: 1682-1777, Volume: XXX IV, Part no.: 5/W3), *International Workshop on Visualization and Animation of Landscape,* Kunming, China, 26 February–1 March 2002.

van Oosterom, P.J.M., Visualiseren van aerodynamische gegevens (in Dutch), M.Sc. Thesis TU Delft, Computer Science, October 1985.

Verbree, E., van Maren, G., Jansen, F., and Kraak, M.-J., Interaction in virtual world views, linking 3D GIS with VR, *International Journal of Geographical Information Science*, 13 (4), 385–396, 1999.

Vosselman, G. and Dijkman, S., 3D Building model reconstruction from point clouds and ground plans, *International Archives of Photogrammetry and Remote Sensing*, XXXIV-3/W4: 37–43, 2001.

W3C, World Wide Web Consortium, OWL Web Ontology Language (Overview), W3c Recommendation, 10 February 2004.

Wonka, P. and Schmalstieg, D., Occluder shadows for fast walkthroughs of urban environments, *Computer Graphics Forum*, 18 (3), Blackwell Publishers, ISSN: 1067-7055, 51–60, 1999.

Zlatanova, S., 3D Modeling for augmented reality, *Proceedings of the 3rd ISPRS Workshop on Dynamic and Multidimensional GIS*, Bangkok, Thailand, 415–420, 23–25 May 2001.

APPENDIX A: DIFFERENCES BETWEEN CAD AND GIS

The "truth" of the following statements on the differences between CAD and GIS (most of them taken from the literature) depends on the perspective of the parties concerned. Note that there is a difference between the most frequent types of use of CAD or GIS versus the system's true capabilities. These statements try to illustrate the general feeling about the differences between CAD and GIS and are hardly ever "absolute truths." Further, it is our opinion that this generally accepted perspective is changing over time, along with the changes in the systems for CAD and GIS (and their definitions). Below, a scale of 1–5 is applied (1 = not true, 2 = sometimes true, 3 = most of the time true, 4 = nearly always true, 5 = always true) to indicate how true the proposition is, or will be generally perceived as such, according to the authors of this chapter at different moments in time.

	Statement Related to CAD and GIS	10 Years Ago	Today	10 Years from Now
1	CAD provides minimal or no thematic attribution; GIS has virtual unlimited attribution (often via a DBMS solution)	5	3	1
2	CAD has 3D geometry with little or no topology (e.g., closed volumes defined by faces in 3D space); GIS has 2D/2.5D geometry with 2D topological structure	5	4	3
3	CAD has no provision for modeling behavior; OO GIS has recently begun to model behavior	4	4	3
4	CAD has data set size limitations (for managing a set of limited objects relevant in the design project); GIS has worldwide size data sets	5	3	2
5	CAD usually deals with man-made objects; GIS deals with both natural and man-made objects	4	4	4

	Statement Related to CAD and GIS	10 Years Ago	Today	10 Years from Now
6	CAD usually deals with one (complex) object or product (possibly consisting of many parts), GIS deals with many (simple) objects embedded in the same space (and some of the objects have explicit relationships)	4	4	4
7	CAD assumes a 2D or 3D orthogonal world; GIS is capable of handling many differing coordinate systems to model a spherical (ellipsoid or even geoide) world	5	5	5
8	CAD may (or may not) be tied to the physical world; GIS must be tied to the physical world	5	5	5
9	CAD supports more complex geometry types (curves, splines, surface patches, etc.); GIS has to do with more simple geometry types (based on straight lines and flat surfaces)	5	4	3
10	GIS and CAD use different concepts and meanings (different semantics based on different, but related, ontologies)	5	4	2
11	CAD is design based (followed by analysis and computation); GIS is based on data collection (survey, remote sensing, photogrammetry, followed by analysis)	5	4	4
12	CAD is project related (design a specific environment followed by adjustments of the environment); GIS is related to constantly changing phenomena (e.g., topography changes); A project-based process leads to a file-based and single-user solution, while an ongoing process leads (registration) to a DBMS and multiuser solution	5	4	3
13	CAD may consider movement of parts of a product in relation to the function of the complete object; GIS considers (change of location and shape over time in) the context of transformations of the real world (both the past and the future) in spatial-temporal models	4	4	4
14	CAD systems have "standard" support for good 3D visualization (on 2D screens); GISs are usually limited to 2D visualizations (and sometimes modest 3D extensions)	5	4	3
15	CAD systems provide 3D coordinate input and digitizing; GISs are (mainly) limited to 2D data entry	5	5	4
16	CAD systems are used to deal with indoor as well as outdoor aspects (of unmoveable objects); GISs only deal with the outdoor (observable from the outside) representation of objects	5	5	4
17	Textures in CAD systems are better supported (for realistic rendering) than in GIS	4	3	2

Part II

Data Handling and Modeling

2 3D Data Acquisition and Object Reconstruction for AEC/CAD

C. Vincent Tao

CONTENTS

2.1 INTRODUCTION

This chapter addresses the major approaches to 3D data collection and object reconstruction. Emphasis is on building objects, which are considered to be the most popular entities for AEC/CAD applications. Many mapping approaches have been developed for collecting 3D building information. In general, these can be grouped as image-based, point cloud–based, and hybrid approaches. The following sections provide an introduction to these approaches. A comparison is provided in terms of resolution, accuracy, turnaround time, and cost. This chapter aims to address the following issues:

- What are the approaches available for large-scale object reconstruction (e.g., buildings)?
- Which approach would be appropriate for the given AEC applications in terms of resolution, accuracy, turnaround time, cost, etc.?
- How much automation has been achieved thus far?

FIGURE 2.1 (See color insert after page 86.) Multiplatform sensing technologies.

Mapping technology has advanced tremendously in the last decade. Modern digital mapping technology is driven largely by advanced capabilities in multiplatform sensing, multisensor integration, and multidata fusion (Figure 2.1). 3D data acquisition has been a challenging issue for many applications, in particular AEC/CAD applications, in terms of time, cost, and quality.

The advancement of sensor technologies has opened up many new avenues for acquiring 3D data. One of the major advancements in mapping is the increasing use of the direct georeferencing technology. Direct georeferencing provides both position and orientation information of onboard sensors using integrated inertial devices (e.g., INS) and positioning systems (e.g., GPS). With direct georeferencing, sensor orientation data (i.e., three position and three direction parameters) can be determined without ground controls. Direct georeferencing technology has enabled the development of a new generation of sensor systems and has also improved the system workflow for 3D data collection and data processing.

2.2 3D BUILDING RECONSTRUCTION APPROACHES

From an information processing perspective, there are three primary approaches to collecting 3D objects, namely, image-based, point cloud–based, and the hybrid approach:

- *Image-based 3D data acquisition*: Use of images, such as close-range, aerial photographs, or satellite images, to collect information about 3D buildings, etc. This approach can derive 3D structural and dimensional information from imagery. The process is well documented, but many components still have to be executed manually.

- *Point cloud–based 3D data acquisition*: Active sensors, such as laser scanning devices, are applied for mapping detailed structures of 3D objects. Both airborne and ground-based laser scanning, or a combination of the two, can produce very dense and accurate 3D point clouds. Extraction of height information is largely automated, but textures from point clouds are often weak.
- *Hybrid approaches*: One of the technological trends is to combine optical images, point cloud data, and other data sources (e.g., maps or GIS/CAD databases). These approaches are generally more robust but require additional data sources.

Each of the above approaches has unique technical characteristics. The following sections describe these in further detail.

2.2.1 IMAGE-BASED 3D DATA ACQUISITION

Image-based 3D data acquisition has been in practice for years. It is well known and well documented in many reference books on photogrammetry (Manual of Photogrammetry, 2004). Based on the number of images used and their settings, image-based 3D data acquisition can be further classified into the following three main categories:

- Stereo image-based
- Single (or monoscopic) image-based
- Multiple image-based

2.2.1.1 Stereo Image Based

3D data acquisition and object reconstruction is conventionally performed using stereo image pairs. Stereo photogrammetry, based on a block of overlapped images, is the primary approach for 3D topographic mapping (Tao, 2002). Figure 2.2 is a typical digital stereo photogrammetric system (also called a "softcopy photogrammetric system") with a dual monitor setup. The fundamental objective of photogrammetry is to rigorously establish the geometric relationship between the object and the image and to derive the information about the object strictly from the image. The employment of close-range photogrammetry has also matured to the level where cameras or digital cameras can be used to capture the close-look images of objects (e.g., buildings) and to reconstruct them using the same theory used with aerial photogrammetry. Photogrammetry is a dominant approach for 3D data acquisition and 3D mapping. It is proven stable, accurate, and operational. The current trend is to improve the automation of object recognition and reconstruction from images. A summary of this method is shown in Table 2.1.

Collection of 3D building models is mainly manual in most commercial photogrammetric systems. Human operators manually drive the 3D mouse (i.e., with a height control) to delineate the building footprints and roof structures under a stereo

FIGURE 2.2 A typical stereo photogrammetric system setup. (Courtesy of Leica Geosystems. Used with Permission.)

viewing environment. Given that the process is very labor intensive, the "standard" 3D building product only includes building footprints and the average (or highest) point of the building roof. Many systems also support texture mapping, where the image textures can be mapped onto the associated building facets.

There is limited progress on automating 3D building extraction from stereo images, although the research is dated to about 20 years ago. A large number of research papers have been published in this area. Following are some typical strategies to automate building reconstruction from stereo images.

Zlatanova et al. (1998) have presented a semi-automatic method for acquiring 3D topologically structured data from aerial stereo images. The process involves the manual digitizing of a minimum number of points necessary for automatically

TABLE 2.1
Stereo Image-Based 3D Data Acquisition

Pros	Accurate and robust
	Widely adopted process for collecting 3D building data
	Roof structure and textures can be obtained
Cons	Expensive in general
	High skill set requirement for users
	Labor-intensive digitizing of objects (largely not automated)
Research Issues	Automation in digitization or feature extraction
	Building true 3D products (highly realistic buildings with textures)
	Use of new digital imaging sensors with direct georeferecing

reconstructing the objects of interest. The 3D topologically structured data are stored in a database and are also used for visualization of the objects. A research system, TOBAGO, reported by Grün and Dan (1997), uses a similar strategy.

Another strategy for semi-automatic building extraction is model-driven-based, whereby initials of the building model are provided to guide the extraction process. Often, corner points, or the initial wire frame of the building model, are provided, and an accurate 3D model is then reconstructed automatically (Sahar and Krupnik, 1999; Zhang and Zhang, 2000; Rottensteiner, 2001). An interaction interface is needed to handle the cases where the semi-automated algorithm might fail. An example of such systems was developed by Hu et al. (2001). In their system, the human operator only needs to provide two corner points of the rectangular or gabled roof. Then an accurate 3D model of the roof can be constructed by using line grouping and deformable least squares template matching techniques. Figure 2.3 illustrates the result of the building extraction.

Fully automatic building reconstruction has received much attention in the research community (Collins et al., 1998; Fischer et al., 1998; Henricsson and

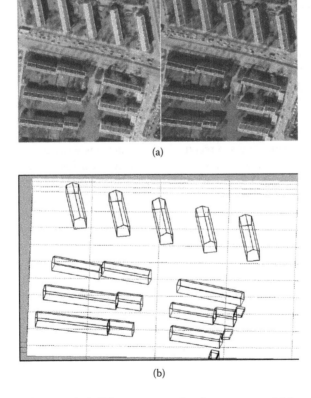

(a)

(b)

FIGURE 2.3 Semi-automatic building reconstruction from stereo aerial images. (Hu et al., 2001. Used with Permission.)

Baltsavias 1997; Henricsson, 1998; Fradkin et al., 2001; Croitoru and Doytsher, 2003; Jaynes et al., 2003). From an algorithmic perspective, automatic building extraction algorithm research has evolved from 2D detection and extraction to 3D reconstruction, from the simplest cubic house model to a complex polyhedral/ multimodel structure, and from a monotonic (data-driven or model-driven) strategy to a hybrid top-down and bottom-up control. For the model-based strategy, knowledge and constraints are developed and integrated into the process of building reconstruction. Though extensive research has been carried out in the area, algorithms are limited to image type and resolution. Development of robust and operational algorithms is still under research.

2.2.1.2 Single (or Monoscopic) Image Based

Single image-based methods utilize the image projection of the geometric perspective of the ground objects. The perspective information can be used to infer 3D information from imagery. To date, little research has been conducted in this field. It is understandable that perspective imaging (i.e., oblique imaging) is much preferred for single image-based 3D information extraction. Single image-based 3D building reconstruction has drawn attention recently due to its rapid turnaround time and no requirements for stereo image pairs. In many applications, such as emergency mapping, where stereo images are not available or too expensive, the single image-based method has considerable advantages. This also applies well to commercial high-resolution satellite images, since stereo satellite images are rarely available.

Extraction of 3D buildings from single images is readily possible, although there are not many publications in this area. The author has developed a viable method for extracting 3D buildings and other 3D objects from single images. This method has been integrated into a commercial software package, SilverEye, developed by GeoTango, Toronto (www.geotango.com). SilverEye is the first product specifically designed for 3D modeling and reconstruction using single images. Figure 2.4 shows a SilverEye software interface for 3D building reconstruction. It utilizes the Rational Function Model (RFM) as the internal sensor model for 3D mapping (Tao and Hu, 2000 and 2004). The added value of using the RFM is that it is widely adopted in the commercial satellite imaging industry and is also applicable to other airborne sensors. Many satellite vendors provide RFM parameters (PRC) as part of the image metadata. For example, IKONOS-2, Quickbird, and OrbView-3 satellite images are all delivered with RPC's metadata files. RFM is an open sensor model that can be used for representing most imaging sensors (Tao and Hu, 2004). With RPCs, 3D extraction process can be made transparent to end users. That is, users are no longer required to understand the sophisticated physical sensor geometry. Once an image with PRCs is loaded, users can start performing their mapping or 3D extraction work immediately. Table 2.2 summarizes the pros and cons of this approach.

Automatic building extraction from single imagery is challenging, due to the lack of 3D cues from stereo pairs. Lin and Nevatia (1998) described a scheme for automatic building reconstruction from a single image. A grouping process was first used to generate 2D roof hypotheses from fragmented linear features extracted from the input image. Good hypotheses were selected based on 2D evidence and some

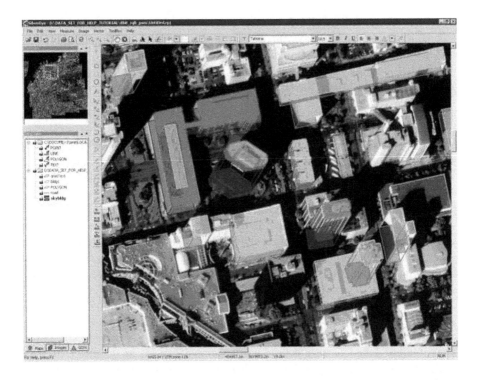

FIGURE 2.4 (See color insert after page 86.) SilverEye software interface for 3D building reconstruction from a single image. (Courtesy of GeoTango International. Used with permission.)

local 3D evidence. They were then verified by searching for 3D evidence consisting of shadow casts by the associated roofs and walls. Finally, overlap and containment relations between 3D structures were analyzed to resolve conflicts.

It required some time for the mapping community to realize that the semi-automatic method is more feasible in an operational environment. Gülch et al. (1998) have reported a system that offers semi-automated building extraction from images.

TABLE 2.2
Single Image-Based 3D Data Acquisition

Pros	No stereo devices are required
	No stereo pairs are needed
	Reduced cost on data acquisition
	Relatively fast turnaround time
	Suitable for defense, intelligence, emergency mapping, urban planning, telecom, utility, and transportation
Cons	Occlusions may occur
	Accuracy depends on the nadir angle
	Manual 3D interpretation required for some cases

The CSG (Constructive Solid Geometry) modeling and the model-image matching techniques were used in the system. The creation of complex buildings is supported by a gluing or docking of volumetric primitives.

2.2.1.3 Multiple Image Based

There are different ways of using multiple images. One is to extend the capabilities of stereo imaging. This is mainly to use multiple images to cover "dead angles." In close-range imaging cases, multiple stereo images are often used for object reconstruction. The other method is to use multiple images to provide different perspective views of the same object. With multiple images, one can alleviate the problem of "occlusions" that often occur in the single and stereo image process. Table 2.3 provides a brief summary of the pros and cons of this approach.

The information obtained from multiple images has high redundancy, which is very useful for developing automated algorithms for 3D object reconstructions. One good example on building extraction using multiple images is by Jaynes et al. (2003). In this research, buildings are first segmented from the image followed by a reconstruction process that makes use of a corresponding digital elevation model (DEM) created from stereo images. Initially, each segmented DEM region likely to contain a building rooftop is indexed into a database of parameterized surface models that represent different building shape classes, such as peaked, flat, or curved roofs. Given a set of indexed models, each is fit to the elevation data using an iterative procedure to determine the precise position and shape of the building rooftop. The indexed model that converges to the data with the lowest residual error is added to the scene. Their method demonstrated the potential in using multiple stereo images for automatic 3D building extraction.

Rather than using a digital elevation model, Lang (2001) presented a 3D corner grouping method in a stepwise procedure. It uses a hierarchical building model in the automatic building reconstruction. Experiments showed that the algorithm can reconstruct generic buildings, since the 3D corner grouping does not require strong constraints of a predefined building model.

Piecewise planar, or facets, is a frequently used cue for building reconstruction. In Baillard and Zisserman (1999), the planar facets are used for line grouping and also the construction of parts of building wireframes. Instead of using lines or corners as 3D cues, Elaksher et al. (2002) made use of image segmentation for obtaining initial

---

TABLE 2.3
Multiple Image-Based 3D Data Acquisition

Pros	More coverage and perspective
	Suitable for close-range applications or for complex buildings
	Complete texture recovery for 3D objects
	Suitable for engineering, urban planning, and architecture design applications
Cons	High cost on data acquisition
	No streamlined workflow process

primitives of possible roof regions (polygons). Polygon correspondence from multiple images is then established geometrically. All possible polygon corresponding sets are considered, and the optimal set is selected. Polygon vertices are then refined using the known geometric properties of buildings to generate the building wireframes.

In a recent study, Kim and Nevatia (2004) focused on the reconstruction of complex buildings with flat or complex rooftops by using multiple, overlapping images. They used a hypotheses-verification strategy. First, 3D features were generated by grouping image features over multiple images, and rooftop hypotheses were generated by neighborhood searches on those features. 3D rooftop hypotheses generated by the above procedures were verified with evidence collected from the images and the elevation data.

Research on building reconstruction from multiple images has made considerable progress. However, due to the lack of a standard workflow for multiple image acquisition, there is a difficulty in developing a software tool capable of handling multiple images in varying situations.

2.2.2 POINT CLOUD-BASED APPROACHES

2.2.2.1 Overview

LIDAR, or laser scanning technology, is becoming a popular approach to acquiring high quality height or distance information. There is significant growth in the LIDAR industry thanks to the integration of direct georeferencing and scanning laser technologies. As each laser pulse can be directly georeferenced, the 3D position of the reflected object can be determined by using a simple distance-angle calculation. With the rapid development of laser scanning technology, airborne Laser scanning, or LIDAR, can acquire dense, accurate, and fast 3D point clouds of urban downtown core or high-rise structures. 3D building height extraction is one of the most popular commercial applications of either airborne LIDAR or ground laser scanning.

3D building extraction from point clouds requires the determination of building cues, ground elevation, building size, rooftop heights, etc. Most buildings can be described to sufficient detail using general polyhedra (i.e., their boundaries can be represented by a set of planar surfaces and straight lines). Further processing, such as expressing building footprints as polygons, is preferable for storing in GIS databases. Like most feature extraction tasks, building extraction can be implemented in either semi-automatic or automatic strategies. Data-driven and model-driven techniques are commonly used. Some algorithms process the raw LIDAR point clouds directly or grid-based images converted from LIDAR point clouds; other algorithms use these two data structures at different processing stages. The semi-automatic building extraction approaches often prepare a set of building primitives for typical house types and roof shapes. There is considerable published research on building extraction from airborne LIDAR data. The process generally consists of two stages: building footprint detection, and 3D building reconstruction, including roof structures. Some methods focus on building detection (i.e., 2D building footprints as output), while others were designed for both detection and reconstruction (i.e., 3D building models as output).

2.2.2.2 Building Detection

Airborne LIDAR research has seen many new developments, largely in automated building detection and reconstruction. Baltsavias et al. (1995) used an edge operator, mathematical morphology, and height bins for the detection of objects higher than the surrounding topographic surfaces. Hug (1997) showed the detection and segmentation of houses from ScaLARS height and intensity data, based on morphological filtering with successive progressive local histogram analysis. Hug also used the laser reflectivity measure for discerning man-made objects from vegetation via binary classifications. In Hu et al. (2003), several algorithms, including the constrained searching in Hough space, enhanced Hough transformation, and sequential linking techniques, are developed to identify building footprints as rectangles, quadrangles, or polygons. These algorithms utilize the hypothesis verification paradigm and an incremental refinement.

Research efforts have also been made to rectify the detected building footprints. Sester (2000) presented a solution to building generalization using least-squares adjustment with a focus on scale-dependent representations. In Vestri and Devernay (2001), angle constraints are applied to refine the corners and junctions of polygon models. The problem is solved by optimizing an objective function to preserve global consistency.

An important task in building detection is to distinguish between buildings and vegetation in point clouds. The discrimination between buildings and vegetation based on a Bayesian nets classification algorithm using local geometric properties is discussed in Brunn and Weidner (1998). Zhan et al. (2002) applied an object-based classification to detect building footprints. First, image segments belonging to the building class are identified by vertical wall analysis. The procedure first examines the sliced LIDAR data, following which the color infrared image is used to calculate the NDVI, which is then assimilated to refine the identified building segments.

2.2.2.3 3D Building Reconstruction

In Maas and Vosselman (1999) and Vosselman (1999), several techniques for the determination of building models are developed. Based on the analysis of invariant moments of point clouds, closed solutions for the parameters of a standard gable roof building model with a rectangular ground plan are derived from 0th, 1st, and 2nd order moments. Models of more complex buildings are determined using a data driven scheme based on intersecting planes that are fitted to triangulated point clouds.

Wang and Schenk (2000) proposed an edge-based building detection and a TIN-based building reconstruction. The building models are reconstructed by triangulating each cluster of identified building points and grouping those fragmentary triangles into piecewise planes. Finally, the tri-intersections of those average planes are used to derive building corners and their relative orientations.

Building surfaces, including roofs and walls, can be roughly approximated by constructing a TIN for points composing a building. The TINs of 3D points sampled on object surfaces, as well as simplification and refinement methods, have been extensively studied for approximating object surfaces (Heckbert and Garland, 1997).

The simplification method is a fine-to-coarse approach, which starts with an exact fit, and then creates approximations of less and less detail (Wang and Schenk, 2000); whereas the refinement method is a coarse-to-fine approach that starts with a minimal approximation, and generates more and more accurate ones (Hu et al., 2003). Most existing roof reconstruction methods are based on the simplification concept. These methods first aggregate the points that possibly belong to separate patches of a complex roof. A plane fitting is then performed to obtain parameter values for each planar patch. The plane detection methods reported in the literature include clustering of triangles, 3D Hough transformation, and clustering of 3D points, with or without using ground plans (Maas and Vosselman, 1999; Vosselman and Dijkman, 2001; Gamba and Houshmand, 2002).

In Rottensteiner (2001), a method for semi-automatic building extraction, together with a concept for storing building models alongside terrain and other topographic data in a topographic information system is presented. His approach is based on the integration of building parameter estimation into the photogrammetric process using a hybrid modeling scheme. A building is decomposed into a set of simple primitives that are reconstructed individually and are then combined by Boolean operators. The internal data structure of both the primitives and the compound building models is based on a boundary representation method.

Hu et al. (2003) have developed an automatic extraction of prismatic and polyhedral building models using airborne LIDAR data. First a digital surface model (DSM) is generated from LIDAR data, and the objects higher than the ground are automatically detected from the DSM. Based on general knowledge about buildings, geometric characteristics such as size, height, and shape information are used to separate buildings from other objects. The extracted building outlines are simplified using an orthogonal algorithm to obtain better cartographic quality. For a LIDAR dataset acquired for downtown Toronto, the reconstructed building models overlaid on the LIDAR-derived digital terrain model (DTM) are shown in Figure 2.5, where the models are colored by their footprint types. The completeness and correctness of the building detection results are 92% and 96%, respectively.

To construct virtual 3D city models, Fruh and Zakhor (2003) present an approach to automatically create textured 3D city models using laser scans and images taken from ground level and a bird's-eye perspective. The aim of this approach is to register and merge the detailed facade models with a complementary airborne model. The airborne modeling process provides a half-meter resolution model with a bird's-eye view of the entire area, containing terrain profile and building tops. The ground-based modeling process results in a detailed model of the building facades. Finally, the two models with different resolutions can be further merged to obtain a 3D realistic model. Table 2.4 gives a summary of point cloud–based 3D data acquisition approach.

2.2.3 Hybrid Approaches

There are many other approaches to 3D data collection and building extraction. The combination of images, LIDAR point clouds, and existing GIS maps is considered valuable in developing a more robust workflow. Use of existing maps or GIS databases

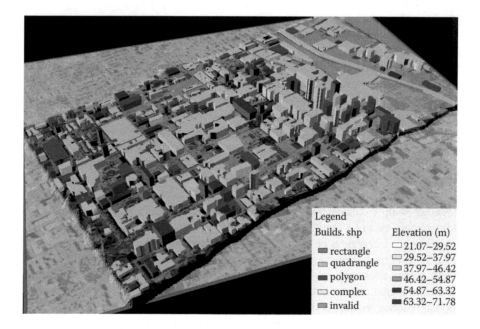

Legend

Builds. shp	Elevation (m)
▬ rectangle	▭ 21.07–29.52
▭ quadrangle	▭ 29.52–37.97
▬ polygon	▭ 37.97–46.42
▭ complex	▬ 46.42–54.87
▭ invalid	▬ 54.87–63.32
	▬ 63.32–71.78

FIGURE 2.5 (See color insert after page 86.) Reconstructed 3D building models of downtown Toronto. (Hu et al., 2003. Used with permission.)

for reconstructing 3D buildings has attracted many researchers. There is some promising published research in this field. Use of existing footprints (i.e., from existing 2D maps or GIS, CAD planning) to fully reconstruct 3D buildings requires additional sources to provide the height information. Again, the height information can be derived from images (i.e, photogrammetry approach) or from laser scanning data or even field surveys.

By integrating knowledge from images and GIS maps, the complexity of the building reconstruction process can be reduced. The integration of LIDAR data and ground plans have been shown to be successful, and detailed reconstruction of buildings can be obtained automatically, even for LIDAR data, with relatively low point densities. This type of approach has the advantage of skipping the building

TABLE 2.4
Point Cloud–Based 3D Data Acquisition

Pros	Dense point clouds
	Direct 3D surface model generation
	Less sensitive to environmental conditions (weather, etc.)
	Suitable for rapid mapping, 3D surface generation, engineering, forest mapping
Cons	Requires conversion from 3D point clouds to objects or features
	Lack of building texture information
	No standard workflow process

detection step and focusing on the building reconstruction stage. These two methods are typical for utilizing maps for 3D object reconstruction. Henricsson et al. (1996) used information from images to separate elevation blobs detected in a DSM from stereo image matching into building and tree classes. Lemmens et al. (1997) showed the fusion of LIDAR altimeter data with 2D digital maps in a topographical database to derive heights for cube-type building primitives.

Haala and Anders (1997) demonstrated two methods for combining DSMs, aerial images, and ground plans for the reconstruction of 3D buildings. The ground plans provide very precise information about the building outlines. The first approach extracts breaklines from both DSMs and image data. Then breaklines of high reliability are combined with gray value edges of high geometric accuracy to reconstruct simple building types. The second approach extracts planar surfaces likely to be roof planes from the DSMs and uses a polyhedron as the building model for reconstruction.

Brenner (1999) combined multispectral information provided by an aerial image with geometric information from a LIDAR DSM. A pixel-based classification is applied for the extraction of buildings, trees, and grass-covered areas, whereby the normalized DSM is used as an additional channel in combination with three spectral bands. Additional constraints are obtained for reconstruction by using the assumption that the given ground plan is correct and exactly defines the borders of the roof. In Brenner (1999), several interactive modeling tools for 3D building reconstruction are reviewed, including ObEx, the "Stuttgart approach," and CC-Modeller. The former two measure building primitives using several aerial images (monoscopic view) or LIDAR data and 2D ground plans, while the latter uses stereo measurement of points in aerial images. CC-Modeller consists of two steps. In the first step, structured point clouds containing all feature points are obtained using manual point measurement. The second step is automatic, and it groups points into planar faces and the generation of roof and wall faces.

Brenner (2000) also presented the reconstruction of buildings with complex structures using LIDAR DSMs and ground plans. Roof surface primitives are segmented, and a rule-based approach decides which segments can be explained by the chosen building model. Finally, the roof is built from the primitives that have been accepted, closing gaps that are caused by the deletion of unexplainable regions. In Ameri (2000), building models are first created based on DSMs and are then verified by back-projecting them to images. By matching the model edges with image edges, the accuracy of the model parameters can be increased with respect to the building outlines.

Suveg and Vosselman's (2001) strategy for 3D reconstruction of buildings is to combine pairs of stereo images with large-scale GIS maps and domain knowledge as an additional information source. The 2D GIS map contains the outline of building footprints. Knowledge about the problem domain is represented by a building library containing primitive building models. Although buildings reveal a high variability in shape, even complex buildings can be generated by combining simple building models with flat or gable-shaped roofs. However, this method must presume the existence of 2D ground plans, which is not valid in some countries. Table 2.5 gives a summary of map-assisted approaches.

TABLE 2.5
Map Assisted 3D Data Acquisition

Pros	Makes use of existing data map sources
	More reliable
	Can be much more automated
	Suitable for urban area mapping
Cons	Height information needs to be extracted from either image sources or point cloud data
	Map dependent (scale, accuracy, currency, etc.)

Sohn (2004) showed a new framework for describing building outlines by combining IKONOS satellite imagery with LIDAR data. A building object is generally represented as a mosaic of convex polygons. Individual buildings are bounded in rectangles by detecting terrain surfaces from a cloud of LIDAR points using RTF (Recursive Terrain Fragmentation) filter (Sohn and Dowman, 2002). Then, those rectangles are partitioned into a number of convex polygons by a recursive intersection of both data-driven and model-driven linear features extracted from IKONOS imagery and LIDAR data. Finally, the building outlines are reconstructed by collecting relevant polygons comprising the building object and merging them.

The quality evaluation for building detection results was initially addressed by Geibel and Stilla (2000), who compared four segmentation procedures using LIDAR data with a density of four points/m^2; based on this, they proposed an evaluation function to estimate the segmentation quality of a complete scene. The evaluation function subjectively weights measures for over-segmentation and under-segmentation. However, at present there is a lack of objective measures concerning reconstruction times, success rates, and reconstruction quality, especially when a human operator is part of a semi-automatic system and different ancillary data are used (Brenner, 1999; Rottensteiner, 2001; Lemmens et al., 1997; Vosselman and Dijkman, 2001).

2.3   COMPARISONS AND ANALYSIS

The above-described approaches have been used in various applications. Selection of the appropriate approach is largely dependent on the end user's specification. Table 2.6 provides a comparison of these approaches to create a 10 km × 10 km city model in terms of accuracy, resolution, turnaround time, cost, and texturing capability, with the given platform.

It is worth noting that Table 2.6 only provides a comparison in a general sense. One observation is that higher cost is always associated with higher accuracy and higher resolution. The major limitation of a point cloud–based approach is its lack of sufficient texture information compared to optical imaging approaches. It is also worth mentioning that LIDAR intensity data (i.e., the magnitude values of laser reflection) continues to be improved. Research has started to look into the possibility of using the LIDAR intensity image as a source of texturing information.

TABLE 2.6
A Comparison of 3D Data Collection Approaches

Performance	Image-Based (Satellite)	Image-Based (airborne)	Image-Based (ground)	Point Cloud–Based (airborne)	Point Cloud–Based (ground)
Accuracy	Low	Medium / High	High	High	High
Resolution	Low	Medium / High	High	Medium	High
Turnaround Time	Fast	Medium	Low	Medium	High
Cost	Low	Medium	High	High	High
Texturing	Low	Medium	High	N/A	N/A

2.4 CONCLUDING REMARKS

This chapter introduced three major approaches towards 3D data acquisition with an emphasis on building reconstruction, namely, image-based, point cloud–based, and hybrid approaches. Selection of these approaches should be based on project specification and end users' requirements. No single approach is best in all contexts.

We have entered an era where the acquisition of 3D data is becoming ubiquitous, inexpensive, and fast. However, automation remains the biggest challenge. This chapter addressed the various state-of-the-art approaches, as well as their current status in terms of automation capabilities. Thus far there are multiple sources for 3D data collection, including high-resolution imagery from aerial photography and satellites; ground-based close-range imaging; 3D point clouds from airborne laser range-finding systems, such as LIDAR or ground laser scanning devices; imagery from synthetic aperture radar (SAR); and other sources. However, converting the data to meaningful 3D features is not straightforward and has been challenging. Each approach has some barriers, and no single acquisition mode is likely to produce complete 3D models in a fully automated way.

As the cost of sensors, hardware, and computing devices decreases, it is the author's view that integrated 3D data collection through the use of multiple sensing technologies will allow a full solution to 3D building reconstruction effectively and efficiently. Since automated acquisition mechanisms will permit repeated collection over time, the initial high costs of acquiring multiple data sources can be balanced and justified.

ACKNOWLEDGMENTS

Dr. Yong Hu has offered partial writings for Section 2.2.2, and Dr. Xianyun Hu and Dr. Gunho Sohn have provided valuable information for several sections. Their assistance to the work is highly appreciated.

REFERENCES

Ameri, B., Feature based model verification: a new concept for hypothesis validation in building reconstruction, *IAPRS*, 33, part B3, 24–35, 2000.

Baillard, C. and Zisserman, A., Automatic reconstruction of piecewise planar models from multiple views, *Proceedings of IEEE Conference on Computer Vision and Pattern Recognition*, 2, 559–565, 1999.

Baltsavias, E.P., Mason, S., and Stallmann, D., Use of DTMs/DSMs and orthoimages to support building extraction, *Workshop on AEMOASI*, 199–210, 1995.

Brenner, C., Interactive modeling tools for 3D building reconstruction, *Photogrammetric Week*, 23–34, 1999.

Brenner, C., Towards fully automatic generation of city models, *IAPRS*, 17–22 July, 33, part B3, 85–92, 2000.

Brunn, A. and Weidner, U., Hierarchical Bayesian nets for building extraction using dense digital surface models, *ISPRS JPRS*, 53, 296–307, 1998.

Collins, R.T., Jaynes, C.O., Cheng, Y., Wang, X., Stolle, F., Riseman, E.M., and Hanson, A.R., The ascender system: automated site modeling from multiple aerial images, *Computer Vision and Image Understanding*, 72 (2), 143–162, 1998.

Croitoru A. and Doytsher, Y., Monocular right angle building hypothesis generation in regularized urban areas by pose clustering, *Photogrammetric Engineering & Remote Sensing*, 69 (2), 151–169, 2003.

Elaksher, A., Bethel, J., and Mikhail, E., Reconstructing 3D building wireframes from multiple images, *Photogrammetric Computer Vision — ISPRS Commission III Symposium*, A–091, 2002.

Fischer A., Kolbe, T.H., Lang, F., Cremers, A.B., Förstner, W., Plümer, L., and Steinhage, V., Extracting buildings from aerial images using hierarchical aggregation in 2D and 3D, *Computer Vision and Image Understanding*, 72 (2), 185–203, 1998.

Fradkin, M., Mâýtre, H., and Roux, M., Building detection from multiple aerial images in dense urban areas, *Computer Vision and Image Understanding*, 82, 181–207, 2001.

Fruh, C. and Zakhor, A., Constructing 3D city models by merging aerial and ground views, *Computer Graphics*, 23 (6), 52–61, 2003.

Gamba, P. and Houshmand, B., Joint analysis of SAR, LIDAR and aerial imagery for simultaneous extraction of land cover, DTM and 3D shape of buildings, *International Journal of Remote Sensing*, 23 (20), 4439–4450, 2002.

Geibel, R. and Stilla, U., Segmentation of laser altimeter data for building reconstruction: different procedures and comparison, *IAPRS*, 17–22 July, 33, part B3, 326–334, 2000.

Grün, A. and Dan, H., TOBAGO — a topology builder for the automated generation of building models, in *Automatic Man-Made Object Extraction from Aerial and Space Images*, Grün, A., Kuebler, O., and Agouris, P., Eds, Birkhaeuser Verlag, Basel, 1997, 149–160.

Gülch, E., Müller, H., Läbe, T., and Ragia, L., On the performance of semi-automatic building extraction, in *Proceedings of ISPRS Commission III Symposium*, Columbus, OH, July 6–10, 1998.

Haala, N. and Anders, K.H., Acquisition of 3-D urban models by analysis of aerial images, digital surface models and existing 2-D building information, *SPIE Conference on Integrating Photogrammetric Techniques with Scene Analysis and Machine Vision*, Orlando, FL, 212–222, 1997.

Heckbert, P.S. and Garland, M., Survey of polygonal surface simplification algorithms, Technical Report, Computer Science Department, Carnegie Mellon University, 29, 1997.

Henricsson O., The role of color attributes and similarity grouping in 3-D building recon-struction, *Computer Vision and Image Understanding,* 72 (2), 163–184, 1998.

Henricsson O. and Baltsavias, E., 3D building reconstruction with ARUBA: a qualitative and quantitative evaluation, *Automatic Man-Made Object Extraction from Aerial and Space Images,* Grün, A., Kuebler, O., and Agouris, P., Eds, Birkhaeuser Verlag, Basel, 65–76, 1997.

Henricsson, O., Bignone, F., Willuhn, W., Ade, F., Kubler, O., Baltsavias, E., Mason, S., and Gruen, A., Project Amobe: strategies, current status and future work, *IAPRS,* 31, 321–330, 1996.

Hu, X., Zhang, Z., and Zhang, J., Object-space based interactive extraction of manmade objects from aerial images, *Proceedings of SPIE International Symposium on Mul-tispectral Image Processing and Pattern Recognition,* 4554, 274–279, 2001.

Hu, Y., Tao, C.V., and Collins, M., Automatic extraction of buildings and generation of 3-D city models from airborne LIDAR data, *ASPRS Annual Conference* (CD ROM), 3–9 May, Anchorage, AK, 12 p., 2003.

Hug, C., Extracting artificial surface objects from airborne laser scanner data, *Workshop on AEMOASI,* Basel, 203–212, 1997.

Jaynes, C., Riseman, E., and Hanson, A., Recognition and reconstruction of buildings from multiple aerial images, *Computer Vision and Image Understanding,* 90, 69–98, 2003.

Kim, Z. and Nevatia, R., Automatic description of complex buildings from multiple images, *Computer Vision and Image Understanding,* 96 (1), 60–95, 2004.

Lang, F., Component-based building reconstruction by structural multi-image correspondence analysis, *Proceedings of ASPRS Year 2001 annual conference,* St. Louis, MO, CD-ROM, 2001.

Lemmens, M., Deijkers, H., and Looman, P., Building detection by fusing airborne laser altimeter DEMs and 2-D digital maps, *IAPRS,* 32, 42–49, 1997.

Lin, C. and Nevatia, R., Building detection and description from a single intensity image, *Computer Vision and Image Understanding,* 72 (2), 101–121, 1998.

Maas, H. and Vosselman, G., Two algorithms for extracting building models from raw altimetry data, *ISPRS JPRS,* 54, 153–163, 1999.

Manual of Photogrammetry, 5th ed., McGlone, C., Mikhail, E., and Bethel, J., ASPRS, 2004.

Rottensteiner, F., *Semi-automatic extraction of buildings based on hybrid adjustment using 3D surface models and management of building data in a TIS,* Ph.D. dissertation, Vienna University of Technology, 2001.

Sahar, L. and Krupnik, A., Semiautomatic extraction of building outlines from large-scale aerial images, *Photogrammetric Engineering & Remote Sensing,* 65 (4), 459–465, 1999.

Sester, M., Generalization based on least squares adjustment, *IAPRS,* 17–22 July, 33, part B4, 931–938, 2000.

Sohn, G, Extraction of buildings from high-resolution satellite data and LIDAR. *ISPRS,* 12–23 July, Istanbul, Turkey, DVD-ROM, 2004.

Sohn, G. and Dowman, I.J., Terrain surface reconstruction by the use of tetrahedron model with the MDL Criterion. *Proceedings of ISPRS Commission III, Symposium 2002 on Photogrammetric Computer Vision,* Graz, Austria, 9–13 September 2002, 34 (3A), 336–344, 2002.

Suveg, I. and Vosselman, G., 3D Reconstruction of Building Models, *International Archives of Photogrammetry and Remote Sensing,* 17–22 July, Amsterdam, Vol. XXXIII, 2000.

Suveg, I. and Vosselman, G., 3D Building Reconstruction by Map Based Generation and Evaluation of Hypotheses, *12th Proceedings of the British Machine Vision Confer-ence,* 10–13 September, Manchester, 643–652, 2001.

Tao, C.V., Digital photogrammetry — the future of spatial data collection, *GeoWorld*, http://www.geoplace.com/gw/2002/0205/0205dp.asp, 30–37, May 2002.

Tao, C.V. and Hu, Y., A comprehensive study on the rational function model for photogrammetric processing, *Photogrammetric Engineering and Remote Sensing*, 67 (12), 1347–1358, 2001.

Tao, C.V. and Hu, Y., RFM: an open sensor model for cross sensor mapping, *ASPRS Annual Conference*, 23–28 May, Denver, CO, 2004.

Vestri, C. and Devernay, F., Using robust methods for automatic extraction of buildings, *CVPR*, 1, 8–14 December, Kanai, HI, 133–138, 2001.

Vosselman, G., Building reconstruction using planar faces in very high-density data, *IAPRS*, 8–10 September, Munich, 32, 1999.

Vosselman, G. and Dijkman, S., 3-D building model reconstruction from point clouds and ground plans, *IAPRS*, 34, part 3/W4, 37–44, 2001.

Wang, Z. and Schenk, T., Building extraction and reconstruction from LIDAR data, *IAPRS*, 17–22 July, Amsterdam, 33, part B3, 958–964, 2000.

Zhan, Q., Molenaar, M., and Tempfli, K., Building extraction from laser data by reasoning on image segments in elevation slices, *IAPRS*, 34, 305–308, 2002.

Zhang, Z. and Zhang, J., Semiautomatic building extraction based on least square template matching with geometrical constraints in object space, *International Archives of Photogrammetry and Remote Sensing*, 32 (B3), 1022–1025, 2000.

Zlatanova, S., Paintsil, J., and Tempfli, K., 3D Object Reconstruction from Aerial Stereo Images, http://www.gdmc.nl/zlatanova/thesis/html/refer/ps/sz_jp_kt98.pdf, 1998.

3 Three-Dimensional Representations and Data Structures in GIS and AEC

Roberto Lattuada

CONTENTS

3.1 INTRODUCTION: A CASE FOR GIS/AEC INTEGRATION

Historically, GIS and AEC have developed as solutions to different problems in different domains — the former optimized for the modeling of new, but well-defined objects; the latter for the reconstruction of existing objects about which only sparse and incomplete information is available.

The modeling of complex systems that go beyond the drawing part of the problem well into the simulation, budgeting, environmental impact analysis, and decision support makes a strong case for a tighter integration of GIS and AEC in a full three-dimensional environment.

A typical example of such complex problems is the construction of a new underground station; the following are just some of the needed modeling requirements:

- Produce detailed drawings of the tube station buildings, rails, and tunnels (Figure 3.1 and Figure 3.2).
- Model the drainage and water systems below the surface to simulate water levels and water flow over a number of variables, such as historical rain levels, terrain, and rock properties (Figure 3.3).
- Produce an accurate rock properties model to simulate the cost of excavation and devise optimal excavation paths.
- Evaluate possible structural damages to neighboring buildings during excavation and operation of the underground rail.
- Produce drawings for the "above ground" buildings; evaluate the architectural impact, run fire and emergency simulations (Figure 3.4 and Figure 3.5).

FIGURE 3.1 (See color insert after page 86.) Underground station: 3D model of above-ground buildings, below-ground structures, and rail tunnels.

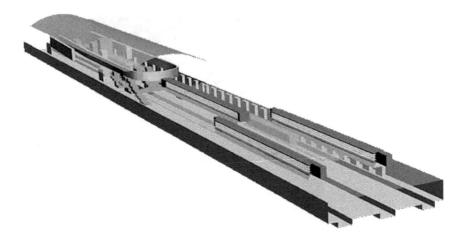

FIGURE 3.2 Detail of underground station: access to platforms and rail tunnels.

In order to have a scientific and effective approach to answering all the questions posed by each of the modeling steps outlined above, the "view" of the problem, or its "scale," needs to be defined. First we model the different objects and visualize them before they are actually manufactured. Next we carry out a simulation in a local context by stressing their resistance to variables such as heat and impact. Then we compute volume and other shape-related properties.

On a smaller scale, we see how these objects relate to each other: the volume of the station underground has a corresponding volume of material that needs to be excavated and removed (this material can be of different types with corresponding different means and costs of excavation).

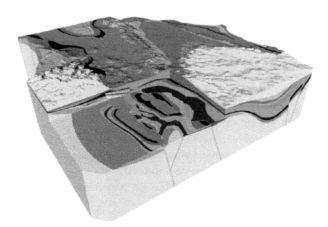

FIGURE 3.3 Water flow and aquifer model. (Model and image generated by CSIRO Exploration and Mining as part of a project sponsored through the Australian Geodynamics Cooperative Research Centre. Used with permission.)

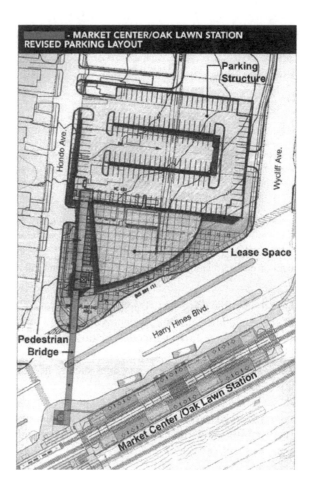

FIGURE 3.4 "Above" ground planning.

On an even smaller scale, we see the station and the subsurface modeling in the context of a modern city, with streets, buildings, other underground works, and a sewage and aquifer system.

The "scale" of the problem has a significant impact in the design of an integrated solution and is the parameter against which each system requirement (i.e., precision, functionalities, data structures) must be validated.

The following sections in this chapter are organized as follows: Section 3.2 through Section 3.5 contain a literature review of data models and current research areas in the 3D modeling field, Section 3.6 and Section 3.7 introduce the research problem of the integration of large 3D models for 3D GIS and AEC, Section 3.8 and Section 3.9 describe a solution to the integration problem that makes the integration step possible while preserving the requirements and modeling features of each system.

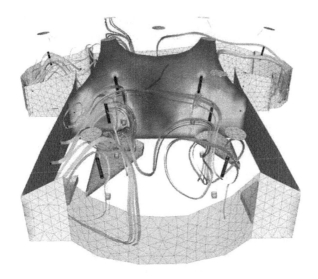

FIGURE 3.5 Finite elements model for fire risk assessment.

3.2 GIS AND AEC OBJECT TYPES

In order to make a valid proposal for a unified data modeling solution, we first need to understand which are the object types that we try to model in AEC and GIS and what are the functionalities and the output that we expect from each system.

In AEC-oriented systems, the main target is to define objects using geometric primitives to design, evaluate, edit, and construct. Classical CAD methods are used to interactively design curves and surfaces. Bezier and spline techniques have been used extensively for this purpose because they generate nice smooth geometries that are storage efficient and easy to manipulate interactively.

For AEC systems:

- We build mathematical descriptions of objects whose shape is well known (if only in the head of the architect, for example).
- The editing and drawing step is crucial as very little data is initially available.
- The modeling process is targeted at manufacturing these objects.
- Well-known, simple-shaped objects, with a corresponding efficient mathematical description, are often used in the modeling process to build more complex structures (as in systems based on Constructive Solid Geometry, for example).
- The final object is well defined, to any degree of precision required.

Most of the initial AEC graphics technology was developed to serve mechanical engineering disciplines; designing car bodies, buildings, machined parts, and other man-made objects. These are not easy tasks but are completely different from modeling natural objects, especially geo-scientific objects. Unlike "designed" objects, geo-scientific objects are revealed by limited samples, or by indicative data that is highly irregular and complex with many more parameters than simple geometry.

For GIS systems:

- We build statistical descriptions of objects whose shape is not well known.
- The capability to handle large amounts of diverse input data is crucial (seismic data, boreholes data, known geo-morphological shapes, etc.).
- Linkages must be maintained between the spatial elements and the original nonspatial data, as often spatial elements must be considered in the source context.
- Spatial functions like adjacency, proximity, connectivity, inclusion/exclusion are required, and complex spatial relationships need to be determined and simulated to place the data in context and truly create a model.
- Only limited editing is usually required.
- A degree of uncertainty is always present both in the initial data and in the result of the modeling process, so the final object is not necessarily well defined and is subject to further analysis, simulation, and interpretation.
- Many models may be created for a particular project, and they should be filed and managed with their respective source data and modeling parameters.

3.2.1 Characteristics of Geo-Scientific Data

Exploration prospects are typically defined by sampling data, which are the result of collating many variables and the combinations of which present nonunique solutions. Existing data collection points may provide detailed information, but this is usually at widely distributed locations.

The geoscientists are faced with the important task of developing predictive models integrating and synthesizing vast quantities of diverse and sometimes ambiguous information. Three-dimensional GIS systems must provide the tools to manage, represent, and display this data in the most appropriate way.

In summary, source data in the geosciences field can be described as diverse, complex, and voluminous. This presents several problems for 3D applications:

- The subset of data to be used in model generation must be extracted and translated from the massive sources available.
- Linkages must be maintained between the spatial elements and the original nonspatial data, as often spatial elements must be considered in the source context.
- Spatial functions like adjacency, proximity, connectivity, inclusion/exclusion are required.
- Many models may be created for a particular project and they should be filed and managed with their respective source data and modeling parameters.

It is clear, therefore, that databases for 3D applications must accommodate considerable quantities of both attribute and spatial data and provide more functions than traditional database management systems.

3.2.2 NOISE, ERRORS, AND DATA UNCERTAINTY

In any modeling process, it is impossible not to incur errors of various kinds. This is particularly true of geoscientific modeling, where the sampling density is usually low and the sampling methods very diverse. The papers of King et al. (1982) and Sides (1992) stress the need to identify, quantify, and control the errors that arise at the different stages of the modeling process.

To understand the rest of this section and the arguments presented, it is necessary to give a full definition of the term "error." The error is the difference between a measurement, or the mean of a set of measurements, and the most reliable estimate of its unknown true value (the true value will always be unknown because its value can only be obtained through some measuring method and every measuring method, no matter how accurate, is limited in its precision). Such differences may be absolute (constant over a range of values) or relative (proportional to the magnitude of the value being measured) (Sides, 1992).

The study of errors associated with sampling for reserve estimation purposes led to the formulation of a comprehensive theoretical background for controlling the errors associated with sampling procedures (Gy, 1989). In a similar way, the development of geostatistics as an estimation technique (Krige, 1976; Matheron, 1963), provided a theoretical basis for predicting the errors associated with the estimation of regionalized variables such as reserve grades. The work done in these two areas provides a firm basis for studying the inherent uncertainties associated with sampling, modeling, and estimating the internal properties of geoscientific objects.

An area that has received less attention is the measurement and prediction of errors associated with the modeling of shapes and estimation of volumes. This aspect is closely related to the work presented here, which is centered on the geometric reconstruction of geoscientific bodies. In this context, two approaches to modeling can be distinguished:

Probabilistic: The values predicted are, in fact, an average value for a volume; these are expressed as a statistical distribution of values within a given volume, specified by a predicted mean and variance.

Deterministic: The model indicates an exact value for any given point, no error estimate is associated with any of the predicted values, but different sets of models can be built from different data sets representing intervals of possible values. More or less weight can be assigned to each of the resulting models, depending on the degree of confidence we have in the data it is built from.

The modeling approach based on triangulations described in Section 3.8 and Section 3.9 is essentially deterministic; most of the subsequent discussion in this section is dedicated to the analysis of deterministic models. Despite the fact that any error information that might be available in the input data is not used in the geometrical reconstruction phase, there is no reason why it could not be used in a following property interpolation phase. Error information is not lost; it can be modeled as any other attribute to represent error distribution throughout the model (for example, to verify measurements procedures in different parts of the model), or it can be used in any further processing if required.

Burrough (1986) identified five potential sources of error associated with geographic information systems:

- **Inaccuracies associated with original data:** These include errors in topographic surveys, and differences between samples collected on different dates or using different methods. The use of graphical displays can facilitate the validation process and help reduce the impact of these kinds of errors on the modeling process.
- **Sampling and analytical errors:** These include the effects of precision and accuracy of different sampling methods, as well as the incorrect use of equipment.
- **Errors due to natural variation:** The presence of natural variations make exact reproducibility of measurements impossible, regardless of the precision and accuracy of measurements.
- **Errors in data capture:** These include errors in data input, data transfer, and translation.
- **Computer processing errors:** These include errors introduced at the processing stage due to hardware and software limitations, limitations of model structures, or errors associated with the interpretation of geoscientific data.

The concept of "fuzzy" data points was introduced by Mallet (1988, 1989) to take into account the differences in the quality of the data points used. For example, a drill hole point is generally regarded as less "fuzzy" than one interpreted from a geophysical survey.

Errors that arise during data collection and interpretation are best quantified by means of duplicate sampling and interpretation studies, expressed as a set of models each representing a different approximation or interpretation.

Deterministic models like the ones described in Section 3.8 and Section 3.9 do not yield any estimate of the potential difference in the quality of the data points. The only way to handle "fuzzy" points is to generate different "deterministic" models for each possible input configuration. Despite this limitation, data inaccuracies should not prevent the user from starting with generating a precise interpolation of the data, whatever the degree of confidence in that data or its density. The geoscientific modeling process is often a trial-and-error procedure, and a first interpolation of the data is exactly what it is — a needed approximation that represents the starting point for further refinement.

3.3 SPATIAL REPRESENTATIONS

Once defined, the AEC and GIS objects need to be stored and logically connected. The way in which spatial data are numerically stored, linked, and processed in a computer constitutes a spatial representation.

Defining a spatial representation requires definitions of three basic components:

- How 3D space is represented
- How data are stored and logically interrelated (data modeling)
- How the model is displayed

A spatial representation can be considered separate from the visualization of the spatial data, which is a set of possible views over the representation (Jones, 1989; Loudon, 1986); similar display techniques can also be applied to different representations in order to produce similar viewable results. Spatial queries and operations are performed against these different representations as required, and different representation techniques have distinct advantages and disadvantages depending on the geoscientific model and spatial operation.

We can roughly divide these representations into two main classes similar to their two-dimensional counterparts — vector and raster. They are: **surface** (or boundary) techniques, which model the boundary or "skin" of objects; and **volume** (or spatial occupancy) techniques, which completely fill the space with elementary shapes (Figure 3.6).

Geoscientific objects often require features of both representations; most products available today reflect those requirements by including elements of both classes of techniques.

The characteristics of the 3D spatial objects to be modeled are the most important factors in the choice of approach to 3D modeling. An important qualitative difference is seen between the identification of geoscientific objects that are believed to have a discrete spatial identity and those that vary in identity in space but that can be visualized by choosing threshold parameter values for inspection. We can define the first kind of geoscientific objects as **sampling-limited** and the second as **definition limited** (Raper, 1989).

Many applications consider geoscientific objects as numerical functions to be estimated and then graphically displayed as, for example, porosity or sound velocity through a layer. However, this approach is not always relevant for geoscientific data. Geometrical and physical properties of geoscientific objects constitute two very distinct characteristics to be modeled differently. It is necessary to draw the distinction between geometry and property data within a geoscientific context because tools that are well suited to model properties, such as, for example, intervals of porosity of an ore body, might not be optimal when we try to model geometric properties like layer intersections or salt body boundaries.

At the end of this chapter, a uniform approach to modeling both types of objects is proposed in an attempt to overcome the limitations of methods designed with only one specific geoscientific object type in mind (Figure 3.7).

3.4 SURFACE MODELING IN 3D GIS

The creation of surfaces is a widespread form of modeling that dates back more than 30 years (Harbaugh and Merriam, 1968), and a wide range of application software is available to create 2.5D visualizations (Muller, 1988). The display of

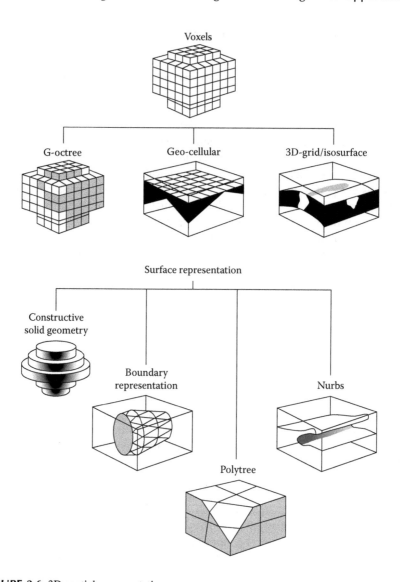

FIGURE 3.6 3D spatial representations.

2.5D surfaces to visualize a 3D representation of reality can only be used within certain limits. One of the major restrictions is that multiple z-values cannot be displayed within the same surface. However, geometrically, surfaces can be thought of as complex spatial objects whose spatial configuration is not limited by the constraints of a 2.5D visualization. The limitation on single z-values is not a limitation of the surface itself but of the method used to build the surface. This constraint originates from the difficulty of defining a neighborhood order among the data points when these are defined on surfaces that fold over themselves, thus generating multivalued z coordinates.

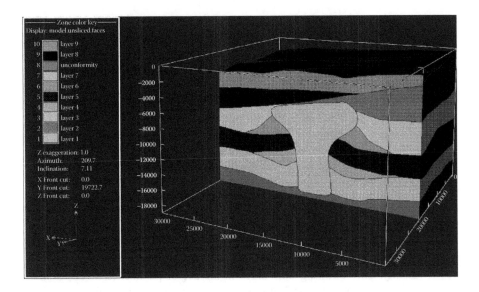

FIGURE 3.7 (See color insert after page 86.) Sampling-limited and definition-limited objects can coexist within the same model.

Surfaces are developed by spatially structuring point- or line-based z-value data using raster (grid-based) or vector (triangulated) techniques, which do not limit *per se* the definition of a surface to single values in z. Therefore, surfaces can be used in a 3D representation as a means of bounding 3D space. This can be achieved by collating together several surfaces to enclose a volume, or by developing new ways to represent and generate surfaces directly in 3D space (Batten, 1989; Fisher and Wales, 1989; Kelk and Challen, 1992).

The most common methods to represent surfaces in 3D space are the following:

- **2D rectangular grids:** These data structures generically consist of a grid of evenly spaced values stored as an array of elements or as a set of irregularly distributed point values. In the latter case, a set of interpolated values must be generated to be later assigned to every cell of the regular grid. Regular grid structures are generally used for surfaces that have a single value for each grid point. Note that lateral boundaries such as discontinuities are difficult to represent due to the lack of explicit connections between grid points. For this reason, they are not well suited to store nearly vertical or steeply dipping surfaces, nor near surfaces with faults where two elevation values are assigned to a single grid point. The same limitations are encountered when we try to model continuous surfaces that enclose a volume, as in the case of ore bodies, since they are also multivalued. Processing inefficiencies might be caused by the fact that shapes have to be represented by a large number of relatively small rectangular elements in order to achieve an acceptable precision in the boundary representation, regardless of the geometry, shape, or origin of the data (Houlding, 1989). Despite the many limitations, the use of rectangular or regular grids can still be a very useful option in cases where the ease of use and implementation are to be preferred to the flexibility of the modeling approach.

- **Parametric functions and NURBS:** This is a valuable solution to the problem of representing free-form surfaces that may be multivalued for particular Cartesian coordinates (Fisher and Wales, 1989) and can adapt well for use with geoscientific applications (Tipper, 1977; Tipper, 1978). The x, y, z coordinates become a function of a 2D mesh coordinate system (u, v) that lies within the surface. Complex surfaces can be subdivided into contiguous patches parallel to the u, v co-ordinate system, each defined locally by low order polynomial functions. This is clearly a valuable technique; surfaces are defined mathematically instead of using a large number of small elements. Complex objects can be stored in small spaces, and spatial operations and intersections can be computed efficiently. The following difficulties in the use of parametric functions as an alternative to the method proposed here have been identified:
- NURBS is an open system; several operations on NURBS objects (composition, intersection, projection) do not inherently result in NURBS objects. The NURBS closure problem makes splitting NURBS difficult when required for contouring or constraints recovery.
- A high order and a high number of knots is required if we want to fit a parametric surface to a number of given, irregularly distributed data points. High order and highly degenerate splines are better avoided for reasons of numerical stability.
- The use of a high number of joined NURBS patches is typically adopted in CAD systems where point distributions are highly regular and can be easily controlled. This construction also requires a number of conditions to be effective, such as tangent continuity of neighboring patches and identical degree and knots along the borders. These conditions are very difficult to meet in a highly variable point distribution scenario.
- NURBS are not easily handled within an efficient space repartition mechanism like the N-tree. Problems may arise when reconciling the parametric space where the NURBS are defined to the geometric space where the N-tree is defined, for example, it may be difficult to calculate points for a NURBS that is guaranteed to be INSIDE the element of the N-tree.

Geologic investigations, like most scientific studies, result in output of some finite amount of data. Suppose we now want to view this data as a series of points through which we wish to fit a curve or surface. This leads to a data-fitting problem. The curve or surface can be arbitrarily approximated by a series of short, straight-line segments or planar polygons. This method becomes insufficient in many contexts, because it requires a large amount of data to obtain the necessary smoothness of fit for complex curves or surfaces that become awkward to manipulate. In some cases it might be more desirable to represent the curve or surface analytically (i.e., using parametric functions and NURBS). This reduces storage, increases precision, and eases the burden of calculation of intermediate points. Analytically fitting a curve through a set of known data points becomes a classical interpolation problem, and interpolation is just a special case of the more general approximation problem (creating a curve or surface that comes near the data points but does not necessarily pass through them). There are a number of cases where geoscientific data are best treated by approximations because they are subject to error or noise (Section 3.2.2). Therefore, using an approximated fitting can be seen as a way of taking this uncertainty into consideration. It is usually difficult to create interpolated models built on NURBS because of the problems inherent in fitting a complex surface through a set of known and fixed points; much better results can be obtained if an approximated representation is acceptable. In this case, the use of NURBS can provide a concise and efficient representation.

In a NURBS-based system, a single **mathematical** representation is used for all different entities; this allows a uniform approach to the geometric and property definition of a model.

As part of this research work, another uniform approach, based on triangulations, has been studied and implemented. When compared to a NURBS-based system, this approach can be regarded as a purely **geometrical** representation. The system developed also provides for efficient spatial indexing for geometrical searches, thereby overcoming the deficiencies of a mathematical approach as described above.

- **Triangulations:** In this geometric representation, a surface is defined by a triangular tessellation based on a given set of nodes, which usually represents original observations. This differs significantly from regular grids where values at the grid points need to be interpolated from the original data points. One advantage of triangulations is that the density of nodes can vary and can be locally adapted if required. Few nodes are required to describe smoothly changing parts of a surface, while highly changing parts can be described by denser sampling (Schroeder et al., 1992). Triangulations incur higher storage overheads for each node than do grids, as all coordinates and connectivity need to be stored explicitly. On the other hand, fewer nodes are usually necessary to represent a surface. As all 3D co-ordinates for each node are stored explicitly, triangulated surfaces in 3D are not constrained to be single valued at any given location as in the 2D and 2.5D cases. Also, triangulated surfaces can fold over themselves in all directions and discontinuities such as faults can be properly represented. Another advantage is that, in most cases, regular grids need to be converted into a triangular representation for display purposes (Lorensen and Cline, 1987), while this is obviously not required when using triangulated surfaces, and shaded images of the surface can be directly calculated from the stored data structure.

Perhaps the most serious disadvantage of triangular schemes is that any location-related search requires the scanning of the whole network of nodes, whereas any part of a regular grid can be addressed directly. This problem can be overcome by including the whole triangulation structure (nodes, connections, boundaries, constraints) within a spatially indexed structure like an octree. If, on the other hand, typical grid-based Boolean operations are required, the triangulation can always be converted into a grid to allow for more efficient processing.

One particular characteristic of geological surfaces is the likely presence of faults that may lead to "steps" in the surface. These steps may be associated with vertical and lateral movement that may juxtapose different materials across the fault. Hence, when creating surfaces to model solid geology, it is necessary to prevent interpolation across a fault and to control interpolation around the ends of faults. Because of the following difficulties: dealing with multiple z coordinate values, extending interpolation across faults, and representing definition-limited objects, the creation of models that use only triangulated surfaces is limited to specific applications. These surfaces are, on the other hand, useful as basic building blocks in 3D modeling to record the boundary surfaces of uniform strata.

3.5 VOLUME MODELING IN 3D GIS

Much of the early experience of solid modeling has been gained in the computer-aided design (CAD) field (Requicha and Rossignac, 1992). In Requicha (1980), Bak and Mill (1989), and Meier (1986), several distinct groups of 3D representation techniques that can produce unambiguous definitions have been identified:

- **Sweep representation:** The sweep technique represents an object by sweeping a defined area or volume along a defined trajectory.
- **Primitive instancing:** This represents an object by a set of predefined shapes or mathematical primitives positioned in space without intersection.
- **Constructive Solid Geometry:** This technique represents an object by combining primitive shapes using Boolean operators (union, intersection, difference).
- **Boundary representation:** This technique defines an object by its bounding surface. This can be easily represented as a set of coordinates and their connectivity, usually triangular or quadrilateral meshes (Mallet, 1988, 1989).
- **Spatial occupancy enumeration:** This represents an object by the union of a set of cells where each cell is a primitive, simple shape that can be regular or irregular. Cells are adjacent, connected, and do not intersect.
- **Cell decomposition:** This method is related to the voxel approach but is much more general; in fact, cells of any shape and size can be considered.

While the first three are oriented more toward building models from predefined parts, the last three schemes listed, namely boundary representations, spatial occupancy enumeration, and cell decomposition, are clearly relevant to geoscientific modeling (Jones, 1989).

These representations implicitly define a set of techniques to create 3D models. Figure 3.1 shows a typology of the representations commonly used in the geosciences;

the suitability of one or another of these depends on the characteristics of the data set, the operations that it is desirable to carry out, and the specific form of spatial indexing employed. Only the latter three will be profiled here to illustrate the scientific principles on which they are based.

3.5.1 BOUNDARY REPRESENTATIONS

In this method, a solid is defined in terms of the geometry of its bounding surface, typically defined by polygonal facets, edges, and vertices. While the most common polygons used are triangles and squares (Tsai and Vonderohe, 1991), in the case of sculptured (free-form) surfaces, spline functions can also be used. Advantages of using such a representation are that they provide an exact spatial representation of known observations and are also well adapted to display with modern graphic libraries that can plot directly the polygonal faces of the model. Shortcomings of this representation, when compared to cell models, lie in the difficulties they present when performing set operations or carrying out spatial searches.

Boundary representations can be integrated with octree data structures that facilitate efficient spatial addressing and improve the performance of the set operations.

Several commercial packages support boundary representations using different techniques, including EarthVision, GoCAD, and Lynx.

3.5.1.1 Boundary Representations Using Iso-Surfaces

A fundamental concept required when modeling the surface S of an object for which there are multiple z values for a given pair (x, y) is the concept of an **iso-value surface** of a function $\xi(x, y, z)$. Iso-surfaces were proposed as a method of 3D modeling by Paradis and Belcher (1990) for a system now called EarthVision. This method is also widely used to model "sampling limited" geological objects in EarthVision, such as salt structures, overfolds, and channels. EarthVision works by first incorporating a multivalued surface into the geospatial model by representing this surface as a three-dimensional grid. Normally, an arbitrary property is assigned to the data points in order to represent the surface with a zero value, which indicates the interface between the surface and the rest of the model. When the grid is calculated, the three-dimensional contour, or iso-shell, of the zero line represents the boundary surface. In order to guide the three-dimensional gridding process, control points to indicate the *inside* and *outside* of the surface need to be added to the data set. These control points have negative values on the inside and positive values on the outside.

This technique works well for relatively smooth surfaces and has been used successfully to model not only salt (Kolarsky, 1996; Lattuada et al., 1997) but also complex overturned folds and thrusts (Hoffman and White, 1996; Mayoraz et al; 1992). However, there are some major limitations to this process. The iso-surface geometry exists because of an objective variation in a property, but when the property value is just an artifact of the interpolation process, the outcome is prone to uncontrollable variations. This can be summarized with the following statement: property data interpolation is a poor tool for geometric reconstruction of sampling limited objects. While defining property values for the surface interface is an easy task and is usually given as input, the process of adding control points to define the inside and outside is often an iterative one. The more complex the shape, the more closely control points need to follow the surface; for a large three-dimensional shape, adding control points can be difficult.

While this method gives interesting graphic results, it has two main drawbacks: it is very time consuming and does not create any direct link between the shape of the surface S and the function $\xi(x, y, z)$. In particular, it is difficult to:

- Modify the surface interactively; While it is possible to change a point, it is then necessary to re-compute the whole 3D grid to be able to see the change in the surface
- Compute intersections of surfaces (for example, intersect a layer with a salt dome)
- Use the surface with seismic or reservoir simulation tools

3.5.1.2 Boundary Representations Using Discrete Smooth Interpolation

Discrete Smooth Interpolation (DSI), the modeling engine behind the GoCAD software, is a new interpolation method specially adapted to model complex 3D geological surfaces, such as salt domes and lenses, that can also handle discontinuities in the surface of the kind required to model normal or reverse faults (Mallet, 1992).

The main characteristics of the DSI method are the following:

- The use of triangulated surfaces (in 2D) with a set of control nodes (whose position is known) and a set of free nodes whose position is calculated according to a minimum roughness function. These surfaces are then embedded in three-dimensional space by the use of control nodes and the global optimization method defined.
- The choice of the mesh is free; any automatic algorithm can be used to build it, even if triangular elements are recommended. The mesh can also be locally adjusted at a later stage.
- The surface can be manipulated in real time by the user.
- It is a global method and does not generate any numerical discontinuities, yet it can handle constraints.
- Linear constraints corresponding to fuzzy information can be accounted for; this is very important in geology where the problem is not to produce nice surfaces but to fit a set of precise and imprecise data.
- It is flexible and can handle a variety of constraints.
- It generates smooth, nice-looking results.
- It is very efficient if few nodes are used but becomes very slow or impractical with more that 10^3 nodes.
- It is a deterministic method, but it may still have an associated error related to the degree of confidence on which the model is built.

While for some applications geologic structures can satisfactorily be described by boundary surfaces, they are in fact true three-dimensional bodies that should, whenever possible, be modeled using full 3D techniques capable of modeling the inside of the structure besides its boundary. In a similar way, a reverse fault that belongs to some 3D layer is not a zero-dimensional surface but a layer with a well-defined depth. To model precisely these types of features and to be able to derive useful information, we will have to resort ultimately to a full 3D model, and despite its usefulness, the DSI method is still a hybrid 2D/3D method.

In general, 3D geoscientific models are based on precise (though not necessarily accurate) representations, rather than fuzzy ones, due to the difficulty of visualizing fuzzy 3D models. A series of models reflecting different estimates is usually constructed, although some fuzziness can be displayed by the use of transparency to blur the edges of the objects. GoCAD has some powerful functionalities developed to handle this type of data. In Mallet (1989), a method is given to incorporate data fuzziness into a model definition. This is probably one of the most interesting features of the DSI method.

3.5.1.3 Boundary Representations Using 3D Component Modeling

In the Lynx system (Houlding, 1994), the ability to define and represent irregular, realistic, geological, and mining shapes with precision has been met by the capabilities of the 3D component modeling technology (Houlding, 1987; Houlding. and Stoakes, 1989). The key features that distinguish this technology from traditional modeling methods are the following:

- The ease and precision with which complex irregular shapes are defined and represented in a computerized geoscientific environment; this is achieved by means of a geometric characterization of shapes based on analytical geometry and solids of integration theory
- The precision with which the enclosed volumes of complex irregular shapes, and the volumes of intersection of two or more shapes, are determined; this is achieved by means of an analytical procedure based on the geometry of intersection of any plane with an irregular shape, and volumetric integration

Within 3D component modeling, the complex irregular shapes of realistic geoscientific units are modeled by sets of one or more solid **components** or modeling elements. The shape of a component is controlled by mid-Plane, fore-plane, and back-plane boundaries, which are defined interactively, and by the links between boundary points on different planes, also defined interactively (Houlding et al., 1991). The volume of a component is that enclosed by the implied polygonal facets formed by the boundaries and links of the component.

The user as appropriate to the application dictates the size and shape of a component and the level of detail incorporated within it. Contiguous components are linked in sets to form modeling "units." A unit can represent, for example, a geologic zone or feature (Houlding, 1989).

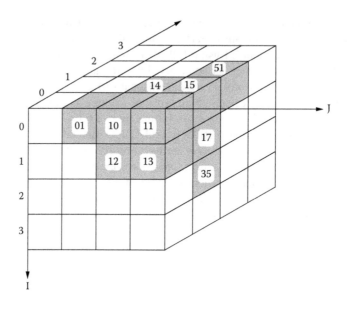

FIGURE 3.8 Spatial occupancy representation.

3.5.2 SPATIAL OCCUPANCY ENUMERATION

Spatial occupancy enumeration represents space as an array of adjacent cells called "voxels," whose cells are occupied by the object to be represented. Typically these data structures are stored as a one-dimensional array of elements, each of which is defined by the *x, y, and z* coordinates of the voxel centroid. Each element can then store a set of attributes, or a Boolean value, to indicate whether it is totally inside, partially inside, or totally outside the object. The interior volume is the union of the cells that are totally inside the body. The boundaries of the object are approximated by staircase boundaries of the cells (Figure 3.8 and Figure 3.9).

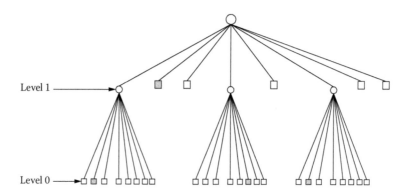

FIGURE 3.9 Octree for object in Figure 3.8.

This representation, also referred to as "volumetric modeling" or "regular tessellation" (Frank and Buyong, 1989), has two distinct advantages:

- Space is uniquely defined.
- Cells are spatially indexed — implicitly, if we use regular grids (cubic), or explicitly, for irregular grids (tetrahedral). This means that each cell is easily addressable, thus allowing efficient spatial searching.

The popularity of spatial enumeration (or volume representation) in its two most common versions, the **cuberille** and the **octree**, lies with the advances of current technology and the improvements in terms of cost of memory and parallel processors. Because in a volume representation the entire object is explicitly stored using the location and size of its main components, large amounts of storage memory are usually required. Since most of the time different parts of an object can be processed independently of one another, parallelism can be used very effectively.

Octrees (Gargantini, 1992) (Figure 3.8) are often used for encoding three-dimensional objects because they enable large object blobs to be represented, addressed, and processed with the same space and time complexities as those of a single volume element or *voxel*. The octree is a rooted, directed graph generated by recursive subdivision of an initial $2^N \times 2^N \times 2^N$ (n > 0) raster (Figure 3.9) into nodes or octants. If all voxels forming a node have the same attribute, that node becomes a leaf with that attribute, and recursive subdivision is stopped for that node. Otherwise, the octant is subdivided into eight suboctants, and the process repeated, at most, N times. Normally, two attributes are considered, "black" or "full," for nodes that belong to the object, and "white" or "empty," for those that do not. **Linear octrees** (Prissang, 1991) (Figure 3.9) are a compressed form of the octrees in which only those leaves that belong to the object are stored ("black" nodes). Each node is labeled with a location code representing the path from the root to the leaf and an integer representing the level in the tree where the node is stored. For the object in Figure 3.8 and the octree in Figure 3.9, the corresponding linear octree is as follows (note: the digits to the left of the comma represent the path from the root to the leaf node, and the digit to the right the level where the node is):

$$<(01,0), \quad (1,1), \quad (35,0), \quad (51,0)>$$

The domain of this representation technique is, theoretically, infinite. However, memory requirements, which increase with an increase in domain, dictate the maximum number of cells that can be stored. For complex and large domains, unlimited resolution of detail cannot be achieved; the representation we have is, therefore, an approximation of the object.

Octrees are of particular interest in several respects:

- They can provide a compressed version of voxel models.
- They can be used to perform Boolean set operations between 3D objects in a very efficient manner.
- They provide the basis of a 3D spatial addressing scheme for creating spatial indexes in geoscientific databases.

Octrees can also be used to represent the boundary of an object by recursively dividing the space at the edge of the modeled object; this has the disadvantage of only approximating the surface with small cubes (Houlding, 1989). If we want to improve on the boundary approximation, poly-trees (Carlbom et al., 1985) can be used, allowing more complex geometries to be represented within a node, resulting in a more accurate representation of surfaces.

3.5.3 CELL DECOMPOSITION

This method is closely related to the voxel approach, but in this case cells of any shape and size can be considered (Requicha, 1980). Given an object defined by a set of vertices on its surface, a possible cell decomposition would be to subdivide it using an irregular tessellation of tetrahedral elements (Boissonnat, 1984). **Irregular tessellations** are based on the concept of irregular subdivision of space; the cells are defined by algebraic topology and are defined as the simplest polyhedron of a given dimension. This irregular decomposition approach can be compared to the regular volumetric decomposition technique employed in octrees, where variable-sized cubes are used to map the spatial extent of an object.

For both regular and irregular tessellations, resolution contributes enormously to the cost of storing and processing data. Representing data of low precision with high resolution is wasteful; data structures should be adaptable to the degree of precision of the data set. Quadtree-like data structures like the N-tree have a natural concept of resolution built in, which can be exploited to represent data with the resolution needed.

3.6 REQUIREMENTS FOR A COMMON 3D GIS/AEC DATA MODELING SOLUTION

In the previous sections, we see how a unified data modeling solution must be functional not only in the aspect of modeling, but also in analysis and visualization. In detail, the most important requirements are the following:

- Integration of spatial and nonspatial objects
- Maintenance of spatial relationships (implicit or calculated topology)
- Fast search and application of spatial, statistical, mathematical, and geometrical functions
- Efficient storage and data handling
- Ability to operate on object composites, join several objects of similar types, apply spatial set operations
- Ability to create and derive different representations for the same conceptual model
- Support for object generalization techniques
- Handling of geometrical and numerical constraints

In particular, a comprehensive handling of geometrical constraints is crucial when we want to merge objects that originated in different systems. A robust procedure to integrate simple geometrical objects (points, edges, facets) into an existing model is needed to effectively merge different models together and ensure that the original characteristics of the different objects are maintained in the final model.

3.7 INADEQUACIES OF CAD SYSTEMS FOR GEO-SCIENTIFIC MODELING

In CAD-oriented systems, the main target is to design objects using geometric primitives to design, evaluate, edit, and construct. Classical CAD methods are used to interactively design curves and surfaces. In 3D GIS systems, on the other hand, objects are often invisible to the human observer and yet still need to be modeled. In this regard, the main goal is to establish, delimit, and characterize them. Because the goals of 3D GIS systems are so different from those of CAD systems, typical CAD tools are often inadequate for 3D geoscientific modeling. Although Bezier and spline functions can generate smooth abstract surfaces, it is much more difficult, if not impossible, to use them to fit complex data, which is the main goal in geoscientific modeling. This difference should not, however, be taken too far, as there is a lot in common between the two approaches. For example, many tasks for engineering geologists require intersecting revealed objects with designed ones (Saksa, 1995).

Following is an attempt to list which are the difficulties we might expect to face when creating geoscientific models, as this can illustrate the differences between a 3D CAD and a 3D geoscientific approach to modeling:

- Normally only incomplete, and sometimes conflicting, information is available concerning the dimensions, geometries, and variabilities of the rock units.
- The natural subsurface environment is characterized by extremely complex spatial relationships.
- Economics prevents the sufficiently dense sampling required to resolve all uncertainties.
- The relationships between rock property values and the volume of rock over which they are being averaged (scale effect) are usually unknown.
- Sample data are usually sparse, random, inadequate, but mostly detailed.
- Complex spatial relationships need to be determined and simulated to place the data in context and truly create a model.
- It is difficult to hold and display information about the internal composition of the geoscientific objects and not just their boundary surfaces.
- It is critical to allow the reconstruction of the model to satisfy different data models.
- The data are heterogeneous; possible sources include well data, dip meter data, seismic data, geological data, temperature probes, and weather balloons.
- Data are more or less reliable (for example, well data is considered more reliable than seismic cross sections).

A classic example of such difficulties is three-dimensional seismic data. Seismic methods are commonly used to locate and map features as anticlines, faults, salt domes, and reefs; it is very important to be able to model accurately many of these features since they are usually associated with the accumulation of oil and gas. Using the seismic reflection method, for example, the structure of subsurface formations is mapped by measuring the time required for a seismic wave (or pulse), generated in the earth by a near-surface explosion of dynamite, mechanical impact, or vibration, to return to the surface after reflection from interfaces between formations having different physical properties. The reflections are recorded by detecting instruments responsive to ground motion; variations in the reflection times from place to place on the surface usually indicate structural features in the strata below. The way these instruments are laid along the ground and the distances from the shot point determine the density and the pattern of the final data set used to reconstruct the formation.

While abundant 3D seismic information has been acquired from salt provinces over the past two decades, these data have, until recently, only been interpreted using two-dimensional analysis. Only the most recent three-dimensional computer visualization (Guglielmo et al., 1997) can exploit the full potential of these data by displaying even highly irregular geological structures such as convoluted salt contacts, strata disrupted by salt tectonics, and discontinuous faults. Salt deforms into irregular, convoluted shapes that can be difficult to represent by computer-generated surfaces generated through CAD-oriented methods. This is the reason why the most successful three-dimensional analysis methods have been developed ad hoc for these kinds of problems and are based on 3D interpolated grids or triangulations.

3.8 EXTENDING 2D GIS SYSTEMS TO THREE DIMENSIONS

Most commercial GIS systems available today (ESRI 3D Analyst, Imagine Virtual GIS, Intergraph's GeoMedia Terrain, and PciGeomatics Topographer) claim 3D GIS capabilities, but considering none of these systems is built on an actual 3D modeling engine, the real extent of 3D support in these systems needs to be critically evaluated. All the systems mentioned above provide little or no support of 3D functionality in terms of 3D modeling, 3D data manipulation, and analysis; most of them handle (very efficiently) the 3D data visualization aspect even if the three-dimensional display and real-time navigation is, in fact, only supported for 2.5D data (Zlatanova et al., 2001). Oracle Spatial, one of the few database products that supports spatial objects as native data types, has virtually no support for 3D spatial entities and no 3D spatial queries nor operators.

Apart from the traditional GIS vendors, some other companies have recently provided GIS modules in their products. For example, the Imagine system, originally developed by ERDAS for remote sensing applications now has a GIS module (Imagine Virtual GIS). This module enables 3D analysis to be carried out together with visualization. Unfortunately, the analysis features themselves are based mainly on visualization instead of object and data evaluation. These solutions suffer from the same limitations of traditional GIS systems, the lack of a fully featured 3D data modeling engine.

Some companies have solved the 3D support (or lack thereof) problem by linking the 2D GIS system to other products that support native 3D data types and functionalities. These "extensions" are often specific to vertical markets, in terms of both the modeling capabilities and operations allowed on 3D data.

A good example of such a solution is the Encom Discover 3D add-on module for MapInfo, an integrated 3D GIS solution for the resource sector mainly targeted at mining and oil exploration applications. The level of integration is still rudimental and lacking the features of systems designed as true 3D GIS, but nevertheless it offers a valid solution to a range of 3D geoscientific problems. The effectiveness of an integrated 2D-3D GIS solution can be measured by the ease of use of 2D and 3D GIS objects when moving between the two systems. Despite the fact that most objects must be imported or exported from one system to the other, various types of gridded objects are natively supported in both packages. This allows 2D grids and raster models to be converted to 3D solids where appropriate (e.g., in the case of cross sections). Major limitations are that 2D vector data can only be visualized in Discover and the only way to export data from Discover to Mapinfo is via views (images) that can be used in presentations.

3.9 THE EXTENDED SIMPLEX MODEL (ESM)

The simplex model utilized as part of the proposed solution evolves from the 3D FDS and TEN models as described in Zlatanova (2001) and Zlatanova et al. (1996). The basic geometric entities or constructive objects are n-dimensional simplices: point, edge, triangle, and tetrahedron. Different from previous work, besides the basic constructive objects, the system is completed with the following:

- An efficient storage structure based on octrees (Figure 3.10)
- A method to build a triangulated model (Delaunay triangulation) from a set of points (0-dimensional simplices)
- Procedures to generate constrained triangulations incorporating one- and two-dimensional simplices (edges and triangles) (Figure 3.11 and Figure 3.12)
- Fast searching routines with bounded "neighborhood" searches
- Minimal storage requirements achieved by separating the geometric information from the triangulation-derived explicit topology information (Figure 3.13)
- Support for both boundary representations, achieved using triangulated surfaces in 3D, and spatial occupancy representations through the use of tetrahedra as volume elements

The triangulation process generates explicit topological information that describes in full the relationship between the tetrahedral elements in the model (Figure 3.13); other relationships (i.e., point on face, edge on face, etc.) are not stored or maintained but can easily be calculated when needed. This approach differs significantly from the one used in most CAD/CAM-oriented systems, which store all geometrical relationships between objects (points, lines, edges, faces, surface, etc.) using a complex object model (i.e., ACIS). While the latter is a good choice for CAD/CAM systems in the

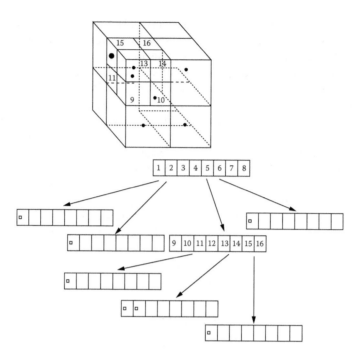

FIGURE 3.10 Octree data structure for point objects.

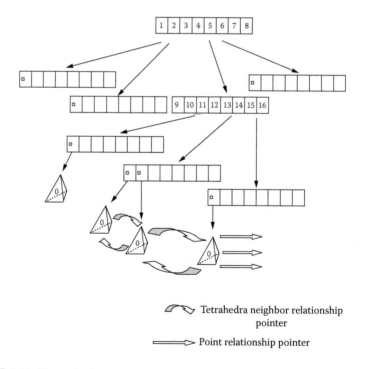

FIGURE 3.11 3D tetrahedral model with 2-dimensional surface constraints.

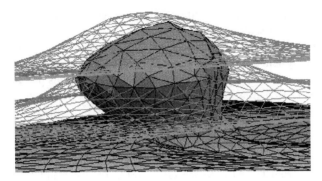

FIGURE 3.12 (See color insert after page 86.) 3- and 2-dimensional triangulations coexist in the same model.

simplex model, a different approach has been used in order to streamline the space requirements and reduce the complexity of the data structure and data management.

3.10 A SOLUTION FOR INTEGRATED AEC/GIS MODELING

Current AEC and GIS tools have developed through the years to satisfy the modeling requirements of each respective field. It would be difficult for a new system to offer the same level of functionalities across all the domains.

The main idea behind the proposed solution for an integrated representation is that we only need to integrate AEC and GIS where and when the two worlds actually meet. Direct consequences of this are that, for example, only the parts that overlap need to be brought into a unified model, and some objects or parts may not be relevant at a certain scale or have a negligible influence in a simulation. A simplified or lower resolution version of the object (i.e., a triangulated surface mesh) can often be used in place of the full version. The use of models at different resolution is a technique already widely used in CAD during the parts assembly phase: parts from different systems are brought together at a lower level of detail for integration and

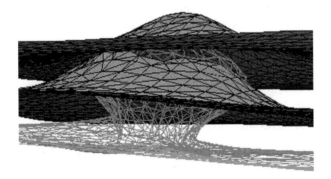

FIGURE 3.13 (See color insert after page 86.) Octree data structure for tetrahedral objects.

testing, but if changes and more editing are required, this is done in the original system using the full-scale model.

For example, if we need to develop an industrial heater, we would probably use a modern CAD system that can describe the geometry of all its parts and its assembly up to the smallest level of detail. When we need to integrate this part into the project of a building (AEC), lots of the details can be safely removed, most likely a representation of the boundary (skin) of the heater is more than enough. Besides, the boundary representation itself can be simplified; for example, converting curved surfaces into triangular flat polygons (triangular mesh). The concept of model decimation and reduction can be widely applied. When we move from the CAD to the AEC world or from the AEC to the GIS world, we can adapt the model to the specifications and scale of the hosting system. This conversion step may involve: removal of detail, removal of hidden parts, and simplification of the geometry.

An approach like this would favor a solution that can easily manipulate and integrate boundary descriptions from a diverse system. As most systems are capable of generating a triangulated boundary mesh of a model, triangular meshes could be used as the optimal exchange data model.

3.11   CRITICAL ANALYSIS OF THE EXTENDED SIMPLEX MODEL

The Extended Simplex Model (ESM) satisfies most of the requirements for an integrated modeling framework where CAD, AEC, and GIS models can be brought together, as:

- It provides an integrated spatial addressing schema (through the use of an octree-like data structure) and an homogenous construction approach for the geometry of surfaces and volumes in three dimensions
- It can handle large models and diverse input data
- It offers a minimal space partitioning solution and fast generation of 3D subdivision of space
- It has the ability to create efficient representations for display purposes (VRML, triangular meshes)
- It offers fast object access and data structure traversal
- Point level editing can be performed on the merged model without a recursive import/export to the original modeling package
- Boundaries and constraints can be easily integrated into a model
- The model generation and constraints recovery processes are automatic
- The simplex model could be easily adopted by the OGC (Open GIS Consortium) by extending the simple-features schema (OGC, 1999)

3.12   CONCLUSIONS

As illustrated in the introduction to this chapter, we have so far reviewed current state-of-the-art solutions in 3D modeling, highlighted the main research problems for the integration of 3D GIS and AEC, and, finally, proposed a modeling infrastructure that can provide a valid solution to the integration problem.

While there is great activity aimed at providing better and more efficient tools that can effectively model three-dimensional problems regardless of their classification as typical GIS, CAD, or AEC, the observations in Section 3.6 and Section 3.7, as well as the characteristics of the proposed solution (Sections 3.8 and Section 3.9), seem to indicate that solutions based on a real 3D modeling engine are better positioned to answer the questions of the GIS and AEC worlds combined.

Future developments of this work include the critical review of what support for data analysis and simulation is required for an integrated 3D GIS/AEC system and what level of support for data analysis is available today in commercial GIS or AEC systems.

REFERENCES

Bak, P.R.G. and Mill, A.J.B, Three dimensional representation in a geoscientific resource management system for the minerals industry, in *GIS, Three Dimensional Applications in Geographic Information Systems,* Raper, J., Ed., Taylor & Francis, London, 1989.

Batten, L., National capital urban planning project: development of a 3-D GIS, in *Proceedings of GIS/LIS'89 ACSM/ASPRS*, Falls Church, VA, 1989, 781–786.

Boissonnat, J.D., Geometric structures for three-dimensional shape representation, *ACM Transactions on Graphics*, No. 3, 266, 1984.

Buchele, S. and Crawford, R., Three-Dimensional Halfspace Constructive Solid Geometry Tree Construction from Implicit Boundary Representations, *SM'03*, Seattle, WA, June 2003.

Burrough, P.A., *Principles of Geographical Information Systems for Land Resources Assessment, Monographs on Soil and Resources Survey, No. 12,* Oxford University Press, Oxford, UK, 1986.

Carlbom, I., Chakravarty, I., and Vanderschel, D., A hierarchical data structure for representing the spatial decomposition of 3D objects, *IEEE Computer Graphics and Applications*, No. 5, 24–31. 1985.

Curry, S., Autodesk Infrastructure Solutions. CAD and GIS Critical Tools, Critical Links, White Paper, May 2003.

Curry, S., Autodesk Infrastructure Solutions. Destroying Seven Myths of Autodesk GIS, White Paper, May 2003.

ESRI, Using CAD in ArcGIS, An ESRI Technical Paper, June 2003.

ESRI, Creating Compatible CAD Data for ArcGIS Software, An ESRI Technical Paper, October 2003.

Fisher, T. and Wales, R., Three dimensional solid modelling of geo-objects using NURBS, in *Three-Dimensional Modeling with Geoscientific Information Systems,* K.A. Turner, Ed., Dept. of Geology and Geological Engineering, Colorado School of Mines, Golden, CO, Kluwer Academic Publishers, Series C, Vol. 356 of the NATO ASI Series, 1989.

Foley and Van Dam, Solid Modelling.

Frank, A. and Buyong, T., Geometry for Three-Dimensional GIS in Geo-scientific Applications, in *Three-Dimensional Modeling with Geoscientific Information Systems,* K.A. Turner, Ed., Dept. of Geology and Geological Engineering, Colorado School of Mines, Golden, CO, Kluwer Academic Publishers, Series C, Vol. 356 of the NATO ASI Series, 1989.

Gargantini, I., Modelling Natural Objects via Octrees, in *Three-Dimensional Modeling with Geoscientific Information Systems,* K.A. Turner, Ed., Dept. of Geology and Geological Engineering, Colorado School of Mines, Golden, CO, Kluwer Academic Publishers, Series C, Vol. 356 of the NATO ASI Series, 1989, 145–157.

GeoEurope, Geofocus: CAD/GIS. Which way to CAD/GIS integration? 2002.

Guglielmo, G., Jackson, M.P.A., and Vendeville, B.C., Three-Dimensional Visualization of Salt Walls and Associated Fault Systems, *The American Association of Petroleum Geologists Bulletin,* 81 (1), 46–6, 1997.

Gy, P., *Sampling of Particulate Materials,* Elsevier Scientific Publishing Company, Amsterdam, 1989.

Harbaugh, J.W. and Merriam, D.F., *Computer Applications in Stratigraphic Analysis,* John Wiley & Sons, New York, 1968.

Hoffman, K.S. and White, P.L., Computer mapping of overthrust structures using a three-dimensional technique, *66th Annual International Meeting of the Society of Exploration Geophysicists,* 1996.

Houlding, S.W., 3D Computer Modelling of Geology and Mine Geometry, Mining Magazine, 226–231, March 1987.

Houlding, S.W., The Application of new 3-D computer modelling techniques to mining, in *Three-Dimensional Modeling with Geoscientific Information Systems,* K.A. Turner, Ed., Dept. of Geology and Geological Engineering, Colorado School of Mines, Golden, CO, Kluwer Academic Publishers, Series C, Vol. 356 of the NATO ASI Series, 1989.

Houlding, S.W., *3D Geoscience Modelling — Computer Techniques for Geological Characterization,* Springer Verlag, Berlin, 1994.

Houlding, S.W. and Stoakes, M.A., Mine Activity and Resources Scheduling Using 3D Component Modelling, in *Transactions of the Institute of Mining and Metallurgy Conference on Computer-Aided Mine Planning and Design,* UK, 1989, A53–A59.

Houlding, S.W., Stoakes, M., and Clark, I., Direct Geostatistical Estimation of Irregular 3D Volumes, in *Computer Graphics in Geology,* R. Pflug and J. Harbaugh, Eds., Springer-Verlag, 1991.

Jachens, R.C., 3D Geologic Map of the San Francisco Bay Area for Seismic Hazard Mitigation, United States Geologic Survey, Menlo Park, CA, May 1999.

Jones, C., Data structures for three-dimensional spatial information systems in geology, *Int. J. Geographical Information Systems,* 3 (1), 15–31, 1989.

Kelk, B. and Challen, K., Experiments with a CAD package for spatial modelling of geoscientific data, *From Digital Map Series in Geosciences to Geo-Information Systems,* R. Vinken, Ed., Geologisches Jahrbuch, Reidhe A., Heft 122, Hanover, 1992, 145–153.

King H.F., McMahon, D.W., and Bujtor, G.J. A guide to the understanding of ore reserve estimation, *Supplement to Proceedings No 281 of the Australasian Institution of Mining and Metallurgy,* Victoria, Australia, 1982.

Kolarsky, R.A., 3-D geospatial modelling and visualization of a salt diaphir based on well control and 3-D salt proximity survey data: an example from Cote Blanche Island Field, Southern Louisiana: Society of Exploration Geophysicists annual meeting, 1996.

Krige, D.G., A review of the development of geostatistics in South Africa, in *Advanced Geo-Statistics in the Mining Industry,* Guarascio, M., David, M., and Huijbregts, C., Eds., Reidel, Dordrect, The Netherlands, 1976, 279–293.

Lattuada, R., Modelling of Salt Domes from Unorganised Sets of Points, Technical Report, Dynamic Graphics Inc., Alameda, CA, September 1996.

Lattuada, R., Building a very large image database using Oracle and the geo-image component, *International Workshop on Integrated Spatial Databases: Digital Images and GIS*, ISD'99, Portland, ME, 14–16 June 1999.

Lattuada, R. and Raper, J., Applications of 3D Delaunay triangulation algorithms in geoscientific modelling, in *Proceedings of the Third International Conference on Integrating GIS and Environmental Modelling*, Santa Fe, NM, January 1996.

Lattuada, R. and Raper, J., Modelling of salt domes from scattered non-regular point sets, XXII General Assembly of the European Geophysical Society, Vienna, Austria, April 1997 (published in the special issue of *Physics and Chemistry of the Earth*) 1997.

Lattuada, R., Hoffman, K.S., and Neave, J.W., Three-dimensional structural modelling of multi-valued salt masses, *67th Society of Exploration Geophysicists International Exposition and Annual Meeting*, Dallas, TX, 2–7 November 1997.

Lyle, D., GIS in exploration, *Oil and Gas World,* June 1999.

Lorensen, W.E., and Cline, H.E., Marching cubes: a high resolution 3D surface construction algorithm, *Computer Graphics,* 21 (4), 1987.

Loudon, T.V., Digital spatial models and geological maps, in *Proceedings of Auto-Carto London*, 14–19 September 1986, Vol. 2, Blakemore, M., Ed., International Cartographic Association, London, available from the Royal Institution of Chartered Surveyors, 1986, 60–66.

Mallet, J., Three-dimensional graphic display of disconnected bodies, *Mathematical Geology,* 10 (8), 977–990, 1988.

Mallet, J., GoCAD: a computer aided design program for geological applications, in *Three-Dimensional Modeling with Geoscientific Information Systems,* K.A. Turner, Ed., Dept. of Geology and Geological Engineering, Colorado School of Mines, Golden, CO, Kluwer Academic Publishers, Series C, Vol. 356 of the NATO ASI Series, 1989.

Mallet, J., Discrete smooth interpolation in geometric modelling, *Computer Aided Design,* 24 (4), 1992.

Mann, C. and Daugherty, K., Bentley/ESRI AEC-GIS Interoperability, White Paper, Bentley Systems, ESRI, March 2003.

Mayoraz, R., Mann, C.E., and Parriaux, A., Three-dimensional modelling of complex geological structures: new development tools for creating 3-D volumes, in *Computer Modelling of Geologic Surfaces and Volumes: AAPG Computer Applications in Geology, No. 1,* Hamilton, D.E. and Jaro, T.A., Eds., 1992, 261–271.

Matheron, G., Principles of geo-statistics, *Economic Geology,* 58, 1246–1266, 1963.

Meier, A., Applying relational database techniques to solid modelling, *Computer Aided Design,* 18, 319–326, 1986.

Muller, J.P., *Digital Image Processing in Remote Sensing,* Muller, J.P., Ed., Taylor & Francis, London, 1988.

OGC, OpenGIS Simple Features Specification for SQL Rev 1.1, Open GIS Consortium Project Document, 99-049, May 1999.

OGC, Data Models and Interoperability, An Open GIS Consortium White Paper, February 2004.

Paradis, A. and Belcher, R., Interactive volume modelling — a new product for 3-D modelling, *Geobyte,* 5 (1), 42–44, 1990.

Prissang, R., Three-dimensional predictive deposit modelling based on the linear octree data structure, in Pflug and Harbaugh, 1991.

Raper, J., Ed., *Three Dimensional Applications in Geographical Information Systems,* Taylor & Francis, London, 1989.

Raper, J., The 3-dimensional geo-scientific mapping and modelling system: a conceptual design, in Raper, 1989, 1989a.

Raper, J., Key 3D modelling concepts for geo-scientific analysis, in Turner, 1989, 1989b.

Requicha, A., Representations for Rigid Solids: Theory, Methods, and Systems, ACM Computing Surveys, No. 12, 1980, 437–464.

Requicha, A. and Rossignac, J., Solid Modelling and Beyond, *IEEE Computer Graphics and Applications,* September 1992.

Sacchi, C., An object-oriented approach to spatial databases, University of Milan Electronics Department, Report No. 92-034, May 1992.

Saksa, P., Rock-CAD, Computer Aided Geological Modelling System, Report YJT-95-18, Nuclear Waste Commission of Finnish Power Companies, December 1995.

Sarkozy, F., Designing an integrated 2.5 and 3 dimensional information system for geo-scientific and engineering purposes, in *Proceedings FIG XIX Congress,* Helsinki, 1990, 6, 131–145, 1990.

Sarkozy, F., The GIS concept and the three-dimensional modelling, *Computers Environment and Urban Systems,* 18 (2), 111–121, 1994.

Schroeder, W., Zarge, J., and Lorensen, W., Decimation of triangle meshes, *Computer Graphics,* 26 (2), 65–70, 1992.

Schutzberg, A., CAD/GIS integration modern technology merges the best of both worlds, *GeoWorld,* 2002.

Sides, E.J., Reconciliation studies and reserve estimation, in *Case Histories and Methods in Mineral Resource Evaluation*, Annels, A.E., Ed., Geological Society Special Publication, No. 63, 1992, 197–218.

Tipper, J.C., Three-dimensional analysis of geological forms, *J. of Geol.,* 85, 591, 1977.

Tipper, J.C., Computerized modelling for shape analysis in geology, In *Recent Advances in Geomathematics, An International Symposium,* Merriam, D.F., Ed., Pergamon Press, Oxford, 1978, 157–170.

Tsai, V. and Vonderohe, A.P., A generalised algorithm for the construction of Delaunay triangulations in Euclidean n-space, Dept. of Civil Environmental Engineering, University of Wisconsin, Madison, GIS/LIS, 1991.

Vieira, A., Sousa, L.R., and Barreto, J., Numerical investigation for the analysis of a large underground station of Lisbon metro, *Int. Conference on Soil Structure Interaction in Civil Engineering*, Darmstadt, Germany, 1999.

Zlatanova, S. and Verbree, E., A 3D topological model for augmented reality, in *Proceedings of the Second International Symposium on Mobile Multimedia Systems & Applications,* 9–10 November, Delft, The Netherlands, 2000, 19–26.

Zlatanova, S., Pilouk, M., and Templfi, K., Building reconstruction from aerial images and creation of 3D topologic data structure, in *Proceedings of the IAPR TC-7,* 2–3 September, Graz, Austria, 1996, 259–275.

Zlatanova, S., Rahman, A.A., and Pilouk, M., 3D GIS: current status and perspectives, in *Proceedings of the Joint Conference on Geo-spatial theory, Processing and Applications,* 8–12 July, Ottawa, Canada, 2001.

4 3D Geo-DBMS

Martin Breunig and Sisi Zlatanova

CONTENTS

4.1 GEO-DBMS: HISTORICAL DEVELOPMENT AND STATE OF THE ART

Historically, one can distinguish between two ways of incorporating database management system (DBMS) in GIS. The first way is that GIS vendors use DBMS mainly to store thematic (i.e., nonspatial) data. The spatial data are managed by single files only, i.e., no DBMS support is provided for spatial data. In this case, the analysis of the data takes place in the GIS, and only database queries on thematic attributes are executed by the DBMS. If data analysis concerns spatial *and* nonspatial data, the geo-objects have to be composed explicitly by their spatial and nonspatial parts. Few GIS vendors (e.g., ESRI) pursued storing both nonspatial and spatial data into DBMS. Both solutions are "top-down approaches," because, from an architectural point of view, the DBMS functionality has been constructed "under" the GIS application and the GIS application accesses "top-down" to the geodata stored in the DBMS.

The second way to integrate DBMS within GIS is DBMS offering support of our spatial data types. This solution is called the "bottom-up approach," because it extends "low level" DBMS data types and indexes to use them in the upper level of GIS applications. Data analysis is then performed by DBMS during the execution of database queries. Data analysis on the spatial *and* nonspatial parts of objects can be executed. Since the 1990s, more and more commercial DBMSs provide such spatial extensions to offer support of spatial objects.

In the field of AEC, the use of DBMS functionality is even more restrictive than in the field of GIS. As the spatial modeling features in DBMS are restricted to single points, edges, and polygons (triangles), there are no complex objects that could be stored consistently in a database. It should be noticed, however, that an increasing number of AEC systems (e.g., GeoGraphics, MicroStation) have already developed extensions that make use of spatial models and functionality provided by Geo-DBMS. We believe the significance of Geo-DBMS in both GIS and AEC worlds will continue to increase.

4.2 BENEFITS OF USING DBMS FOR GIS AND AEC APPLICATIONS

Clearly, there are a lot of reasons to use Geo-DBMSs in both GIS and CAD/AEC systems: multiuser control on shared data and crash recovery, automatic locks of single objects while using database transactions, advanced database protocol mechanisms to prevent the loss of data, data security, data integrity and operations that comfortably retrieve, insert, and update data. This section will provide an argumentation for wider utilization of geo-DBMS in GIS and AEC applications.

4.2.1 PROVIDING DBMS STANDARD FUNCTIONALITY

Most GIS and CAD system users would be concerned if there was no multiuser access possible on data during design processes. There is no question that the results of their work being constructed on shared data should be automatically stored within the database periodically. Furthermore, unpredictable events, such as power breakdown, wrong operation by the user, hardware error, etc., should not cause the loss of data. Fortunately, multiuser control and crash recovery are two of the standard functions in today's DBMSs. The user does not have to care about obtaining exclusive data access. The DBMS automatically locks single objects or tables using database transactions so that several users can access the same objects, reading or even updating them at the same time. Furthermore, advanced database protocol mechanisms prevent the loss of data by writing the data on disk beforehand.

Other useful DBMS functions concern data security and the checking of data integrity. Thus the correctness and the consistency of thematic and spatial data can be automatically checked during the input of the data and during the execution of database queries. Typical examples are the checking of the data types for input data and the checking of their domains. Finally, DBMSs offer operations for the comfortable retrieval, insertion, and update of nonspatial data. Therefore, standard relational or object-relational DBMSs are well suited to store and retrieve the values of nonspatial attributes of geo-objects.

4.2.2 EXTENDING THE DBMS TO A GEO-DBMS (2D AND 3D)

Many DBMSs have evolved to offer spatial functionality, which brings further benefits for GIS and AEC applications. The spatial functionality concerns the support of spatial data types in the data model, the implementation of spatial access methods, and the execution of spatial database queries (see Güting, 1994). Therefore, a Geo-DBMS manages both thematic *and* spatial data. Typical geo-database queries, such as "select the <u>names</u> of all buildings which are higher than 20 m and whose <u>distance</u> is smaller than 1 km from Frankfurt Airport" concern thematic *and* spatial attributes and functions of geo-objects.

Geo-DBMSs provide spatial *data types* and spatial *functions (and operations)* on them that define the *spatial functionality* of a Geo-DBMS. A Geo-DBMS knows primitive (simple) and composed geometric data types in the same way as its standard data types such as character, string, integer, real, etc. Currently, many DBMSs offer support of spatial data types, but most of them are only 2D types, i.e., point, line, and polygon. In contrast to the nonspatial data types, spatial data types have to be organized in a model (topological or geometrical), where a number of spatial rules have to be fulfilled. For example, "lines should not self-intersect," "two points on one line cannot be the same," etc. (see next section).

Following this order of thoughts, a Geo-DBMS is a 3D Geo-DBMS if it:

- Supports 3D data types, i.e., point, line, surface, and volume in 3D Euclidean space
- Maintains 3D (topological and/or geometrical) models
- Offers 3D spatial functionality, i.e., spatial operations and functions that can operate with the 3D data types

Having in mind the higher complexity of 3D objects, a 3D Geo-DBMS may need to support even different geometric and topological models needed in different GIS and AEC application classes. The primitive and composed 3D geometric data types differ between GIS and AEC applications, because the requirements of these two application fields vary from standardized geometries of buildings to complex nature-formed objects in the geosciences.

An important aspect of 3D Geo-DBMS is the amount of data to be processed. The access problem can be resolved by extending well-known spatial access methods like the R-tree (Guttman, 1984) or the R*-tree (Beckmann et al., 1990) for the third spatial dimension (z-coordinates). The procedure is the same as in the two-dimensional case: in the first step (filter or approximation step), the data set is reduced by using a spatial search function of the spatial access method computing the intersection between approximated objects — in most cases minimal circumscribing 3D-boxes of the object geometries — and a 3D query box. In the second step (refinement-step) the real geometric operation (e.g., intersection between the exact geometries of 3D objects and the 3D query box) is executed on the reduced data set. At present, Geo-DBMSs support several types of 3D spatial indexing.

3D Geo-DBMS has to offer an appropriate 3D user interface. To date, 3D user interfaces have not yet been exhaustively examined. Future 3D query interfaces should support the formulation of complex SQL-like mixed spatial and nonspatial database queries as well as 3D graphical input supporting the intuitive graphical formulation of 3D queries. Existing VRML/X3D interfaces are not flexible enough to support the manipulation and database update of 3D objects. Potential solutions are to be sought in coupling AEC software with Geo-DBMS. AEC applications offer a rich set of 3D modeling and visualization tools that can be further extended toward specifying 3D spatial (SQL) queries.

4.2.3 GEO-DBMS MODELS: GEOMETRY VS. TOPOLOGY

Geometry and topology are often used in Geo-DBMS terminology (in contrast to Open Geospatial specifications) as synonyms to denote the two ways of describing spatial data types. Geometry data types are defined by the x, y, z coordinates of the points composing a data type. Topology data types have references to the unique identifiers of low-dimensional data types.

Apparently, for some period of time, two models (topology and geometry) will be maintained in the Geo-DBMS. Although there is belief that a topological model might be sufficient (geometry can be derived from topology), in the same way, one could argue that the same is true for a geometry model, because topology can be derived from geometry. In this respect, one can choose between three different options:

- Storing the topological model in the 3D Geo-DBMS (and deriving geometry from it)
- Storing the geometric model in the 3D Geo-DBMS (and deriving topology from it)
- Storing both models in the 3D Geo-DBMS.

In approach 1, the topological relationships between object parts, such as "all surfaces belonging to the boundary of a 3D volume object" are stored in the topology model of the DBMS. The location of objects, i.e., the x, y, z coordinates of its defining points, are not part of the topology model. The advantage of this approach is that objects can quickly be identified by their topological properties, such as the Euler characteristics for triangle nets. However, geometric database queries, such as "return the intersecting geometry of two objects," cannot profit from the explicit knowledge of the objects' topology. What they need is the geometry, i.e., the "shape" of the objects given by plane equations, individual x, y, z coordinates of the vertices, etc.

Approach 2 prevents the disadvantage of approach 1; however, topological database queries cannot be answered efficiently by providing only a geometric model. As the topological relationships between single polygons (surfaces) or polyhedra (volumes) are missing, 3D spatial queries have to be completed using computational algorithms (which might become very complex and, thus, slow). For example, constructing a new triangulated irregualr network (TIN) object (geometrically computed by the intersection between two TIN objects) can profit from the neighborhood information of triangles while testing for intersecting triangles between the two TIN objects.

Approach 3 still seems to be the best solution: it allows flexible topological and geometric database queries executed efficiently by accessing the topology and geometry model in the 3D Geo-DBMS. With these two models, all relevant types of spatial database queries can be executed, including:

- Topological database queries (e.g., neighborhoods)
- Geometric database queries (e.g., spatial search inside a 3D box)

Topologically based analysis will be beneficial for consistency checks and all kinds of operations making use of neighborhood relationships. Geometric-based analyses will be necessary for constructing new objects (e.g., buffer, aggregations), to build the topology and perform metric operations (distance, area, spatial search). CAD and AEC applications, being more visualization- than analysis-oriented, will largely benefit from geometry models, which will allow fast retrieval of coordinates (having the coordinates stored with the data types). GIS applications will be ensured with consistent models (topology).

4.2.4 OBJECT-RELATIONAL VS. OBJECT-ORIENTED DBMS

There are two different database system architectures to be considered for Geo-DBMS: object-relational and object-oriented. The third possibility, i.e., XML-DBMS, does not seem to be appropriate, because most 3D geodata are well structured, containing complex geometric and topological structures. XML-DMBSs are specialized to manage semi-structured and text data instead. Both object-relational and object-oriented DBMSs allow their users to model data as objects. Of course, object-databases can export their objects also as XML-structures by using appropriate adapters.

In contrast to object-relational database management systems (ORDBMSs), an object-oriented database management system (OODBMS) does not only support objects as its data model, but it also physically stores the objects on disk. In contrast to ORDBMSs, OODBMSs are not based upon existing relational database technology. OODBMSs are newly developed DBMSs for the management of objects.

Most of today's object databases such as Oracle®, Informix®, etc., are solutions on top of relational DBMS (ORDBMS), but there are also some native OODBMS on the market, such as ObjectStore®, FastObjects®, etc.

The conceptual data modeling in object-relational and object-oriented DBMSs is the same: data are modeled as classes, which are the generalization of objects with the same or similar properties and operations. ORDBMSs are based on the well-proven technology of 30 years of relational DBMS experience. They are using sophisticated query optimization strategies based on the well-founded relational algebra. What makes the difference is the internal physical data model. ORDBMSs store their data in tables that are coupled by referential integrity, with relationships between primary and secondary keys of different tables. This change of the data model from user-defined classes to internal "flat" tables leads to the impedance mismatch, which must be paid by a performance loss during the "object" retrieval of very large data sets.

OODBMSs allow the "native" storage of objects in their data model. This is mostly done by an overriding of the new operator of object-oriented programming languages like C++ or Java. Furthermore, cluster strategies for the optimized storage of objects in one class are provided. OODBMSs are flexible and can be extended by new spatial data types and spatial indexes. However, 15 years after their birth, OODBMSs still are a research subject and the idea of having standardized OODBMSs (ODMG, 1993) seems to be far in the future. Unfortunately, they do not provide comfortable data modeling and I/O-tools. OODBMSs have not succeeded on the market yet, in spite of their undisputed advantages concerning the management of complex 2D and 3D geo-objects.

GIS and AEC applications are currently offering support to data types provided by object-relational DBMS. One of the reasons is, of course, that most of the mainstream Geo-DBMS are object-relational; the other is that the objects can be defined in a different way by OODBMS.

4.3 TOWARD 3D GEO-DBMS

3D Geo-DBMS has to be able to provide the necessary data types to maintain as many as possible representations, to be able to serve both GIS and ACE applications. Several possibilities will be discussed here.

4.3.1 Geometry

4.3.1.1 Simple Nature-Formed Objects

Depending on the system architecture of the DBMS (see Section 4.4), the 3D geo-objects are internally stored as tables or as objects by overriding the new operator of the object-oriented application programming interface of the Geo-DBMS.

We pick up one of the representations to model simple 3D (vector) objects demonstrating their design and implementation in Geo-DBMS. The following primitive

3D geometric data types are appropriate to be implemented in Geo-DBMSs, if *nature-formed objects* shall be modeled:

```
- type Point3D = (xᵢ:double, yᵢ:double, zᵢ:double)
with (i = 0);

- type Segment3D = (xᵢ:double, yᵢ:double,
zᵢ:double) with (0 ≤ i ≤ 1);

- type Triangle3D = (xᵢ:double, yᵢ:double, zᵢ:double)
with (0 ≤ i ≤ 2);

- type Tetrahedron3D = (xᵢ:double, yᵢ:double,
zᵢ:double) with(0 ≤ i ≤ 3).
```

We summarize the special properties of these primitive 3D geometric data types as follows:

They are defined in 3D Euclidean space and are pairwise independent, i.e., the following consistency conditions hold: the two points of a segment must not have the same coordinates, the three points of a triangle must not be on one line, and the four points of a tetrahedron must not lie on one plane.

Each primitive 3D geometric data type with dimension i (0 i 3) contains those spatial objects of dimension i with the most simple geometry in dimension i. Notice that there is a primitive 3D geometric data type — Tetrahedron3D — for the explicit modeling of volumetric objects. Thus, thematic information can be attached to single or groups of tetrahedron objects.

4.3.1.2 Complex Nature-Formed Objects

Complex nature-formed objects can be easily constructed by composing adjacent primitive objects. Thus, the following composed 3D geometric data types are appropriate:

```
- type Line3D = (xᵢ:double, yᵢ:double, zᵢ:double) with
(0 ≤ i ≤ 1);

- type Surface3D = (triᵢ:Triangle3D) with (0 ≤ i ≤ p);

- type Volume3D = (tetᵢ:Tetrahedron3D) with
(0 ≤ i ≤ s).
```

The left side of the data type definition is the abstract interface (line, surface, volume). The right side, however, gives a possible implementation that can be exchanged by other implementations. In the given example, Surface3D is implemented as a list of triangles and Volume3D as a list of tetrahedrons, respectively.

4.3.1.3 Simple Man-Made Objects

In many cases, this approach is not appropriate due to data collection procedures (e.g., many real-world objects are measured only from the outside), modeling considerations (e.g., unnecessary subdivisions), or volume of data. The problems are mostly in the 3D primitive. A simple box (e.g., representing a building) will require six tetrahedrons to model it. Furthermore, CAD software can model a spatial object very realistically with curved surfaces, but curved surfaces produce a large number of tetrahedrons. Such arguments give preference to the polyhedron option.

The data types in Geo-DBMS will then become point3D, line3D, polygon3D, and polyhedron3D. However, extending the freedom in the shape requires rules defining which shapes are allowed in the model. Examples of widely implemented rules are related to constraints on self-intersection and planarity of polygons. The polyhedron is restricted to a polyhedron composed of flat faces.

The representations of the data types then will be:

- type Point3D = (x_i:double, y_i:double, z_i:double) with ($i = 0$);

- type Line3D = (x_i:double, y_i:double, z_i:double) with ($0 \leq i \leq 1$);

- type Polygon3D = (x_i:double, y_i:double, z_i:double) with ($0 \leq i \leq p$);

- type Polyhedron3D = (x_i:double, y_i:double, z_i:double) with ($0 \leq i \leq s$).

The need of a rule for such data types is apparent. Any polygon with $i > 2$ is not planar by default. A polyhedron is defined as "a bounded subset of 3D coordinate space enclosed by a finite set of flat polygons (called faces) such that every edge of a polygon is shared by exactly one other polygon." The polyhedron should bound a single volume, i.e., from every point (can be on boundary), every other point (can be on boundary) can be reached via the interior. The characteristics of a polyhedron primitive are given in Arens et al. (2005) as:

- Flatness: The polygons that make up the polyhedron have to be flat. This means that all points that make up the polygon must be in the same plane (Figure 4.1).
- 2-Manifold: The polyhedron should bound only one volume. This means that from every point on the boundary, one should be able to reach every other point on the boundary via the interior. For the object to be valid, the faces where the hole starts and ends have to be modeled as a face with one or more inner rings.
- Simplicity: The polyhedron has to be composed of simple features, i.e., closed polygons that are not self-intersecting and have no inner rings. The faces of a polyhedron, however, are allowed to have inner rings, if the polygons together form a closed polyhedron.
- The inner rings of polygons are not allowed to interact with the outer ring, except for touching boundaries. The vertices that span a face are not allowed to lie all on a straight line, i.e., the face has to have an area. A face has exactly one outer ring, each edge has exactly two vertices. Only edges with two points are allowed. Note that two or more (but not all) edges are allowed to lie on a straight line, if this is more convenient for modeling an object.

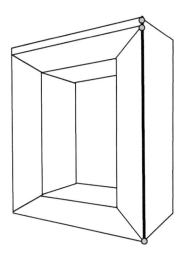

FIGURE 4.1 Two edges in a line (Arens et al., 2003).

- Orientable: The outside and inside of the polyhedron has to be specified. Basic rules in computer graphics related to the normal vector are used for orientation. This means that the vertices in a face must be specified in counter-clockwise order seen from the outside of the object. The vertices in inner rings of faces need to be ordered in the opposite direction (clockwise).

Implementation of such a data type is given in Section 4.4.2.2.

4.3.1.4 Complex Man-Made Objects

Representations with only flat polygons are usually insufficient for modeling many AEC 3D free-form curves and surfaces. Introduction of complex data types based on free-form mathematical curves and surfaces is required.

The representations of the data types will then be:

- type Point3D = (x_i:double, y_i:double, z_i:double) with (i = 0);

- type Curve3D = (x_i:double, y_i:double, z_i:double, r_{ij}: double) with ($0 \leq i \leq k$) and ($0 \leq j \leq k$);

- type Surface3D = (x_i:double, y_i:double, z_i:double, r_{ij}: double) with ($0 \leq i \leq 1$) and ($0 \leq j \leq k$);

- type Polyhedron3D = (x_i:double, y_i:double, z_i:double, r_{ij}:double) with ($0 \leq i \leq m$) and ($0 \leq j \leq k$);

where r_i is a parameter denoting a property (one or many) of a free-form shape.

NURBS can be an option for representing man-made objects. NURBS are approved as industry standards for the representation and design of geometry. Important characteristics of NURBS are listed below (Rogers and Earnshaw, 1991).

- NURBS offer a common mathematical form for both standard analytical shapes (e.g., cones, spheres) and free-form shapes.
- They provide a flexible way of designing a large variety of shapes.
- The shapes described by NURBS can be evaluated reasonably fast by numerically stable and accurate algorithms.

Important characteristics for modeling real-world objects is that they are invariant under affine as well as perspective transformations.

The general drawback of NURBS is the extra storage needed to define traditional shapes (e.g., circles). See also the discussion of NURBS in Chapter 3. NURBS shapes are defined by control points, weights associated with each control point, and knots. A NURBS curve $C(u)$, is defined as (Piegl, 1991):

$$C(u) = \frac{\sum_{i+0}^{n} \{w_i * P_i * N_{i,k}(u)\}}{\sum_{i=0}^{n} \{w_i * N_{i,k}(u)\}}$$

where

w_i: = weights
P_i = control points (vector)
$N_{i,k}$ = normalized B-spline basis functions of degree k.

These B-splines are defined recursively as:

$$N_{i,k}(u) = \frac{u - t_i}{t_{i+k} - t_i} * N_{i,k-1}(u) + \frac{t_{i+k+1} - u}{t_{i+k+1} - t_{i+1}} * N_{i+1,k-1}(u)$$

and

$$N_{i,0}(u) = 1 \text{ if } t_i <= u < t_{i+1}$$

and

$$N_{i,0}(u) = 0 \text{ else}$$

where t_i are the knot points forming a knot vector $U = \{t_0, t_1, ..., t_m\}$ (see Figure 4.2). Then the data type will be:

```
- type NURBS3D = (x_i:double, y_i:double, z_i:double,
  w_i:double, t_ij:double) with (0 ≤ i ≤ k) and
  (0 ≤ j ≤ k);
```

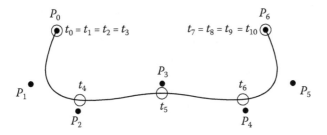

FIGURE 4.2 B-spline (courtesy of http://mathworld.wolfram.com/B-Spline.html).

NURBS surface can be defined in a similar way:

$$S(u,v) = \sum_{i=0}^{n} \sum_{j=0}^{m} P_{i,j} * R_{i,k,j,l}(u,v)$$

where

$$R_{i,k,j,l}(u,v) = \frac{w_{i,j} * N_{j,k}(u) * N_{j,l}(v)}{\sum_{r=0}^{n} \sum_{s=0}^{m} w_{r,s} * N_{r,k}(u) * N_{s,l}(u)}$$

The definition of NURBS requires a number of parameters to be included in the data type. Examples of such parameters are knots sequence, number of control points, coordinates of control points, etc. In case of surfaces, the parameter doubles.

4.3.2 TOPOLOGY

Similar to geometry data types, topology data types can be different with respect to the objects to be modeled. Discussing topological data structures, many application-related issues have to be taken into consideration, e.g., the space partitioning (full, embedding), the object components (volumes, faces), the construction rules (planarity, intersection constraints, etc.). The 3D topological data structures reported currently in the literature can be subdivided into two large groups: structures maintaining objects and those maintaining relationships. While in the first group (object-oriented), most of the relationships between the objects have to be derived, in the second group (topology-oriented), the representation of the objects has to be derived. Many structures that are typical examples of the explicit storage of objects also maintain explicit storage of relationships, i.e., singularities.

4.3.2.1 Nature-Made Geo-Objects

The kind of geometric or topological data model presented here is known as "cell decomposition" (Requicha and Voelcker, 1982). Cell decomposition is taken here as an example to show the design and implementation of topology and geometry in Geo-DBMS. Being a special case of a cell decomposition, a TIN is known as "a collection of adjacent triangles with the topological consistency requirement that two pairwise adjacent triangles must completely touch in their adjacent edges by their whole length." There are no "dangling" triangles allowed in the TIN. Thematic attributes can be attached to whole TIN objects as well as to its parts, i.e., to single points, edges, and triangles. Analogously, tetrahedron nets can be joined together by adjacent tetrahedra with the topological consistency requirement that two pairwise tetrahedra are touching completely at their adjacent triangle faces. Thematic attributes can be attached to whole tetrahedron net objects or to its parts, i.e., to single points, edges, triangles, and tetrahedra.

The theory behind the implementation of topological or composed data types like "point set," "polylines," "surfaces," and "volumes" are the simplicial complexes that have been introduced into the field of GIS by Egenhofer (1989) and Egenhofer et al. (1990). The advantages of implementing simplicial complex data types in Geo-DBMSs are the following:

Unified treatment for 0-, 1-, 2-, and 3-dimensional objects, i.e., all objects are defined in one unified topology and geometry model.

Simplicial complexes are composed objects so that thematic attributes can also be attached to single points, edges, surfaces, and volumes of simplicial complex objects. Simplicial complexes provide a good approximation for the shape of complex nature-formed 2D and 3D objects, like the earth's surface or geological strata. Geometric database queries like the intersection query between a set of complex 3D objects executed on simplicial complexes internally profit from using the relatively simple intersection algorithms between points, segments, triangles, and tetrahedra, all being members of the introduced primitive 3D geometric data types.

To choose a suitable 3D primitive, some criteria have to be evaluated. The implementation should lead to valid objects. And once an object is modeled, there cannot be any ambiguities. A representation of an object should make clear how the object looks in reality. It should be easy to create and enable efficient algorithms. Furthermore, the size and redundancy of storage (conciseness) should be taken into consideration.

Figure 4.3 shows a conceptual 3D Geo-DBMS topology and geometry model for complex nature-formed objects. The simple topological data types are *Point, Segment, Triangle,* and *Tetrahedron.* Notice the following topological extension of the "traditional" simplicial complex approach: Each segment internally knows its start and end point, each triangle is aware of the list of its maximum three neighboring triangles, and each tetrahedron knows its maximum four neighboring tetrahedra.

The complex objects *PolyLine, TriangleNet,* and *TetraNet* are composed by a list of segments, triangles, and tetrahedra, respectively. However, a segment, a triangle, and a tetrahedron can belong to one or more polylines, triangle nets, or tetra nets to avoid data redundancy of primitive topological objects.

GeoPoint, GeoSegment, GeoTriangle, and *GeoTetrahedron* are the corresponding 3D geometric data types that contain the x-, y-, z-coordinate information and additional thematic information.

Finally, *GeoObject3D* is a polyline, triangle net, or tetra net attached with thematic information for application-specific thematic information. A *Group* is a collection of GeoObject3D objects that are allowed to have different dimensions. Group objects are

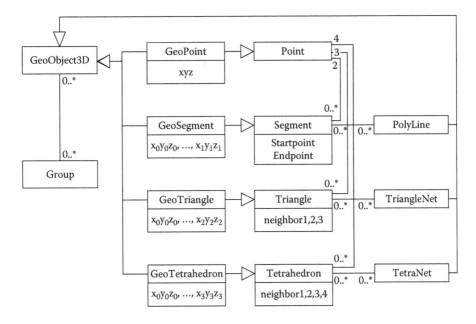

FIGURE 4.3 Conceptual 3D Geo-DBMS topology and geometry model for complex nature-formed objects.

generated during the execution of geometric 3D operations, e.g., if the intersection between two intersecting and touching tetra nets is computed as mixed triangle (two-dimensional) and tetra nets (three-dimensional objects).

In the future, it must be discussed whether advanced topology models such as the "GMaps" (Lienhardt, 1994; Levy, 1999) being used in the gOcad® 3D geological modeling software (Mallet, 1992, 2002) should be implemented in 3D Geo-DBMS. Obviously GMaps serve as an abstract framework as well as a flexible instrument to attach thematic and geometric attributes to 3D geo-objects.

4.3.2.2 Man-Made Geo-Objects

The existence of many topological models for man-made objects clearly indicates the complexity of the issue. A large number of topological structures have been developed through the years (Zlatanova et al., 2004). To distinguish between geometry and topology, often different names are used for the primitives, (e.g., TEN):

- type Node3D = (pointID$_i$, x$_j$, y$_j$, z$_j$) with (j = 0);

- type Arc3D = (arcID$_i$, pointID$_{i,j}$) with (0 ≤ j ≤ 1);

- type Face3D = (faceID$_i$, arcID$_{i,j}$) with (0 ≤ j ≤ 2);

- type Body3D = (bodyID$_i$, faceID$_{i,j}$) with (0 ≤ j ≤ 3);

Furthermore, the type of primitive varies from simplexes as described above (Pilouk, 1996; Coors 2003) to more free representations (Molenaar, 1992, Zlatanova 2000, de la

Losa and Cervelle 1999). Clearly, advantages of a topological representation in one of the aspects occur as disadvantages in another aspect. For example, the arbitrary number of nodes per face can be seen as advantage and disadvantage for different applications. It is very convenient for modeling complex 3D objects (e.g., buildings), since an inappropriate partitioning (into triangles) is not required, but the operators for consistency checks become very complex.

The subdivision into triangles furnishes the data needed to display graphic information in the most appropriate way. In this respect, TEN and UDM (Coors, 2003) are perhaps the optimal models for visualization of surfaces. Maintenance of triangles solves other modeling problems as holes or explicit storage of relationships (such as arc-on-face and node-on-face). An additional disadvantage for TEN is the much larger database compared to other representations and the need for special processing of the tetrahedrons that are not needed for visualization.

Some of the primitives (e.g., arcs) are suggested to be left out of the model to accelerate the visualization (Zlatanova, Holweg, and Coors, 2003). Those usually stored with Arcs BeginNode EndNode can be derived from ordered nodes in faces. However, some topological queries, such as navigating trough surfaces (e.g., "follow shortest path"), can become time-consuming.

The relationships stored per object also differ: a body can be explicitly described by faces, but body can also be implicitly derived from references stored with the faces (i.e., "left" and "right" body). "Left" and "right" body stored per face is a very convenient manner for navigating through 3D objects, but requires reference to a body "open air." The major problem with TEN (see above) refers to the modeling stage. Since the space is completely subdivided into tetrahedrons, the interiors of objects (e.g., buildings), as well as the open space, are also decomposed into tetrahedrons. Such subdivision is rather inconvenient for 3D man-made objects. Pilouk 1996 suggests a combination of TEN and TIN when appropriate.

Pigot (1995) elaborates on a cell tuple data structure, which provides the largest spectrum of topological relations between cells and complex cells. From a database point of view, this model promises an easy maintenance, due to the solid mathematical foundations and the simple representation. In the visualization respect, the extraction of faces and points is a simple operation, due to the explicitly stored link between the cells. In addition to the tuples, some supplementary information is needed, such as order (clockwise or counter-clockwise) of cells (note that the cycle is ensured). Assuming a relational implementation, the entire tuple information is available in one relational table, which has advantages and disadvantages. On the one hand, there is no need to perform JOIN operations to select any data. On the other hand, the size of the table grows tremendously, which slows down the speed of SELECT operations. For example, the records for a simple box occupy double space compared to other representations.

Presently, no agreement on a 3D topological representation exists. Van Oosterom et al. (2002) suggest an alternative approach. Instead of looking for an appropriate 3D topological representation, it is suggested to extend the DBMS kernel with meta information describing different topological structures in the DBMS.

This topological meta information can then be used both within the DBMS and outside the DBMS. In general, meta information (or system catalogs) of a DBMS contains descriptions of the data stored in the database: tables, attributes, and types, and also contains descriptions of the available types and operators. The different topological structures can be characterized by the following "parameters":

- Dimension of the embedding space: 2D, 2.5D, 3D, time added
- Topological primitives are used: node, edge, face, volume
- If the elements considered are directed (oriented) or not
- Explicit topological relationships (part_ of, in, on) are stored
- Topological "rules" — crossing edges allowed? dangling elements allowed? same topological primitive on both sides of boundary allowed? etc.

In general, such an approach may resolve many 3D modeling and visualization problems but requires robust consistency management. Such an approach is not completely unfamiliar for Geo-DBMS. For example, Oracle Spatial also uses a specific meta data table to describe geometric attributes in more detail: USER_SDO_GEOM_METADATA, which contains information about the number of dimensions, the extent of the domain, and the resolution.

Similarly Geo-DBMS supporting topology management has to store (and supply to the applications) the topological information: e.g. topological layer name, which table plays the role of the boundary table, which table plays the role of the area table, and how are the relevant attributes, with metrical and topological information called, within these tables. A drawback of this solution is that the topology elements (object ids, references and also the metric attributes) have fixed names. A better approach is storing this information in a meta data table. Again, somewhere it must be declared which tables and which attributes carry the topological information. An example of the extension of the meta information of the DBMS is given in Vijlbrief and van Oosterom, 1992.

4.3.3 3D SPATIAL ACCESS METHODS

3D spatial access methods implemented in a Geo-DBMS have the task to speed up database queries referring to the spatial position of objects in 3D Euclidean space. They support the 3D region query (3D-box query), i.e., all objects containing or intersecting a given 3D query box are selected. The SQL-like formulation of the 3D region query runs as follows:

```
SELECT  *

  FROM GeoObject3D

  WHERE 3DQUERYBOX intersects GeoObject.boundingBox;
```

To support the spatial search query efficiently, spatial index structures such as the R-tree (Guttman, 1984) or the R*-tree (Beckmann et al., 1990) are used. Such index structures are based on the hierarchical decomposition of the data space. The objects in the database are divided into subsets (buckets) that correspond to a partition of the data space, respectively. The buckets are accessed by a search tree. Typically all buckets belonging to an R-tree or R*-tree node are stored together on one database page. That is why a spatial preclustering is guaranteed in the database. For each object in the database, a minimal 3D axe-directed bounding box must exist, because the spatial index structure only takes these "approximated objects" to determine a possible intersection between a given 3D query box and the minimal bounding boxes of the objects in the database.

4.3.4 3D Spatial Predicates, Functions, and Operations

An important question is which spatial functionality should be allocated to a Geo-DBMS. Apparently, the functionality will be distributed between DBMS and front end, but how? In general, GIS functionalities that are generic for the geodata should be provided by the DBMS. Arguments for this are maintenance of logical consistency and data integrity. Following these arguments, we appreciate the development of generic geo-database kernel systems and front ends. They provide 3D data types, 3D access methods, and a 3D query user interface. First prototype systems have been developed with the DASDBS-Geokernel (Schek and Waterfeld, 1986; Waterfeld and Breunig, 1992), GEO++ (Vijlbrief and van Oosterom, 1992), Geo₂ (David et al., 1993), OMS (Breunig et al., 1994), GeoToolKit (Balovnev et al. 2004), and others. Front ends can build a further specific functionality. On the other hand, 3D topological analyses are of higher computational complexity compared to 2D. If performed at object-relational DBMS level — e.g., on top of SQL — this might have a negative effect on the database performance. This would speak for the direct embedding into the programming language of an OODBMS instead.

Moreover, the question arises whether the Geo-DBMS is an appropriate place to organize level of detail (LOD). ORDBMSs or OODBMSs could be extended by new spatial access methods supporting LOD.

Obviously, there are many specialized 3D geometric functions and operations needed in GIS and AEC applications. Therefore, a Geo-DBMS should provide the possibility to embed user-defined procedures for the computation of such operators (see Günther, 1991; Breunig et al., 1994). Of course, the efficiency of the computing in these operators depends on the geometry and topology model, as well as on the spatial access methods internally used in the geometric operators (Günther, 1988; Güting, 1994).

4.3.5 3D Extensions for Spatial Query Languages

To support 3D spatial database queries, query languages like SQL have to be extended by 3D predicates, functions, and operations. We give two examples for 3D database queries in geology using the 3D spatial function and operation introduced in the last section:

```
SELECT *

 FROM drilling

   WHERE distance3D(DRILLING, drilling.geometry) <
100m;
```

Query 1 uses the *distance3D* function. It selects all drillings in 3D Euclidean space that have a distance of less than 100 m to the specified DRILLING. One could also think of an additional geometric 3D query that projects the drillings selected by query 1 on a vertical plane (Breunig et al., 2004). Such projections are very useful for the construction of geological profile sections.

```
DEFINE VIEW AS

    SELECT intersection3D(fault.geometry)

    FROM fault

    WHERE STRATUM intersects3D fault.geometry ;
```

Query 2 uses the spatial predicate *intersects3D* and the spatial operation *intersection3D*. It creates new objects being computed by the intersection between the current geometry of STRATUM and the geometry of all faults in the database. In each step of the query execution the intersection is only computed if the *intersects3D* predicate returns the Boolean value TRUE.

4.4   3D IN PRESENT DBMS

The currently offered functionality by Geo-DBMS is not 3D with respect to the background provided in Section 4.3, but 3D objects can be stored and a number of spatial operations can be performed on 3D objects. The following sections provide examples.

4.4.1   3D OBJECTS IN OBJECT-ORIENTED DBMS

Kay, the inventor of Smalltalk object-oriented programming language, summarized five essential characteristics of pure object-oriented modeling and programming (Eckel, 2002):

- Everything is an object.
- A program is a bunch of objects telling each other what to do by sending messages.
- Each object has its own memory made up of other objects.
- Every object has a type.
- All objects of a particular type can receive the same messages.

The requests that may be sent to an object are defined by its *interface*. The data type determines the interface. The idea that the data type is quasi equivalent to the interface is fundamental to object-oriented modeling. Thus, the implementation, i.e., all internal structures are hidden from the user and are separated from the interface. In the database context, the interface is called *database schema*.

We speak of an OODBMS if the DBMS completely "understands" objects as its data model. Thus, the database schema is defined by classes (collections of objects) and the DBMS is in the position to store extensions of a class, i.e., arbitrary objects (instances). The OODBMS can return the instances by its object query language (OQL). This implies facilities for the description of the schema and for the hierarchical navigation between objects in classes.

The design of the topology and geometry model (see Figure 4.3) can be directly transferred to the physical database schema OODBMS is used. The structure of the spatial data type hierarchy consisting of primitive and composed data types can be directly maintained by inheritance relationships between the corresponding classes. The attributes of the 3D data types are implemented as properties of the classes (class variables), and their geometric and topological operations are realized as class methods. Therefore, every 3D object knows to which class it belongs and which properties and methods it owns. The multiplicities of the relationships between two classes (such as n:m-relationship) are implemented as properties of classes that again are allowed to be of type "class." Furthermore, every class is responsible for checking the input data if generating a valid geometry of this class (see *valid* method in the following example).

Example — part of class code demonstrating some methods for class Tetrahedron3D:

```
PUBLIC MEMBERS:

static int valid (const pointRep& P1, const pointRep&
P2,

  const pointRep& P3, const pointRep& P4);

// Description: this function checks if the points
P1, P2, P3 and P4 form a valid tetrahedron.

// Parameter: the points of the tetrahedron.

// Return value: 1 if the tetrahedron is valid, else 0.


Tetrahedron3D();

// Description: generates a "default-" Tetrahedron3D
with the points (0,0,0), (1,0,0), (0,1,0), (0,0,1).


Tetrahedron3D (const pointRep& P1, const pointRep&
P2,

  const pointRep& P3, const pointRep& P4);

// Description: generates a Tetrahedron3D with the
points P1, P2, P3 and P4.

// Parameter: the four points of the tetrahedron.

// Integrity constraint: The four points must define
a tetrahedron, i.e. they must not be

// equal and they must not be situated on a single
plane.
```

In the above example, we have only shown the methods for the integrity check of the geometry and two constructors generating a new Tetrahedron3D object. Beyond the presented code, the Tetrahedron3D class provides other methods such as cloning and geometric intersection with other Tetrahedron3D objects.

From an architectural point of view, we can distinguish between two types of OODBMS: page-based OODBMS vs. object-based OODBMS. Page-based OODBMS allows the loading of all objects that are located on one database page in one call. Therefore, they use the advantage of an object cached in main memory instead of reloading single objects. Against that, object-based OODMBS allow the loading of single objects from a disk. This type of OODBMS is well suited for the retrieval of individual objects or small sets of objects.

4.4.2 3D Objects in Object-Relational DBMS

Object-relational approach is based on defining new objects (data types) that can be stored in one record of relational tables. DBMS knows the meaning of the new data types and threads them in the same way as the simple data types. The spatial data types are complex, easily resulting in the relationship 1:m. This multiplicity can be represented in different ways, e.g., Oracle Spatial offers *Varrays* and *Nested tables*.

The data types and the validity rules are only the first step in providing spatial functionality. Geo-DBMS offers a set of spatial functions. For example, Oracle Spatial, SDO_RELATE operator implements the 9-intersection model for categorizing binary topological relations between points, lines, and polygons. The 9-intersection model investigates the intersection between the interiors, boundaries, and exteriors of two objects. The intersections are recorded in a 3×3 matrix, which results in 9 intersections. In general, Oracle, IBM DB2, Informix, and PostGIS support geometric functions defined by OGC — and often more functions than these.

The major problem of the implementations of spatial features and operators in mainstream DBMSs is that they differ from each other. The statement "select attribute_a from table_b where a < 100" is the same in every DBMS. However, if geometries have to be found within a certain distance, different types of queries have to be executed in the different DBMSs. For example, Oracle Spatial has implemented data types that do not have explicit names such as point, line, and polygon. There is one complex data type, sdo_geometry, composed of several parameters indicating type geometry, dimension, and an array with the x, y, z coordinates.

3D objects can be organized in Geo-DBMS in different ways: using existing 2D data types or defining a new 3D data type.

4.4.2.1 Using 2D Data Types

Mainstream DBMSs maintain 2D data types (point, line, polygon) but with their 3D coordinates. Using 3D polygons, 3D objects can be represented as polyhedrons in two ways: as a list of data type *polygons* or as data type *multipolygon/collection*.

The first option (defining a 3D objects as a list of 3D polygons) will be completed by creating two tables: a table BODY and a table FACE. In the table BODY the 3D spatial object is defined by a set of records containing a unique pointer to the faces closing the volume of a body. The table FACE contains geometry of faces stored as 3D polygons. This model is partly a topological model; since the body is defined by references to the faces (faces share two bodies).

In the second representation, a body is stored, using the data type *multipolygon/collection*, as one record. In this case, only one table is necessary, i.e., BODY. Note that the type of geometry used is not visible in the *create* statement.

An apparent advantage of the 3D multipolygon approach is the one-to-one correspondence between a record and an object. Furthermore, the 3D multipolygon (compare to a list of polygons) is that it is recognized as one object by front-end applications (GIS/CAD). For example, a 3D multipolygon is visualized as a "group" of objects in Microstation Geographics. However, in case of editing the objects, it still has to be ungrouped into composing faces (Figure 4.4).

A disadvantage of both representations is the redundant storage of coordinates (also in the case of 3D multipolygons). The coordinates of vertex of the body are stored at least three times either in the 3D multipolygon or in the FACE table.

Moreover, both representations are not recognized by DBMS as a volumetric object, i.e., they are still polygons and, thus, the 3D objects cannot be validated (as specified in Section 4.3.1). The objects can be indexed as 3D polygons but not as 3D volumetric objects.

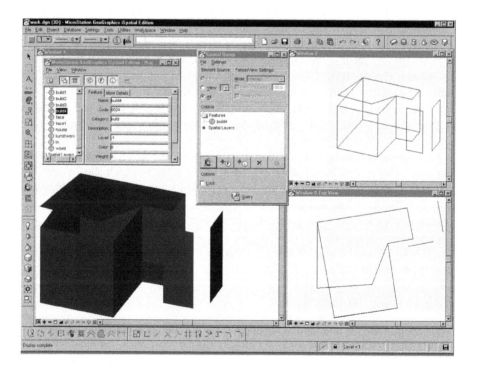

FIGURE 4.4 Visualization of 3D object stored in the Oracle Spatial.

4.4.2.2 Using a New 3D Data Type

The only way to resolve these drawbacks is by defining a true 3D data type. Arens at el. (2003) implemented a 3D data type polyhedron (as described in Section 4.3.1.3) using the Oracle Spatial object relational model. The new data is given sdo_gtype = 3008. Instead of listing all the coordinates composing a face, the structure of mdsys.sdo_ordinate array is suggested to have two parts — one with the coordinates of all the vertices (listed only once) and, second, a list with references to the triple coordinates.

The rules for validity of polyhedra are used as basis for a validation function. This function as well as some other interesting functions such as 3D area, volume, etc., are implemented and tested with different data sets. More details can be found in Arens (2003).

4.5 CASE STUDIES

Two case studies from man-made objects and nature-made objects reveal some of the problems with maintaining large-scale 3D objects, which are used to draw conclusions and requirements for 3D developments.

4.5.1 AEC CASE STUDY, "MODELING THE INTERIOR OF THE AULA, THE CONGRESS CENTER OF TUDELFT"

3D modeling of man-made objects usually results in large amounts of data and has always required careful consideration of details (with or without texture), thematic and spatial structuring of individual sections of large public buildings, etc. With the advances of technology (as discussed in Chapter 2), new sensors and 3D reconstruction methods are becoming available, which allows complex construction to be modeled with centimeter accuracy. This progress brings new opportunities for creating high-resolution models of real-world objects, which look as detailed as the construction plans at design stage.

For the purpose of experimenting with 3D indoor navigation, a 3D interior model of the congress Centrum (the Aula) at TUDelft has to be created (Figure 4.5). The entire Aula building was scanned from inside. This resulted in a 25 million point cloud obtained from 237 scans (Figure 4.6). Such a data set poses new challenges to the database. It was decided to organize the point cloud in Oracle Spatial for the purpose of simplifying the modeling process and preserving the points for later use. It should be noticed, that for the purpose of 3D navigation, only walls, floors, ceilings, windows, and doors were modeled. Many other objects such as tables, chairs, plants, curtains, etc., were left out. However, the points from these objects still can be appropriately organized in the database for future consideration. Furthermore, a proper organization of points (segmentation into scans or rooms, floors) would allow many users to have access to only a part of the point cloud, which will simplify the modeling process. Finally, each modeled object (wall, room, etc.) will know the points it was created from.

Tests with this point cloud revealed drawbacks of the offered data types. The supported data type for a point is very expensive; one point is stored in one record.

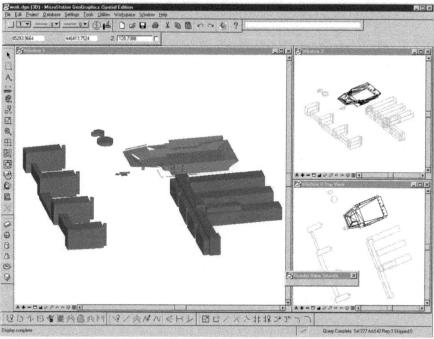

FIGURE 4.5 TUDelft, the Aula: photo (above) and 3D model (below).

Operations on such a point cloud are time-consuming (loading, 10 hours; indexing, 13 hours; etc.). Spatial indexing is not optimal for point data types. If multiple point data types are used, the identity of the points are lost. Apparently, point data type has to be reconsidered, or a new point data type has to be created.

FIGURE 4.6 (See color insert after page 86.) Point cloud of the scanned interior of the Aula.

Furthermore, many sections of the interior can be modeled in CAD software (Cyclone, CloudWorx) with predefined primitives such a cones, cylinders, spheres, etc. Such objects, however, cannot be organized later in the database. Data storage of each representation can be based on free-form shapes, NURBS, Bezier, or B-splines as suggested in Section 4.3.1.4. Storage of NURBS requires space nearly twice as large as Bezier or B-spline. However, certain costs in data storage should be acceptable in order to get more realistic results.

4.5.2 GIS CASE STUDY, "3D GEOLOGICAL MODELING OF AN OPEN CAST MINE IN THE LOWER RHINE BASIN"

The following sections summarize the description first given by Thomsen and Siehl (2002). Geological objects are, by nature, three-dimensional. In the case of almost undisturbed, and not much inclined strata, 2.5-D "flying carpet" models using a stack of stratum boundary surfaces as basic elements of a geometry model may be sufficient. But in the general case of folded and faulted strata, or of intrusionary orebodies, salt domes, etc., only a true 3D model is adequate. As an example, the 3D modeling of the Bergheim open cast mine near Cologne, Germany, is presented (Figure 4.7). For further details of this application, we refer to Thomsen and Siehl (2002).

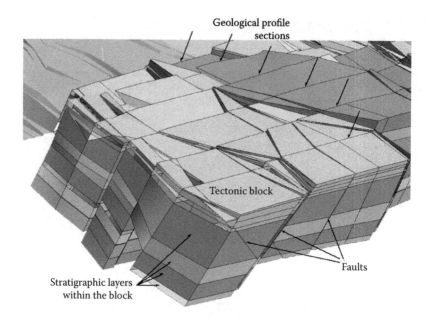

FIGURE 4.7 Structure of the Bergheim 3D geometry model.

This 3D model has been constructed to support a new kind of geological map. The objective is to gain deeper insight into the structural evolution of the Lower Rhine Basin from the Tertiary period until today, by modeling the kinematics of the Bergheim lignite mine, a small and intensely faulted region with an extension of about 2 km and a maximal depth of 500m.

The Bergheim open cast mine 3D model was designed to accommodate about 400 fault blocks, with about 2000 stratum surfaces, 800 fault surfaces, and 800 artificial boundary surfaces, each surface consisting of a small number of triangles.

For future spatio-temporal analysis (Breunig, 2001), an estimated total of 10,000 time-dependent surfaces have to be managed with an estimated 50,000 small timestep surfaces. Whereas the Bergheim kinematic model may serve as an example of a very discontinuous space-time model, experience from other static 3D-models of parts of the Lower Rhine Basin showed that individual stratum surfaces may comprise as many as 100,000 triangles.

Tectonic blocks are separated by layer boundaries, fault surfaces, and artificial boundaries at the location of the geological sections. Each block combines three types of triangulated surfaces, namely layer boundaries, faults, and artificial boundaries, following the original geological profile sections.

Starting with 20 parallel geological sections in SW–NE direction at a scale of 1:2000 supplied by Rheinbraun AG, Cologne, the gOcad 3D® modeler (Mallet, 1992) was used to construct the 3D volume model. For the data management, an extension of the 3D Geo-DBMS kernel GeoToolKit (Balovnev et al., 2004) was used, based on OODBMS ObjectStore®.

The geoscientific 3D geometry model must obey certain *consistency constraints,* whether strict geometrical and topological (e.g., the exclusion of gaps and overlaps between neighboring objects) or weaker and more problem specific (e.g., inverse correspondence of age and vertical position of strata, with certain exceptions). Therefore the Geo-DBMS must enforce *geometric and topological consistency* between strata, faults, and other geological objects. It should also permit formulating integrity checks based on application specific constraints.

The 3D topology and geometry model of the Bergheim open cast mine are implemented in GeoToolKit, using an extension with 3D data types in boundary representation. Thus, the topology and geometry of the geological profile sections, faults, and tectonic blocks are implemented by GeoToolKit classes, inherited by persistent ObjectStore classes.

The 3D geometric operations are realized as methods of GeoToolKit's 3D topological and geometric classes. This means that they are narrowly coupled with the OODBMS, also using ObjectStore's clustering and object management facilities. The methods are embedded into calls of 3D database queries realized with the C++ API of ObjectStore. Until now, no optimization rules determining the order of their execution have been implemented. This would be a difficult task, because the execution of arbitrary 3D geometric operations would lead far beyond the rules known from relational algebra applied in relational or object-relational DBMSs. To support the efficient execution of 3D database queries, the 3D geometric intersection operations, for example, are using an R*-tree index internally. Thus, the search of the "entry point" in the intersection algorithm, i.e., searching the first two intersecting primitive geometries (triangles or tetrahedra), is executed efficiently.

As GeoToolKit does not provide a complete spatial query language, the 3D database queries are implemented in C++ code supported by the object browser and the 3D visualization interface. Typical 3D database queries being implemented for this application scenario are:

- "Return the spatial part of the subsurface model specified by the 3D query box."
- "Compute the distance between all faults and the geological profile section No. 10A."
- "Return the fault surfaces intersecting the tectonic block No. 4."

To support a flexible client–server connection between geoscientific applications and the Geo-DBMS, a client interface was developed in Java, using CORBA technology (OMG, 1998) and an extension to a commercial VRML browser for visualization of geometry (Shumilov et al., 2002; Thomsen and Siehl, 2002).

4.6 SUMMARY AND OUTLOOK: TOWARD BRIDGING AEC AND GIS

In the last several years, many changes affected DBMS toward providing spatial functionality. Still, many developments at the DBMS level have to be completed, e.g., a 3D geometrical model should be fully supported by DBMS, based on standardized specifications. The native support of a polyhedron by DBMS will have significant consequences for 3D modeling in the coming years. Many questions related to CAD-like features have to be addressed: how to maintain curved faces, how to store para-metric shapes (cone, sphere, etc.), how to store texture and other components used to create realistic 3D scenes, mechanisms to maintain levels of detail in DBMS, etc.

Maintenance of topology (especially 3D topology) at the DBMS level is still in an infant stage. In both application fields, GIS and AEC, there are no agreements on a standard 3D topological model. The current implementations are mostly 2D with small exceptions (e.g., radius topology, which uses z-tolerance). The problems with the unification of 3D topology models are relatively high compared to the 2D topology. It is likely that several topologies have to be maintained in the database. The description of the models and transition from one to another may be described in meta-data tables.

Learning from the case studies, we can summarize the following requirements to 3D Geo-DBMS:

- 3D object management of 0D-, 1D-, 2D-, and 3D-objects, such as point clouds of buildings, drillings, profile sections, faults, and tectonic blocks
- 3D data visualization for whole scenes and for results of 3D database queries
- Database support for spatio-temporal planning and processes such as city planning and geological analysis of kinematic modeling

Obviously, most of the requirements cannot be accomplished by today's standard DBMSs.

Clearly DBMS can be used as a bridge between AEC and GIS applications. Currently, many AEC vendors (Bentley, AutoCAD), as well as many GIS vendors (ESRI, MapInfo, Intergraph), use the spatial models of Geo-DBMSs. Although many interoperability issues (maintenance of color, texture, attributes) still have to be developed, the experiments show promising results, i.e., models stored on Geo-DBMS can be visualized and edited from both GIS and AEC applications.

To be able to provide a stronger management of objects from AEC and GIS, Geo-DBMSs have to extend their spatial support to accommodate design objects (coming from AEC) and real-world objects (considering new data collection and modeling techniques). Some of the required developments are listed below:

- Real 3D geometry types and corresponding 3D validity operations: Many objects coming from AEC applications are well-defined closed spaces and their integrity has to be recognized by Geo-DBMSs.
- Free-form curves and surfaces: AEC applications have a large number of free-form curves and surfaces, basically not used in GIS. To be able to combine 3D design models (modeled in CAD) with existing situations (modeled in GIS), specialized data types for free-form sur-faces are needed. Among a large amount of mathematical representa-tions of 3D space, NURBS could be one possible solution. NURBS are approved as industry standards for the representation and design of geometry.

- Point cloud data types: With the progress of data collection techniques, existing data types and spatial indexing appeared to be insufficient. Today, laser-scanned technology easily generates millions of points for a single building. DBMSs fail to efficiently handle such amounts of data.
- TIN data type: Most of the terrain representations presently maintained in GIS, as well as many CAD designs (meshes), are TIN representations. TINs can be stored in DBMS using the polygon data type. This data type is generally assumed for multiple vertices and thus contains many attributes. Thus, a simpler adapted data type is required.
- Maintenance of multiple representations to be used as LOD: The management of multiple representations is still far from formalized. Users take care of their own implementations, which, however, cannot benefit from the indexing mechanisms in the Geo-DBMS.
- Management of texture and mechanism for texture mapping and texture draping: 3D objects usually need more physical attributes compared to 2D objects. Often 3D objects are textured with images from the real world. As AEC and GIS applications come together, the question of linking textures to geometries will appear. Textures have to serve as attributes of 3D objects decoded in the data types.

Questions such as 3D functionality are the next to be considered. It should not be forgotten that Geo-DBMS, in the first place, is a DBMS, i.e., the location for storage and management. The 3D functionality should not be completely taken away from GIS and CAD/AEC applications. 3D Geo-DBMSs should provide the basic (simple) 3D functions, such as computing volumes and finding neighbors. Complex analysis has to be attributed to the applications.

REFERENCES

Aguilera, A., *Orthogonal polyhedra: study and application*, Ph.D. Thesis, Universitat Politechica de Catalunya, Barcelona, Spain. 2001.

Arens, C.A., Maintaining reality, modelling 3D spatial objects in a Geo-DBMS using a 3D primitive, M.Sc. Thesis, TU Delft, The Netherlands, available at http://www.gdmc.nl/, 2003.

Arens, C., Stoter, J., and van Oosterom, P., Modelling 3D spatial objects in a Geo-DBMS using a 3D primitive, *Computers & Geosciences*, 31 (2), 165–177, 2005.

Balovnev, O., Bode, T., Breunig, M. Cremers, A.B., Müller, W., Pogodaev, G., Shumilov, S., Siebeck, J., Siehl, A., and Thomsen, A., The story of the GeoToolKit — an object-oriented geodatabase kernel system. *GeoInformatica,* 8 (1), 5–47, 2004.

Beckmann, N., Kriegel, H.P., Schneider, R., and Seeger, B., The R-tree: An efficient and robust access method for points and rectangles, *SIGMOD Conference*, 322–331, 1990.

Breunig, M., *On the Way to Component-Based 3D/4D Geoinformation Systems. Lecture Notes in Earth Sciences,* Springer, Heidelberg, 2001.

Breunig, M., Thomsen, A., and Bär, W. Advancement of Geoservices — Services for Geoscientific Applications Based on a 3D-Geodatabase Kernel. Geotechnologies Science Report No. 4, Information Systems in Earth Management, Potsdam, Germany, 35–39, 2004.

Breunig, M., Bode, T., and Cremers, A.B., Implementation of elementary geometric database operations for a 3D-GIS, in *Proceedings of the 6th International Symposium on Spatial Data Handling SDH*, Edinburgh, Scotland, 604–617, 1994.

Coors, V., 3D GIS in Networking Environments, CEUS, 27 (4), 345–357, 2003.

David, B., Rayal, L., Schorter, G., and Mansart, V., GeO2: why objects in a geographical DBMS? in *Proceedings of the 3rd International Symposium on Large Spatial Databases*, Singapore, 264–276, 1993.

de la Losa, A. and Cervelle, B., 3D topological modelling and visualisation for 3D GIS, *Computer&Graphics*, Vol. 23, 1999.

Eckel, B., *Thinking in Java*, 3rd Edition, Prentice Hall, free electronic book, http://www.BruceEckel.com, 2002.

Egenhofer, M.J., A formal definition of binary topological relationships, in *Foundations of Data Organisation and Algorithms, Proceedings FODO*, Paris, Lecture Notes in Computer Science No. 367, Springer, Berlin, 457–472, 1989.

Egenhofer, M.J., Frank, A.U., and Jackson, J.P., A topological data model for spatial databases, in *Proc. 1st Symp. on Design and Implementation of Large Spatial Databases*, Vol. 409 of Lecture Notes in Computer Science, Buchmann, A., Günther, O., Smith,T.R., and Wang, Y.-F., Eds., Springer, Berlin, 271–286, 1990.

Günther, O. Efficient structures for geometric data management. *Lecture Notes in Computer Science* No. 337, Springer, Berlin, 1988.

Günther, O. Spatial databases (in German), *Informatik Spektrum*, 14 (4), 218–220, 1991.

Güting, R.H., An introduction to spatial database systems, *VLDB Journal*, 3 (4), 357–399, 1994.

Guttman, A., R-trees, a dynamic data structure for spatial searching, in *ACM SIGMOD* 13, 47–57, 1984.

Levy, B., *Modélisation à base topologique: Combinatoire et Plongement*, Ph.D. Thesis, Institut National Polytechnique de Lorraine, Nancy, France, 1999.

Lienhardt, P., N-dimensional generalized combinatorial maps and cellular quasi-manifolds. *Journal on Computational Geometry and Applications* 4 (3), 261–274, 1994.

Mallet, J.-L., GOCAD — a computer aided design program for geological applications, in *Three-Dimensional Modeling with Geoscientific Information Systems. NATO ASI Vol. 354*, Turner, A.K., Ed., Kluwer Academic Publishers, Dordrecht, The Netherlands, 123–142, 1992.

Mallet, J.-L., *Geomodeling*, Oxford University Press, Oxford, U.K., 599 S, 2002.

Molenaar, M., A formal data structure for 3D vector maps, in *Proceedings of EGIS"90*, Vol. 2, Amsterdam, The Netherlands, 770–781, 1990.

ODMG, *Cattell RGG, the Object Database Standard: ODMB-93*. Morgan Kaufman Publishers, San Mateo, CA, 1993.

OMG, Object Management Group, The Common Object Request Broker: Architecture and Specification, Revision 2.2., 1998.

Piegl, L, On NURBS: a survey, *IEEE Computer Graphics and Applications*, 11 (1), 55–71, 1991.

Pigot, S., *A topological model for a 3-dimensional, Spatial Information System*, Ph.D. Thesis, University of Tasmania, Australia, 1995.

Pilouk, M., *Integrated modelling for 3D GIS*, Ph.D. Thesis, ITC, The Netherlands, 1996.

Requicha, A.A.G. and Voelcker, H.B., Solid Modeling: A Historical Summary and Contemporary Assessment. *IEEE Computer Graphics and Applications*, 9–24, 1982.

Rogers, D.F and Earnshaw, R.A., Eds., *State of the Art in Computer Graphics — Visualization and Modeling*, Springer-Verlag, New York, 1991.

Schek, H.-J. and Waterfeld, W., A database kernel system for geoscientific applications. in *Proceedings of the 2nd Symposium on Spatial Data Handling SDH*, Seattle, 1986.

Shumilov, S., Thomsen, A., Cremers, A.B., and Koos, B., Management and visualisation of large, complex and time-dependent 3D objects in distributed GIS, in *Proceedings of the 10th ACM International Symposium on Advances in Geographic Information Systems*, McLean, VA, 2002.

Stoter, J. and Zlatanova, S., Visualisation and editing of 3D objects organised in a DBMS, *Proceedings of the EuroSDR Com V. Workshop on Visualisation and Rendering*, 22–24 January 2003, Enschede, The Netherlands, 2003.

Thomsen, A. and Siehl, A., Towards a balanced 3D kinematic model of a faulted domain — the Bergheim open pit mine, Lower Rhine Basin, *Netherlands Journal of Geosciences/ Geol. Mijnbouw,* 81 (2), 241–250, 2002.

van Oosterom, P., Stoter, J., Quak, W., and Zlatanova, S., The balance between geometry and topology, in *Advances in Spatial Data Handling, 10th International Symposium on Spatial Data Handling,* Richardson, D. and van Oosterom, P., Eds., Springer-Verlag, Berlin, 2002, 209–224.

Vijlbrief, T. and van Oosterom, P., The Geo++ System: an extensible GIS, in *Proceedings of the 5th International Symposium on Spatial Data Handling SDH*, Charleston, SC, Vol. 1, 44–50, 1992.

Waterfeld, W. and Breunig, M., Experiences with the DASDBS Geokernel: Extensibility and Applications, in *From Geoscientific Map Series to Geo-Information Systems*, Geolog. Jahrbuch, A(122), Hannover, Germany, 77–90, 1992.

Zlatanova, S., Holweg, D., and Coors, V., Geometrical and topological models for real-time GIS, *International Workshop on Next Generation Geospatial Information*, 19–21 October 2003, Cambridge, MA, 2003.

Zlatanova, S., Rahman, A.A., and Shi, W., Topological models and frameworks for 3D spatial objects, *Journal of Computers & Geosciences,* 30 (4), 419–428, 2004.

5 Interaction and Visualization of 3D City Models for Location-Based Services

Heiko Blechschmied, Volker Coors, and Markus Etz

CONTENTS

5.1 INTRODUCTION

Augmented reality (AR) is a technology emerging in computer aided design (CAD), industrial service, and maintenance applications. In contrast to virtual reality (VR), where the user interactively explores an entirely artificial environment, AR aims to supplement the real world. For example, computer-generated information is blended in the field of view of a technician, so that it appears overlaid to the real scene and demonstrates step-by-step complex reparation tasks (ARVIKA, 2004). Another example is AR-CAD allowing engineers to model in a real environment context (Dunston et al., 2002).

Besides CAD-driven industrial planning and maintenance applications, AR technology is increasingly used as a powerful user interface in geospatial applications such as navigation systems, tourist information Services (Malaka and Zipf, 2000), disaster management systems, or in presentation of cultural heritage sites (Ioannidis, 2002; Holweg and Schneider, 2004), and more. These geospatial applications are truly mobile settings, away from special purpose work areas as they will be used in industrial applications. Quite a few technologies must be combined to enable mobile AR technology: global tracking technologies, wireless communication, multimodal human computer interaction (speech, pen-based, gestures), and wearable computing (Höllerer and Feiner 2004). As a result, existing solutions require bulky hardware, severely limiting their usability.

On the other hand, new mobile and ubiquitous computing applications are rapidly becoming feasible, providing people with access to online resources, at any time and everywhere. Location-based Computing (LBC) (Zadorozhny and Chrysanthis, 2004) infrastructure comprises a distributed mobile computing environment where each mobile device is location aware and wirelessly linked. As location awareness is the core of LBC, most Location-based Services (LBS) and applications rely on a global tracking technology and a large portion of geospatial information as provided by GIS. Typical location-based services are city guide applications and mostly deal with three major problems:

- Where am I?
- How do I get there?
- Where can I find something?

Today, LBS provide feasible answers to these questions; the problems are solved. New aspects come up in the context of mobile services like personalizing, and provisioning of attractive content and up-to-date information, but the usability and graphic rendition in presenting these services also gain in importance.

The user wants to have — besides navigation and orientation support — background information and more detailed visualizations to objects located on his or her route. Thus, a new problem comes up that the service has to satisfy: Can I have more information about something?

In order to cope with all tasks, you need information out of a map. As according to Hake, 2002, a map emphasizes important information for the user and decreases irrelevant data. Different maps are needed due to the varying information needs between the tasks. Primarily, interactive points of interest have to be provided on the map, which are linked to further information or to realize the capability of using the object as an initial point in other applications. Additionally, the value of a map can also be increased by presenting the user with a three-dimensional map. In a 3D map, the navigational value increases due to the highly visual correspondence between map objects and real-world objects. This correspondence allows the user to recognize buildings easily (Coors et al., 2004), which leads to a more intuitive navigation inside the map in comparison to a 2D map. Combined with an AR user interface, a 3D map with a dynamically created content fitting the information needs will be the ultimate navigational aid for location-based services.

In the following sections, we will take a closer look at some research projects leading to prototypes in the area of geospatial AR and location-aware systems. Within the ARCHEOGUIDE project (ARCHEOGUIDE, 2002), an outdoor AR cultural heritage on-site guide was developed. The GEIST project (GEIST 2004), combined outdoor AR with digital storytelling in 17th century Heidelberg, Germany. To our knowledge, the first 3D maps for the mobiles, running on Nokia communicator, were developed in the Tellmaris project (TELLMARIS, 2003). Finally, the LoVEUS project (LoVEUS, 2004) creating multimedia location-based services for a variety of mobile devices. The LoVEUS project will be presented in more detail because it is a perfect system for further research and development in AR user interfaces for location-based services.

5.2 AUGMENTED REALITY AND LOCATION-BASED SERVICE PROJECTS

5.2.1 ARCHEOGUIDE

ARCHEOGUIDE (Augmented Reality based Cultural Heritage On-site Guide) uses outdoor AR to guide tourists to Ancient Olympia in Greece while visiting this historic site. Visitors, upon arrival on the site, use a wearable computer equipped with a head mounted display (HMD), camera, and speaker. The hardware components of the system include a site information server, a wearable computer, and a wireless local area network (WLAN). In this project, the wearable computer used is a Qbe Vivo Webpad equipped with PIII CPU at 600 MHz, 128MB RAM, 10 GB HD, TFT touch screen and camera, Sony Glasstron HMD, GPS, and compass.

The system guides tourists through the site, acting as a personal tourist guide and giving them audio/visual information. Where appropriate, the system renders images of 3D models of reconstructions of the monuments and displays them to the user's HMD. In order to integrate virtual objects into the real environment, i.e., augment the user's view, the exact position and viewing direction have to be tracked. In ARCHEOGUIDE, an image-based tracking technique was used. A first rough position of the user will be given by using GPS and compass. The exact tracking will be done by comparing images taken from the user's camera with a large number of geo-referenced images of the real site stored in a database. Using GPS and compass, a first filter of candidate images will be performed. The matching is done by considering the image as a whole (global matching) instead of identifying land-marks in each image (local method). This output is then fed to the rendering algorithm for producing the final augmented view seen by the user. The renderer is capable of real-time rendering of 2D images; VRML models, or transparent back-ground video on static images and live video. It communicates directly with the image tracker and receives in response a 3 × 3 matrix with geometric parameters for the rendering.

For further details on the ARCHEOGUIDE project see Ioannidis et al. (2002) and ARCHEOGUIDE (2005).

5.2.2 GEIST

In the GEIST project, a system has been developed to educate students and adults in the history of a place by offering a personalized and lively tour (Holweg and Schneider, 2004; GEIST, 2004). GEIST is an edutainment system using outdoor augmented reality. Augmented reality, as a medium in historical education, can be defined as a digital mobile tool in a historical location that offers data and is able to combine both authentic resources (e.g., buildings) with interpreted resources such as former parts of a particular building that were destroyed in the past and then rebuilt digitally through paintings or other authentic resources. Instead of a guide, the students are equipped with the "magic equipment" of GEIST (see Figure 5.1). It mainly consists of a see-through display and interaction utilities; additionally, a PDA can be part of the equipment. As GEIST is a location-based service using outdoor AR for 3D visualization, the main and basic user interaction is moving.

The basic idea of GEIST is to allow the users to move freely through the city of Heidelberg, Germany. They are equipped with a laptop, a wearable see-through display, and tracking sensors. Via headphones, ghosts from the past contact the pupils as soon as they enter a place of historical evidence. They appear in the AR display in front of reconstructions from the past and tell pupils facts about the history of the place that played a certain role in the Thirty Years War. The whole game forms a story, which is composed according to the particular pupil and his or her choices. The story is divided into scenes acting at several locations within the city of Heidelberg. Each scene consists of a mixture of real and virtual objects. Real objects exist in reality, while virtual objects and representations of real objects are managed in a 3D geospatial database. The user's position is tracked the whole time using GPS. The user's movement in the real world can be transformed to movements of the

FIGURE 5.1 Magic equipment of GEIST in Heidelberg.

user's representation in the 3D virtual environment. To ensure correct overlaying of virtual objects within the real world, a highly accurate line-of-sight tracking using a video-based approach has been developed.

5.2.3 TELLMARIS

The development of a tourist information system for mobile clients that makes use of 3D maps was the main objective of the project TellMaris (TELLMARIS, 2003). The system is targeted to boat tourists on the Baltic Sea. For this group, relevant information as well as Location-based Services are integrated. A relatively large number of boat tourists already have a laptop computer or PC on board. Together with GPS and network access, the conditions are given to provide them with tailor-made services. From the user's point of view, two applications can be distinguished.

The TellMarisOnBoard (TOB) application supports the boat tourist directly during his trip on the sea. The system runs on a laptop and provides 3D services for navigation and current harbor information. Basic services, such as weather forecasts, are also regarded as important for boat tourists. The interactive 3D visualization helps to explore areas where the boat tourist plans to go and also supports the orientation when he or she enters a harbor. The virtual viewpoint can either be moved to the current boat position, presenting views from the boat perspective, or it can be moved freely through the scene.

The TellMarisGuide (TG), developed for PDAs and smart phones, assists the boat tourists when they disembark and explore the larger-scale harbor surroundings. It can be used to receive tourist information, for example, about sights or hotels, and it can find the closest restaurants or other facilities of interest. From user-selected positions or, if connected to a GPS receiver, from the current position, the tourists can be guided dynamically to their targets of interest.

Compared to desktop computers, the capabilities of mobile devices are limited, and the development of 3D graphics on such devices is just beginning. Geospatial data, especially, requires lots of resources. For 3D maps for LBS, several limitations must be considered. Besides the small screen size and the restricted interaction possibilities, the rendering capabilities are very restricted and are far behind those of desktop PCs.

The 3D graphics of the Nokia Communicator, shown in Figure 5.2, uses NokiaGL, a graphics library similar to OpenGL and optimized for the Symbian OS.

FIGURE 5.2 3D display of the TellMarisGuide on the Nokia Communicator.

3D maps are not seen as static documents but as dynamic visualizations, comprised of an elevation model and GIS data. Since the whole data set for one city is too large in order to be stored on the device, all the data is managed by a database on the server side. The client only contains meta-information like spatial extent and available layers for the area of interest. For regions in the background that will be possibly visited by the user, spatial queries in the form of Web service calls are constructed and sent to the server. As soon as the user approaches, the regions become visible. As a certain amount of geodata can also be cached on the device, additionally an initial download of a larger region is thinkable when the user has access to a faster network like Wireless Local Area Network (WLAN). Nonetheless, typical LBS functions such as guiding the user to the next Chinese restaurant, displaying interesting locations in the near surroundings and the like can only be accomplished with an underlying GIS, which resides on the server.

For more information on technical issues of the TellmarisGuide please refer to Schilling et al. (2003 and 2004) and Coors et al. (2004).

5.2.4 LoVEUS

The LoVEUS (Location- aware Visually Enhanced Ubiquitous Services) project is developing a mobile service that provides personalized, tourism-oriented multimedia information enriched with relevant advertisement (Karagiozidis et al., 2002). The intention of the project is to provide exciting extra information about the actual location of the user in order to guide him in terms of available points of interests and to present visually enhanced information about significant details. Thereby, the service provides active maps with city navigation (see Figure 5.3), active panoramic views and visually enhanced content regarding specific subjects, and more. The entire service is developed for supporting next-generation mobile terminals enhanced with the Global Positioning System (GPS) and a digital compass.

Using LoVEUS, a visitor can discover sights in a pleasant and informative way using the mobile terminal while strolling through an area. Instead of checking facts of interest in a printed city guide, the visitor can directly view desired information (e.g., about history or architecture) to specific objects on the display of the Smartphone or PDA. The advantage of using a service as implemented in the LoVEUS project is that there is no longer a need for irksome leafing through a book-based city guide. The information can be requested by a key press and then presented in an interest-related way by streaming audio and video, panoramic views, or simply by text and images. The presentation of the information is only limited by the capabilities of the used mobile terminal. Due to the rapid development in the mobile market, the use of videos, audio streams, or three-dimensional visualization becomes more and more limitless. The client application, written in J2ME, is completely independent of the content and connects the application server for map and content requests. As a response, the server provides only the content, in a format that the terminal can handle but in an individual and attractive way for the user.

Within the project a "MultimediaGIS" is designed, which combines in one system a location server, a map server, and a multimedia managing system. It can handle navigation and map requests as well as the managing of the multimedia content

FIGURE 5.3 (See color insert after page 86.) User interface mockup of LoVEUS on an iPAQ.

regarding freely defined spatial objects or areas. Based on a content filtering tool, the provided content is adjusted to the user's interests and the used mobile terminal.

For more information on architecture issues of LoVEUS, please refer to Karagiozidis et al. (2002) and the Web site of the LoVEUS project (2004).

5.3 LBS ARCHITECTURE USED IN LoVEUS

5.3.1 System Architecture

In the case of the developed MultimediaGIS, the common GIS functionality is extended by a multimedia managing system (Blechschmied et al., 2004). This allows the system to provide enhanced content about stored points of interest that do not only contain the information required for realization of the GIS functionality, but also information and content for the realization of multimedia. Therefore, multiple representations of spatial features have to be available in combination with the providing of user-friendly information. For example, a restaurant is usually stored within the GIS database by its coordinates or address and the name and an icon might also be available, but with these few data it is not possible to generate a multimedia representation. Hereby, it is only feasible to integrate the restaurant in

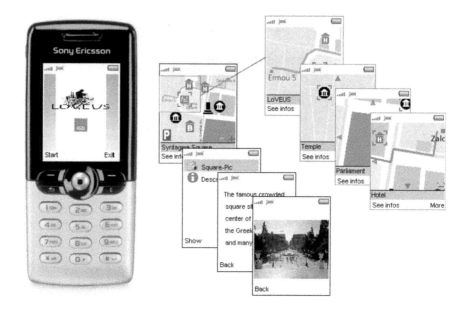

FIGURE 5.4 (See color insert after page 86.) Typical scenario on a cell phone.

the data analyses of the GIS in terms of routing, area selections, and so on. The desired multimedia representation obviously requires data for different kinds of restaurant representations, such as an image or 3D visualization (see Figure 5.4). Furthermore, descriptive information should also be available in order to satisfy different demands of implemented applications or the personal interests of the end users.

The software architecture of the GIS is subdivided in different main components, which are responsible for the realization of predefined tasks. The system is primarily based on a database that contains all data structured in a geometric and topologic data model. Linked to the database is a component that realizes the data insertion into the database and comprises mostly data preparation. Further on, an information server is directly linked to the database, which provides, by data queries, the stored data from the database. The information server is controlled by different applications of the GIS, which can be composed to a component of data analyzing and processing. As the end point in the data flow, a component presents the presentation of the processed data in a numerical or graphical form.

In order to handle the content for the multimedia capability within a GIS, we first have to extend all the architecture of the data repository by a component that intelligently integrates multimedia content into the structure of the common GIS data model (see Figure 5.5). The multimedia component in LoVEUS is defined in such a way that data of different types can be managed, such as images, audio files, and videos, as well as three-dimensional visualizations. In addition to this enhanced content handling, the proposed database can also deal with the real geometry of provided objects in order to generate individual location-based representations on the fly.

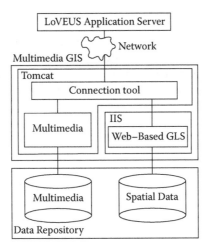

FIGURE 5.5 General architecture of the MultimediaGIS developed in LoVEUS.

The general unit within the multimedia component is the definition of supported features, which the enhanced content will be related to. This part is relatively independent of fixed spatial objects that are available within the GIS database. On the other hand, the used GIS is uncoupled from the multimedia database in order to satisfy a flexible utilization of the applied GIS and its common functionality, such as area selection or routing.

A simple linking between objects based on the GIS database and the enhanced content is not taken into consideration, although this seems workable at first view. In the case of a complex application with many representations of different types, as it is realized in LoVEUS, the resulting data structure will be disordered without an inner fixed structure. Furthermore, the data handling will be very difficult if enhanced content to single objects will be provided, and if the data structure of the GIS database limits the capability of the multimedia application, because the application is completely subjected to the constraints of the GIS and its data structure. In addition, we cannot assume that the objects that will be equipped by enhanced content are explicitly defined within the GIS database. Problems have occurred because single objects are often stored by several parts, based on the definition of the floor plans and the differentiation of building types. On the other hand, features extended by multimedia content comprise several buildings and other urban objects. Consequently, the covering of objects in a GIS is often inhomogeneous and dissimilar to the demands of a multimedia city guide. However, the proposed scheme offers, besides the independent multimedia data model used in the database, the possibility to set links to a file system.

The proposed architecture offers a simple upgrading if further types of multimedia content are required. A new attribute table is then to be specified that accommodates the related attributes according to the data type. So the system can be simply adapted to the demands of the application, concerning system environment and application area, e.g., a mobile City Guide has to handle totally different content and data types than an application for mobile workers.

5.3.2 Multimedia Database

The core unit within the multimedia database is the definition of a feature to which one or more multimedia representations exist. A hierarchical structure in the feature definition can be built up by index linking to other existing features. This categorization allows uniform and easy handling of complex and simple features, because objects, like buildings with a closed spatial relation can be compounded to a new feature.

The creation of a feature offers a further advantage because all data of enhanced content are linked to the features in a closed environment of the multimedia database. Hence, the implementation of GIS functionality is strictly independent of the multimedia content, and changes in the data model or implementation have no impact on the multimedia data. Furthermore, the GIS data and the multimedia content can be handled as independent components within the database and during the creation of the application modules. This separation also supports a flexible data architecture, especially with respect to the modular systems, and offers a wide range of feasible query implementations.

All multimedia content will be related to single features. It is not important if the feature represents a single object like a building, monument, or a complex imaginary compounded object related to a topic like an old city center. All multimedia data available are stored related to such a feature that is not necessarily equivalent to a defined feature within the GIS database. Therefore, features can be defined independently of the GIS database and can be optimally adapted to the application that will be developed. It is, however, reasonable to use the hierarchical structure if features will be represented that are compounded through several single features, because these can be related directly with the GIS database. The complex feature also will be available by multimedia queries for a single object that is included in the complex feature and representation.

For example, a 3D model of the central market of a town will be provided by an Internet-based city guide service. The model will be referenced to the feature "central market" and can be specified in the database. A more favorable implementation is when the market is specified as a complex feature, based on the objects that compose it. Generally, a marketplace consists of a square and closed buildings such as the town hall, church, commercial buildings, and apartment houses. Obviously, the town hall and church are common tourist targets, and therefore, it is conceivable that these objects also will be represented in the multimedia database by their own multimedia-based representations. On the basis of the feature structuring, a compact data structure will be built, whereby, for example, queries about all available representations of one feature can also take into account all representations of complex features, to which the feature is associated.

5.3.3 Representation

Each enhanced content that is available to a specific feature — whatever its multimedia type — can be regarded as representation. Each feature can be associated with several representations, whereby a representation characterizes all types of multimedia data including images, videos, and audio streams, as well as 3D visualizations or PDF documents. The representations are stored directly related to corresponding features, embodied by an m..n relation in the data model. This option is profitable, for instance, in the handling of images, because this type of representation often covers several real objects. The image can then be related to all relevant features without the constraint to define an upper-level feature.

On the basis of the proposed concept, we also must differentiate between representations available in different languages, even though they comprise similar information. For instance, an audio stream in different languages but similar content originates from different files with different properties, particularly audio length and file size.

5.3.4 DATA REPOSITORY

The basic component of a GIS is the data repository that contains all spatial, business, and multimedia data that are required for the realization of such an application. The capability of a GIS basically depends on how the very extensive data are stored and how they can be handled by the system. The data have to be intelligently stored in a data model by structuring and preprocessing so that a logical concept yields an optimal use of the available data in applications with a pure spatial context.

The managing of the representations is split into two components. The first component represents the available content as instance and the subject of it. The second component contains the data file, or a URL if the content is external and is attributed to the corresponding file (e.g., file size, dimension, etc.). According to Figure 5.6, the first component is defined in order to support a flexible handling of the different representations and contains general items about the representation (e.g., a short title, the language, and keywords that describe the kind of representation). In combination with this representation component, the second component contains

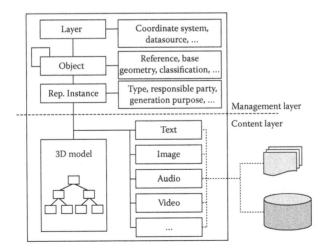

FIGURE 5.6 Scheme of the developed multimedia database.

the data and its corresponding attributes. For each kind of content, an independent module can be specified depending on the storage and availability of it — local or distributed. If a file has to be directly stored within the database, a module can be specified that uses a BLOB field for storing up to 4 gigabytes of unstructured binary data. A URL field can be defined in order to access an external data source. In addition, each kind of multimedia or enhanced content type has its own descriptive attributes. This is why an independent attribute table needs to be specified, e.g., images have a pixel dimension, 3D models are specified by their amount of triangles. The descriptive attributes are essential in mobile applications with their limits in data traffic, display of the terminal, user interaction, and other environmental characteristics, because based on the attributes, it is feasible to control the provided multimedia content within the service utilization.

5.3.5 CONNECTION BETWEEN MULTIMEDIA DB AND GIS DB

As mentioned before, representations in the multimedia database are not directly linked to objects stored in the database of a GIS. All representations are referred to as a defined feature within the multimedia database, because specified features are not necessarily identical with single spatial objects. The connection is realized by an m..n connection between the features of the multimedia database and the corresponding spatial objects stored in the GIS database. The table consists of three columns, one for the index of the feature and two for the position of the object within the GIS database. These two columns are implemented, because it cannot be assumed that all spatial objects are stored in the same table inside the GIS database like the features in the multimedia data model.

5.3.6 HANDLING OF THREE-DIMENSIONAL VISUALIZATIONS

The handling of three-dimensional visualizations of interesting and requested areas and objects is realized through two options. First, a created presentation can be handled like the other representations in a video or VRML file, even by using a different file format. The file of the 3D visualization is then directly stored in the database or via URL linked to the file system. On the other hand, the presentation request can be forwarded to the 3D geometry database, which includes the real feature geometry. Based on this data a visualization can then be generated on the fly to Java3D models or VRML files.

We propose a query-oriented data model for 3D GIS that supports, integrated in the multimedia database, an efficient handling of 3D visualizations, because it stores the real geometry of urban objects independently of the representation. Thus, it is possible to generate individual representations requested from the end user, depending on the location, orientation, and his or her preferences. The advantage of this solution is that it does not require prefabricated 3D visualizations, and each user gets a real location-based representation. Using intelligent data queries, furthermore, allows the user to run the service on mobile devices with its limitation in terminal memory and network bandwidth. The created 3D visualizations can contain only visible objects, as well as a graded level of details that results in small files. Additionally, the 3D scenes can easily be integrated into the concept of personalization with respect to the preferences of the end users.

Another advantage of the storage and access to the real 3D geometry within the database is that data extending and changing are completely independent of the application. Consequently, urban changes can be handled and provided for the LBS within a relatively short time.

5.4   J2ME MOBILE 3D GRAPHICS

To visualize three-dimensional maps on mobile devices, the Mobile 3D Graphics API (M3G) is used. This optional package for J2ME (Java 2 Micro Edition, 2005) was developed under Java Specification Request 184 (JSR-184) by an expert group consisting of leading manufacturers of mobile phones and telecommunication companies and released at the end of 2003. As a non-proprietary system implemented in mobile devices of different manufacturers, we can assume this API will be the standard for three-dimensional visualization on mobile devices.

As an add-on to the Java libraries CLDC and MIDP, M3G is developed to work on devices with slow processors, limited memory, and no hardware-based 3D-rendering support. To work successfully on these systems, the API is implemented in less then 150 kByte of memory.

In the developed system, the "Retained-Mode of M3G" is used to visualize the data. In this mode all geometries are structured hierarchically and managed in a scenegraph. The scenegraph is composed of group objects that specify the entire three-dimensional scene with its geometric objects, the virtual spectator, and light sources. Additionally, M3G supports the handling of files that contain single geometries, complete scenes, and animations. This is done by loading files in the .m3g file format, which can be created by a 3D-modeling software like 3D Studio MAX.

So, highly computational calculations like routing between two points or the modeling of highly detailed models can be done on high-performance machines; the result of these calculations can be loaded on the mobile device and can be shown there. As the construction of a scene in a 3D-rendering software is done one time for all users, and by this being not variable to one user's needs, a system for dynamic map construction was developed. In this system, the user can send a parameterized request for a map to a server, which dynamically constructs a map adapted to the user request. Due to the similarity between Java 3D for stationary computers and Mobile 3D Graphics, the creation of the map is done on the server side in a Java 3D scenegraph, which afterward is converted into a M3G scenegraph. The following section will address this process of map construction in Java 3D and the conversion from Java 3D to M3G.

5.5   CREATING AND TRANSMITTING A 3D MAP
TO MOBILE DEVICES

As described in the last section, there are two ways to generate a three-dimensional map to be shown on a mobile device (see also Figure 5.7). The first one is to create a scene with a 3D-modeling software. This scene will be stored in an .m3g file, which can easily be loaded by an M3G application on a mobile device. One application example would be a route description, which a user can download from

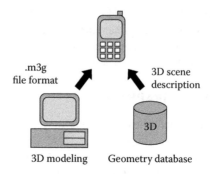

FIGURE 5.7 Sources of 3D data for mobile devices.

a Web server and show on a mobile device. As the scene has to be created manually with the modeling software, there is no way to make this scene depend on the user. In other words, it is possible to create a scene showing the user the way from one fixed point, such as a railway station, to another fixed point, such as a hotel, but it is not possible to adapt the scene to the current position of the user or to his or her personal interests or knowledge.

In this section, we present a system that allows the user to retrieve a dynamically created map fitting his or her needs. To achieve this, a three-layered system is used (see Figure 5.8). On the uppermost level, the mobile device querying a map with a specific content is located. On the lowermost layer, the data needed to create this map is stored in an object-relational database containing the geometries as points,

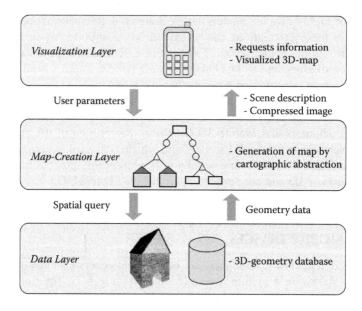

FIGURE 5.8 System for dynamic 3D-map creation.

lines, and faces. As the user query, and so the map, varies due to different users and different information needs, the geodata have to be manipulated in order to create a suitable map. This is done in the middle layer — the map-creation layer — where the visual representation of the data is created by using methods of cartographic abstraction. These methods allow the system to visually emphasize important map objects and reduce irrelevant objects by manipulating their geometric attributes and their visual appearance (e.g., color and texturing). These map objects are generated by creating a Java 3D scenegraph containing the geodata loaded from the database. Every object is stored inside the scenegraph as a single subgraph. By using Java 3D methods to manipulate the scenegraph objects, the appearance of every object can be varied according to the user request. After creating the map, the data in the Java 3D scenegraph must be converted to a format readable on the mobile device and transmitted.

At present, there is no conversion tool between Java 3D and the .m3g file format; we developed a pseudo-.m3g format describing the scene has been developed. This format, based on VRML, is used to store the geometrical and visual attributes, such as colors and textures, of the map objects and is transmitted to the mobile device where it is parsed and its data are visualized.

To create this scene description file, the Java 3D scenegraph is parsed, and its structure and data are written into the file. Due to the memory limitations on mobile devices, some facts have to be observed while creating the scene description. In the used database, the object geometries are stored, geo-referenced in Gauss-Krueger coordinates. In this meter-based coordinate system, the position of an object is given by two values in the magnitude of $n \cdot 10^6$. As in M3G, only short-type integers between -32.768 and 32.767 can be used to describe the position of a vertex (and by this, of a geometry); the coordinates of the geometries have to be scaled and translated in order to be shown on the mobile device. By scaling the coordinates (using decimeter instead of meter as unit length), we achieve sufficient exactness without using decimal numbers. Due to this scaling and the above mentioned coordinate limitation, we theoretically have a maximum map size (maximum distance between two points) of 6553.5 meters. The real maximum map size presentable on a mobile device depends on its hardware performance and, hence, must be transmitted as an additional parameter with the map query.

By translating the scene with all its objects in the direction of the origin of the world coordinate system, the size of the coordinates is reduced to the above-mentioned interval. Consider this example: A scene consists of one object with the vertices $V\,1 = (99999.5, 0, 0)$; $V\,2 = (100000.5, 0, 0)$; $V\,3 = (100001.5, 0, 0)$. After scaling the object, its vertices are located at $V1_{scale} = (999995, 0, 0)$; $V2_{scale} = (1000005, 0, 0)$; $V3_{scale} = (1000015, 0, 0)$. As the x-values of the coordinates are outside of a shorttype variables range, the center of the scene is translated to the origin of the world coordinate system, so the coordinates of the points after translation are $P1_{trans} = (-10, 0, 0)$; $P2_{trans} = (0, 0, 0)$; $P3_{trans} = (10, 0, 0)$, and by this, usable as coordinates in M3G.

The previously described process of dynamically creating a map out of data from a database is also used to create a map for low-performance mobile devices not supporting the M3G-API or devices with a small bandwidth. For this, the "off-screen" rendering ability of Java 3D is used. In this rendering mode, the visual objects inside the scenegraph are written into an image, which can be converted to a compressed image file and transmitted to the mobile device. In comparison to a "real" 3D map, the user cannot navigate inside the map. In order to minimize this disadvantage, the desired position and orientation inside the map can be passed as a parameter to the map-creation layer.

5.6 EXAMPLES

In this section, application examples will show how the presented technologies are used to provide a map containing the information desired by the user.

Figure 5.9 shows how objects important for the user inside the 3D map are highlighted visually by changing their color in comparison to the surrounding buildings. The highlighted objects can be navigational aids ("Change direction at the marked building") as well as requested objects in the map ("The marked objects are the ones you are looking for"). The crosshairs in the middle of the mobile device screen are used to allow the user to select single objects on the map. Reconsider the example of the introduction: The user of the map is standing in front of a historical building and wants to get additional information about it. Now he can select this building on the map, which will start a new query concerning the specified object, and he will get additional information either as an informational text or as a highly detailed image (see Figure 5.10).

FIGURE 5.9 (See color insert after page 86.) Navigational aids in a map.

FIGURE 5.10 (See color insert after page 86.) Highly detailed visualization of an object.

5.7 CONCLUSIONS

In this chapter, we presented an overview of 3D urban models and an AR user interface for location-based services. AR and mobile computing are rapidly growing fields, and this available technology is powerful enough for an increasing number of impressive research prototypes. The ARCHEOGUIDE and the GEIST project give an impression of the possibilities of mobile geospatial AR. On the other side, the projects TellMaris and LoVEUS give impressive examples of the power of multimedia and 3D visualization of currently available mobile phones.

It will take more time and further technical developments, however, for the mobile AR user interface in location-based computing to reach the mainstream. One of the major obstacles is the bulky hardware needs for accurate position and especially line of sight tracking. However, necessary components like GPS and camera and optical see-through displays are integrated into currently available mobiles. This is taken into account in the project ULTRA, started in 2004 (ULTRA, 2004). The objective of this project is to develop an "ultra portable" system by applying AR techniques to handheld-PCs. This will offer a comfortable and unobtrusive solution, integrating AR functionalities with near-the-eye display, wireless connection, and remote support over integrated mobile phones.

Besides further progress in hardware, one big challenge is the integration of large-scale GIS and CAD databases. In LBS, a large amount of geospatial data is needed, mainly traditional 2D GIS data. However, for camera-based line of sight tracking in AR, there is a strong need for a 3D-environmental model. In addition, for 3D visualization and augmented display, a similar 3D model of the environment is necessary. This 3D model is not only used for displaying, but it is also needed for analysis, such as, for instance, calculating occlusions of virtual objects by real ones.

To summarize, if we are heading for ultra portable AR user interfaces for location-based services that offer a large amount of fascinating applications, there is a strong need for very large integrated GIS/CAD 3D databases on the server side.

REFERENCES

ARCHEOGUIDE, 2002, project Web site, http://archeoguide.intranet.gr/, accessed 24 January 2005.

ARVIKA project Web site, http://www.arvika.de/www/index.htm, accessed 24 January 2005.

Blechschmied, H. et al., *LoVEUS — Multimedia geführte Stadtrundgänge,* in Raubal, M. (Hrsg.) u.a.; Institut für Geoinformatik, Münster: Geoinformation und Mobilität — von der Forschung zur praktischen Anwendung: Beiträge zu den Münsteraner GI-Tagen 01./02. Juli 2004, Münster.

Coors, V., Elting, C., Kray, C., and Laakso, K., Presenting Route Instructions on Mobile Devices — From Textual Directions to 3D Visualization, in *Exploring Geovisualization,* Dykes, J., MacEachren, A.M. and Kraak, M.J., Eds., Elsevier, Amsterdam, 2004.

Dunston, P., Wang, X., Billinghurst, M., and Hampson, B., Mixed Reality Benefits For Design Perception, *19th International Symposium on Automation and Robotics Construction* (ISARC 2002), NIST, Gaithersburg, MD, 191–196, 2002.

GEIST, 2004, project Web site, http://www.tourgeist.de, accessed 24 January 2005.

Hake, G., Grüneich, D., and Meng, L., Kartographie, de Gruyter, Sammlung Göschen, 2002.

Holweg, D. and Schneider, O., GEIST: Mobile Outdoor AR-Informations System for Historical Education with Digital Storytelling, in *Federal Ministry of Education and Research: Virtual and Augmented Reality Status Conference Proceedings 2004,* CD-ROM, Leipzig, Germany, 2004.

Höllerer, T.H. and Feiner, S.K., Mobile augmented reality, in *Telegeoinformatics Location-Based Computing and Services,* Karimi, H.A. and Hammad, A., Eds., CRC Press, Boca Raton, FL, 2004.

Ioannidis, N., Ed., *ARCHEOGUIDE — Augmented Reality-Based Cultural Heritage On-Site Guide,* GITC, Lemmer, 2002.

Jawa 2 Platform, Micro Edition (J2ME), Sun Developer Network, Sun Microsystems, Inc., 2005, http://java.sun.com/j2me/index.jsp, accessed 24 January 2005.

Karagiozidis, M., Ed., Location Aware Visually Enhanced Ubiquitous Services, *IST Mobile & Wireless Telecommunications Summit 2002,* 16–19 June 2002, Thessaloniki, Greece, 2002.

Karagiozidis, M., Xenakis, D., Demiris, A.M., and Ioannidis, N., LOVEUS: Software Architecture, *41st FITCE Congress,* 4–7 September 2002, Genoa, Italy, 2002.

LoVEUS, 2004, project Web site, http://loveus.intranet.gr, accessed 24 January 2005.

Malaka, R. and Zipf, A., DEEP MAP — Challenging IT research in the framework of a tourist information system, in *Information and Communication Technologies in Tourism 2000,* Fesenmaier, D., Klein, S. and Buhalis, D., Eds., Proceedings of ENTER 2000, 7th International Congress on Tourism and Communications Technologies in Tourism, Barcelona, Spain, Springer Computer Science, Wien, New York, 2000, 15–27.

Schilling, A., Coors, V., and Laakso, K., Dynamic 3D maps for tourism applications, in *Design of Map-Based Mobile Services,* Zipf, A. et al., Eds., Springer, Heidelberg, Germany, 2004.

Schilling, A., Coors, V., Giersich, M., and Aasgaard, R., Introducing 3D GIS for the Mobile Community Technical Aspects in the Case of TellMaris in *International Workshop on Mobile Computing*, "Assistance, Mobility, Applications" (IMC 2003), Proceedings 2003, Rostock, Germany, 2003, 86–92.

Schilling, A. and Coors, V. (2004): *3D Maps on Mobile Devices,* in Branki, C.; Unland, R.; Wanner, G. (Hrsg.): Multikonferenz Wirtschaftsinformatik (MKWI) 2004, Universität Duisburg-Essen, 9.–11. März 2004, Band 3: Mobile Business Systems, Mobile and Collaborative Business, Techniques and Applications for Mobile Commerce (TAMoCO), Essen 2004.

TELLMARIS, 2003, project Web site, http://www.tellmaris.com, accessed 24 January 2005.

ULTRA, 2004, project Web site, http://ist-ultra.org/index.shtml, accessed 24 January 2005.

Zadorozhny, V. and Chrysanthis, P., Location-based computing, in *Telegeoinformatics Location-Based Computing and Services,* Karimi, H.A. and Hammad, A., Eds., CRC Press, Boca Raton, FL, 2004.

Part III

Interoperability

6 Ontology and Semantic Interoperability

Thomas Bittner, Maureen Donnelly,
and Stephan Winter

CONTENTS

6.1 INTRODUCTION

One of the major problems facing systems for computer aided design (CAD); architecture, engineering, and construction (AEC); and geographic information systems (GIS) applications today is the lack of interoperability among the various systems. When integrating software applications, substantial difficulties can arise in translating information from one application to the other. In this paper, we focus on *semantic* difficulties that arise in software integration. Applications may use different terminologies to describe the same domain. Even when applications use the same terminology, they often associate different semantics with the terms. This obstructs information exchange among applications. To circumvent this obstacle, we need some way of explicitly specifying the semantics for each terminology in an unambiguous fashion. Ontologies can provide such specification. It will be the task of this paper to explain what ontologies are and how they can be used to facilitate interoperability between software systems used in computer aided design; architecture, engineering, and construction; and geographic information processing.

6.2 LANGUAGES AND COMMUNICATION PROCESSES

Communication is an exchange of information about entities and relations between a sender and a receiver. Information is formulated in some language. A language consists of symbols arranged in a well-defined manner. The symbols of a language are not meaningful *per se*. The meaning of a symbol needs to be made explicit by specifying its intended interpretation, i.e., by specifying to which entity (entities) or relation it refers to.

We can think of information exchange from a sender to a receiver as a sequence of distinct processes: (i) translating the symbols of the language in terms of which the sender expresses his information into a language that can be sent through a communication channel; (ii) sending the information encoded in this intermediate language through a channel to the receiver; (iii) translating the received symbols into symbols of a language in terms of which the receiver represents its information; and (iv) interpreting the symbols by identifying the entities and relations they refer to in the way intended by the sender. The (partial or complete) failure of any of these processes may result in a loss of information (Shannon and Weaver, 1949).

Spatial information, i.e., information about spatial entities and spatial relations between them, can be communicated, e.g., via intermediate languages such as natural language, graphical languages, and formalized computer languages. Today, natural language is used mainly in communication between — or to — human beings. Natural language is used, for example, to communicate route directions, i.e., information about how to find a route in a spatial environment. Car navigation systems, for example, give route directions in natural language. Graphical languages are used in sketches and maps. Car navigation systems may give route directions not only in verbal form but may also use maps or graphical direction symbols on a screen. For the communication of spatial information between computers, languages of underlying data exchange formats such as *shapefiles* or *dxf* are used. Particularly desirable in this context are languages that are standardized and whose specifications are available to the public, e.g., *GML* or *VRML*.

Every language is characterized by its syntax and its semantics. The syntax concerns the symbols a language recognizes and the rules that govern how to construct well-formed sentences using those symbols. For languages used to communicate information, agreement about the rules of syntax is assumed as part of the accepted procedures between the communicating partners (Austin, 1975). In the specific case of spatial information, this agreement might mean that the sender uses grammatically correct natural language in verbal route directions, maps that conform to cartographic accepted procedures, or a VRML file with proper XML syntax. Deviations from a mutually accepted syntax complicate the decoding of the message (understanding) by the receiver and can lead to communication failure. For example, an error-tolerant Web browser might be able to repair some breaches of XML syntax but will fail to read the transmitted information if other breaches occur.

The semantics of a language fixes the meaning of its expressions (symbols, terms, or sentences). Usually this is done by specifying interpretations for the language expressions in a given domain. The interpretation of a name is the individual it refers to. For example in most contexts in the English language the name "The Eiffel Tower" refers to a specific steel construction in the center of Paris. The interpretation of a predicate is a set of entities, e.g., the interpretation of the predicate "is blue" is the set of all blue things in the domain of interpretation. The interpretation of an n-ary relation symbol is a set of n-tuples of entities. For example, the interpretation of the relation symbol "is part of" is the set of all ordered pairs (x, y) such that the individual x is a part of the individual y. If we constrain our attention, for example, to Tom's body parts, then the interpretation of "is part of" contains ordered pairs like (*Tom's left thumb, Tom's left hand*), (*Tom's left hand, Tom's left arm*), (*Tom's left arm, Tom's body*), etc.

The meaning of an atomic sentence determines its truth value: "Tom's arm is part of Tom's body" is true since Tom's arm is part of Tom's body, i.e., there is an ordered pair (*Tom's left arm, Tom's body*) in the relation denoted by the relation symbol "is part of." Atomic sentences can be combined to complex sentences using logical connections such as "and" and "or." Let A and B be atomic sentences. The complex sentence "A and B" is true if and only if A is true and B is true. Similarly, the complex sentence "A or B" is true if and only if A is true or B is true.

6.3 SEMANTIC HETEROGENEITY

Communication obstructions arise from the fact that sender and receiver employ different languages for representing information internally. In the case of information systems, these languages might have been established in different contexts and for a wide variety of purposes. As a result, it might happen that the same symbol might have different meanings in different languages, or distinct symbols in different languages might have the same or overlapping meanings (Bishr, 1998; Vckovski et al., 1999). This semantic heterogeneity causes serious problems, since it is often not clear how to interpret expressions properly in a communication process.

As a very simple example of semantic heterogeneity, consider the term "tank." In an information system used in a military context, it usually refers to a certain kind of armored vehicle. In an information system used to store information about zoological equipment, the term "tank" refers to a kind of container that can hold water and serve as a habitat for fish. Now suppose that both an information system about armored vehicles and an information system about zoological equipment are used on a military basis and that the two information systems are to interoperate within a base-wide facility management system. In this case, it is not obvious how to interpret the expression "three tanks."

Comparing the two terminology systems reveals, for example, that ATKIS has a term "forest," but CORINE has no term of the same meaning. A close match in CORINE is the term "mixed forest," whose meaning overlaps but is not identical to that of ATKIS's "forest" (Visser et al., 2001). To determine whether a data item classified as "mixed forest" according to the CORINE terminology can also be classified as a forest according to the ATKIS terminology, we need definitions that state the meaning of each term in some language that is more expressive than either ATKIS or CORINE.

To use terminology systems within a single domain or across domains in an unambiguous manner, it is important to make the semantics (i.e., the meaning) of the terms constituting the systems explicit. Assigning an explicit semantics to every terminology system enables us to interpret data items such as "three tanks" differently, depending on whether the data is structured by a military terminology system or by a zoological terminology system. Similarly, explicit semantics for the CORINE and ATKIS terminologies are essential for integrating data entries like Auenwald-Leipzig is a "mixed forest" (in CORINE) with data entries like Auenwald-Leipzig is a "forest" (in ATKIS).

6.4 ONTOLOGIES

Ontologies are tools for specifying the semantics of terminology systems in a well-defined and unambiguous manner (Gruber, 1993; Guarino, 1998). Ontologies are used to improve communication either between humans or computers by specifying the semantics of the symbolic apparatus used in the communication process. More specifically, Jasper and Uschold (1999) identify three major uses of ontologies: (i) to assist in communication between human beings, (ii) to achieve interoperability (communication) among software systems, and (iii) to improve the design and the quality of software systems. In this paper, we focus on (i) and (ii) and distinguish two major kinds of ontologies: logic-based and nonlogic-based ontologies.

6.4.1 LOGIC-BASED ONTOLOGIES

A *logic-based* ontology is a logical theory (Copi, 1979). The terms of the terminology, whose semantics is to be specified, appear as names, predicate and relation symbols of the formal language. Logical axioms and definitions are then added to express relationships between the entities, classes, and relations denoted by those symbols. Through the axioms and definitions, the semantics of the terminology is specified by admitting or rejecting certain interpretations.

Consider again the symbol "is part of" interpreted as the (proper) "part of" relation as described above. An ontology can explicate the meaning of this symbol by stating that: (A1) if x is part of y, the y is not a part of x, i.e., stipulating that the "is part of" relation is asymmetric, and (A2) if x is part of y, and y is part of z, then x is part of z, i.e., stipulating that the "is part of" relation is transitive. The statements (A1) and (A2) can be used as axioms of a logical theory of parthood. (A1) and (A2) specify meaning by excluding nonintended interpretations of the relation symbol "is part of."

Consider the relation *as tall as,* which is constituted by ordered pairs like *(Tom, Jerry), (Jerry, Tom)*, etc., where Tom and Jerry are two people who are equally tall. Since axiom (A1) stipulates that the symbol "is part of" must be interpreted as a relation that is asymmetric, it cannot be interpreted as the relation as tall as. This is because *as tall as* has the pairs *(Tom, Jerry)* and *(Jerry, Tom)* as members, which taken together violate the asymmetry axiom (A1). The axioms of a logic-based ontology specify meaning by rejecting interpretations that do not conform with the intended use of the terms of the underlying terminology. Notice that the technique of specifying the semantics of a terminology by *constraining* possible interpretations using an axiomatic theory is very general and not limited to a particular domain. For an extended discussion see Guarino (1998).

6.4.2 Nonlogic-Based Ontologies

Often, the semantics of terminology systems are specified using *nonlogical* ontologies. Examples are ontologies stated in natural language as in the various ISO standards or in semiformal languages such as UML.

Nonlogical ontologies do not specify the semantics of a terminology system by constraining the permissible interpretations of the terms by means of logical axioms. An important class of nonlogic-based ontologies are *standards*. A standard specifies the meaning of a terminology by fixing the interpretation of the terms with respect to a single, well defined, and fixed domain of interpretation. Disambiguity of terms is achieved, since cases in which the same symbol has different meanings cannot occur and cases in which distinct symbols have the same meaning are avoided by agreeing on the use of terms.

Consider the standard specifying the semantics of the ATKIS terminology system. The semantics of the term "forest," for example, is defined informally as a kind of vegetation area that has forest plants or cultivated grass as vegetation, and in addition, has a size of at least ten hectares (this example was taken from Visser et al., 2001). This definition is very specific and meaningful only in the relatively narrow scope of the standard and with respect to the other terms specified within the standard. In a similarly specific way, another standard specifies the intended meaning of the CORINE terminology.

Standards often appear where legislating bodies had the power to establish a common terminology for the scope of application of a law. Prototypical examples are ATKIS and CORINE. ATKIS is an established standard in the Federal Republic of Germany, and for official geographic data of the scale 1:25,000. Similar standards exist in nearly every country. With the CORINE project, the European Commission defined a common terminology for land cover classifications in the area of the European Union to collect, coordinate and ensure the consistency of information about the environment and the natural resources in the European Community.

Similar catalogues of shared terminology are established in numerous application areas of CAD. It is the economic pressure to share data in larger projects that drives this development. One arbitrary example is the body of rules defined jointly by the district heating industries of Germany, Austria, and Switzerland (see, e.g., http://www.agfw.de). These rules are adopted by CAD systems for their layers for the utility industry. Some problems with standardization in these application areas are the rapid technological progress and the lack of obligation to follow agreed rules.

6.4.3 META-STANDARDS VS. REFERENCE ONTOLOGIES

Consider the ATKIS and the CORINE terminology systems. Since the domains of interpretation of the two terminologies overlap, complex cases of semantic heterogeneity, as discussed above, might occur. Due to their informal and specific characters, the standards specifying the semantics of the terminologies are not powerful enough to resolve those heterogeneities. For the integration of the two terminologies a third, more expressive, terminology is required. The semantics of this terminology may be specified by a logic-based ontology, which then is called a *reference ontology*. The semantics of the reference terminology may be specified by a standard, which then is often called a *meta*-standard.

Suppose we have a meta-standard or a reference ontology covering the terminology used in environmental planning. We can then establish semantic relationships between the terms in specific terminologies like ATKIS and CORINE and the terms defined in the broader terminology of environmental planning. The relationships between terms in ATKIS and CORINE are established, by translating first from one specific terminology to the broader terminology and then from the broader terminology to the other specific terminology. This strategy has been used with a rudimentary reference ontology in Stuckenschmidt et al. (1999).

One advantage of the strategy of using a meta-standard or a reference ontology is that we do not need to establish direct links between all of the various terminology systems but only between each terminology system and the terminology specified by the relevant meta-standard or reference ontology. Also, the terminology of the meta-standard or the reference ontology will ideally be formulated in expressive languages that enable us to make distinctions (e.g. between CORINE's "mixed forest" and ATKIS' "forest") that cannot be made within the terminology systems.

(Meta) standard-based ontologies are useful in restricted domains and relatively homogeneous environments, while the use of logic-based reference ontologies is more suitable for the integration of large terminologies in nonrestricted domains and heterogeneous environments (Ciocoiu et al., 2000). Reference ontologies can be used to specify the semantics of rather general terminology systems and to integrate a broader variety of standards for at least two reasons. First, the underlying semantics of logic-based ontologies is not limited to a single domain but is specified in a rather general manner by means of logical axioms. Second, due to the underlying logic, the consistency of the ontology can be verified and intended and nonintended consequences can be discovered. The second point is important especially for large terminologies (Rector, 2003).

6.4.4 LOGIC-BASED REASONING

The reasoning facilities of the logical apparatus underlying a logic-based ontology can be used to compute consequences of the assumptions that have been made. For example, from the facts "Tom's left thumb is part of Tom's left hand" and "Tom's left hand is part of Tom's left arm," a computer can, using axiom (A2), derive that Tom's left thumb is also part of Tom's left arm.

The reasoning facilities can also be used to discover nonintended consequences and inconsistencies. For example, in our ontology we might have "door handle part of door" and "door part of house." By (A2) we then have "door handle part of house." This consequence might not necessarily be intended, since a door handle is not, in the same sense, a part of a house as the door, the roof, the walls, or the windows, which are parts that have a direct *function* for the house as a whole (Winston et al., 1987). If this consequence is unacceptable, then more complex notions of parthood, such as functional parthood or constitutional parthood, are required in our ontology (Artale et al., 1996).

The specification of the semantics of a terminology system by means of a nonlogic-based ontology may be sufficient for human communication, since (i) humans understand natural language, and (ii) reasoning-based axioms like (A1) and (A2) are part of human common-sense reasoning (Davis, 1990). Computers, however, do not have this kind of background knowledge and built-in reasoning facilities. For this reason, ontologies that are intended as support for communication among computer programs or between humans and computers need to be specified in a language of formal logic that supports deductive reasoning and can be implemented on a computer.

6.4.5 INTEROPERABILITY

There are at least two different ontology-based types of solutions to the problem of enabling different software applications to communicate: In the first type of solution, all applications *share a common terminology* in the communication process. The semantics of this shared terminology is often specified by a (meta) standard and all applications that adhere to the (meta) standard communicate using the same terminology in an unambiguous fashion. If an application internally uses a terminology that is different from the terminology of the standard, then transformation mappings need to be established. If the application terminology has a well-defined semantics (for example, given by a different, more narrow standard) then semantic heterogeneity can be resolved by the human specialists who write the software that performs the transformation.

The second type of solution is more flexible. Here, applications use different terminology systems whose semantics are specified using logic-based ontologies. A broader terminology, whose semantics is also specified by a logic-based ontology, is used as an interlingua or reference terminology. Relationships between the terminologies are indirect: each terminology can be mapped into, or from, the reference terminology. Since the semantics of the more specific terminologies are specified using logic-based ontologies, the mappings from and to the reference terminology can often be computed automatically (Stuckenschmidt et al., 2004). To enable computer programs to automatically generate transformations between different terminology systems is the core of the dream of the Semantic Web (Berners-Lee et al., 2001; Egenhofer, 2002).

With the growth of the Semantic Web, the specification of the semantics of terminology systems using *description logic*-based ontologies has become popular. A description logic is a specific form of formal logic that can be run efficiently on a computer (Baader et al., 2002). In ontologies specified using a description logic, axioms like (A1) and (A2) can be represented, and automatic reasoning can be performed without human assistance by a computer program.

6.5 STANDARDS AND REFERENCE ONTOLOGIES FOR SPATIAL INFORMATION SYSTEMS

In the following sections, we discuss potential uses of standards and reference ontologies for interoperating software applications in CAD, AEC, and GI processing. Note that, in the remainder, we use phrases like "CAD, AEC, and GI systems" or simply "spatial information systems" to refer to software systems used in CAD, AEC, and GI processing.

6.5.1 SPATIAL DATA STANDARDS AND THEIR LIMITATIONS

In principle, both ontology-based solutions based on standards as well as solutions based on logic-based reference ontologies can be exploited to provide the foundations for systems that facilitate interoperability between the distinct software systems used in CAD, AEC, and GI processing. However, standardization will be most successful in cases where software systems share "common ground" that can be made explicit as a standard. This standard then enables interoperability by ensuring that all applications share a common terminology with an unambiguous semantics in communication processes, as described above.

For spatial information systems, this means that there can be a large degree of standardization of the *spatial component* that can be exploited for facilitating interoperability. This is because the spatial components of these systems are based on terminologies that underlie the processing and communication of information about spatial location. Already, today, data standards are applied quite successfully in the processing of this kind of spatial information.

Some prominent de-facto standards for communicating spatial information are the file formats *shapefile* and *dxf* (owned by the companies ESRI and Autodesk, respectively). The specification of each file format defines a language with a terminology for expressing spatial information and rules of grammar that determine how to form well-formed expressions. However, the provided terminology is rather narrow and limited to expressing relatively simple information about the geometry of spatial entities. Moreover, the specification of the semantics is rudimentary and informal. Nevertheless, both file formats are accepted as standards for the communication of spatial information, and most other vendors have enabled their products to directly read and write files in those formats.

It is important to recognize that, strictly speaking, the spatial components of CAD, AEC, and GIS only provide a means for processing and communicating information about the *location* of spatio-temporal entities. However, information about location is only one aspect of spatio-temporal information. Spatio-temporal information covers information of all aspects of the wide variety of entities ranging from table-top scale (auto parts, computers) to large scale (rivers, continents), from human artifacts (cars) to natural phenomena (wetlands), from crisp entities with well-defined boundaries (land parcels) to entities subject to vagueness and boundary indeterminacy (wetlands, mountains). We hold that to specify the semantics of a terminology system that is general enough to support the communication of information about entities characterized by a corresponding vast variety of different properties and relations by means of a standard is very difficult, if not impossible.

Notice that this does not mean that there cannot be standards for attribute data. Standardized product catalogues are quite common, and ATKIS and CORINE certainly are standardized terminology systems for attribute data. Our point is that there is not likely to be a (meta-) standard that incorporates all (or sufficiently many) product catalogues used to annotate CAD and AEC data, or a meta-standard that incorporates all the (standardized) terminology systems used in AEC and standardized GIS terminologies, including ATKIS and CORINE, etc. This is because the strength of a standard is that it is based on a well constrained terminology and the specification of the meaning of those terms within a limited and well-defined domain. In such a framework, there are no resources to deal, for example, with phenomena like vagueness, indeterminacy, and granularity in a way that is valid across different scales or different kinds of spatial entities.

To specify the semantics of a terminology system that is general enough to integrate a wide variety of different standards and to support the communication of information between heterogeneous sources such as CAD, AEC, and GI systems, a reference ontology is required.

6.5.2 STANDARDS FOR THE SPATIAL COMPONENT

Standardization is sufficient for providing the basis for semantic interoperability among the *spatial* components of CAD, AEC, and GI systems. This is because the domain of interpretation of the terminology systems used to describe the spatial aspect of the entities represented in CAD, AEC, and GI systems is well understood, i.e., good mathematical models exist. As pointed out in Chomicki and Revesz (1999a) and Kanellakis et al. (1990), the mathematical models that provide the semantics for any computer-implemented geometry language, no matter what dimension, are *semi-algebraic sets*: point sets forming lines, surfaces, and volumes, which are described using polynomial formulae in which only numbers that can be processed on a computer occur (Kanellakis et al., 1990). Thus, the aim of any spatial data standard is to find a commonly accepted way of describing a well-defined class of objects: semi-algebraic sets.

Notice, however, that because of the particularities of computer arithmetic, the representation of semi-algebraic sets on a computer is far from trivial. However, these problems are well known (Herring, 1991) and a variety of solutions have been proposed (Gueting and Schneider, 1995; Chomicki and Revesz, 1999b; Miller and Wentz, 2003). Eventually, these solutions will find their way into a standard.

Standards are established in CAD and AEC, as well as in GIS. An example for the previous is *Extensible* 3D (ISO, 2004), an XML-enabled format for the exchange of three-dimensional CAD data developed by the Web3D Consortium. An example for the latter is the *Simple Feature Specification* of the Open Geospatial Consortium (OGC) (Beddoe et al., 1999), which is also the basis for GML, the XML-enabled exchange format for two-dimensional geographic data. CAD/AEC and GIS standards differ not only in dimensions, but also in their primitives. CAD/AEC, and Extensible 3D in particular, offers boundary representations and parametric geometry (constructive solid geometry, CSG). GIS allow only boundary representations. The following paragraphs discuss some properties of standards taking OGC's simple feature specification as an example.

Simple features. The simple feature specification introduces a terminology and specifies its semantics. Parts of the terminology are shown in Figure 6.1. The terminology includes terms like "geometry," "point," "line," etc. The standard organizes these terms into a subsumption (is a) hierarchy, i.e., the term "geometry" subsumes the more specific terms "point," "curve," "surface," etc. The interpretation of the term "point" is specified informally as "A zero-dimensional geometry and represents a single location in coordinate space. A point has an x-coordinate value and a y-coordinate value."(Beddoe et al., 1999).

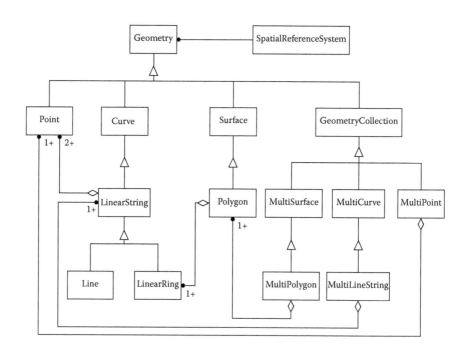

FIGURE 6.1 The geometry class hierarchy of OGC (from Beddoe et al., 1999).

The semantics of the term "curve" is specified as "a one-dimensional geometric object usually stored as a sequence of points, with the subtype of the curve specifying the form of the interpolation between the points (Beddoe et al., 1999). Currently, there is only one term subsuming "curve": "LineString," which is interpreted as a linear interpolation between the points. The specification then continues to distinguish open and closed, and simple and nonsimple (self-intersecting) curves, etc. (For more details see Beddoe et al., 1999.)

Topological relations. Besides providing a terminology for expressing information about semi-algebraic sets (simple features), the OGC also provides a terminology for expressing information about *topological relations* between those sets. For that purpose, the OGC standard utilizes the nine-intersection model (Egenhofer and Franzosa, 1991). Using this formalism, the standard provides a semantics for terms like *disjoint, touches, crosses, within,* and *overlaps.*

Let a and b be semi-algebraic sets denoted by geometric features according to the OGC standard, e.g., two areas or a line and an area, etc. We can identify the boundary of a, the interior of a, the complement of a, and for b, respectively. The semantics of terms referring to topological relations that can hold between a and b is specified by characterizing the intersection of the sets classified as interior, boundary, and complement, with respect to a and to b. Between a and b a total of nine intersections can be built: the interior of a intersected with the interior of b, the interior of a intersected with the boundary of b, and so on. The resulting intersections are sets, which may be empty or nonempty. Nonempty intersection sets maybe of dimension 0 (i.e., points), 1 (lines), etc. The semantics of the term *disjoint,* is then, for example, defined as follows. If it holds that (i) an empty intersection of the interiors of a and b, (ii) an empty intersection of the boundary of a with the interior of b, (iii) an empty intersection of the interior of a with the boundary of b, (iv) an empty intersection between the boundary of a and the boundary of b, and (v) let the remaining five intersection sets be of any dimension, then, according to the standard, the relation that holds between a and b is the relation denoted by the term "disjoint."

Note that the nine-intersection model is able to distinguish more relations than named in the standard. This causes semantic heterogeneity when different terminologies name the relations not covered by the standard differently (Riedemann, 2004).

Conformance testing. The question now is how to establish the relationship between terms in a terminology and abstract mathematical structures in a nonlogic-based framework. OGC's answer to this problem is *conformance testing*. Since the standard is not based on logic, no logical axioms can be employed to specify the intended interpretation of a symbol like "equal." What the standard does provide are test procedures that partly enumerate the relation that is the intended interpretation of a relation symbol like "equal." These enumerations are called *test data*. Using test data, it can be verified if a term like "equal," used by a given application, denotes the right relation. This is done by comparing the test data provided by the standard with the relation denoted by the term at hand.

To see how conformance testing works, consider the symbol "equal." The relation denoted by this symbol is, according to the standard, supposed to contain ordered pairs of numbers such as (0, 0) and (1.234, 1.234), but it should not contain pairs such as (2, 5) or (0.00001, 0.0001). If the relation denoted by the application term "equal" contains the pair (0.00001, 0.0001) or fails to contain the pair (1.234, 1.234), then this interpretation is not the one specified by the standard. Notice, however, that often relations denoted by terms like "equal," "greater than," etc. are infinite or very large so that test data never can exhaustively ensure conformance with the standard.

Since the scope of the standard includes semi-algebraic sets, the relation denoted by the term "equal" also holds between semi-algebraic sets. As in the case of numbers, the standard provides test data for verifying the correct interpretation of the symbol "equal" in the domain of semi-algebraic sets. The specification of the semantics of terms like "disjoint," "overlaps," etc. follows the same methodology.

OGC provides guidelines for conformance testing software implementing its simple feature specification (OGC, 1998). An implementation of an abstract speci-fication (e.g., the relation denoted by a term like "equal") is fed with a given test data set (e.g., "Joe's Blue Lake Vicinity Map") to verify its conformity with the specification of the standard. In this way, a conformance test accomplishes alignment with the semantics of a standard.

Exchange formats. Together with the terminology and its semantics, the OGC standard also specifies the grammar that describes how to form well-formed expres-sions based on the given terminology. Using this language, programs can read and write the well-known binary and text formats to communicate, i.e., to export or import, information about geospatial features.

The OGC standard as meta-standard. The OGC standard is a meta-standard. Internally, each software application can describe semi-algebraic sets using quite different terminologies. Applications, for example, can use a language based on a polar coordinate system instead of a language based on Cartesian coordinates, or use a language of constraints on intersecting half-planes, etc. In the process of communication, the internal terminology needs to be transformed into the terminol-ogy of the standard in a way that preserves the semantics. These translations are well known from mathematics (although not necessarily unique).

Notice that the terminology used by the software internally may be richer than the terminology covered by the standard. A software could, for example, represent internally other types of curves than linearly interpolated ones. In such cases, not all internal distinctions can be communicated from the sender to a receiver by means of the terminology provided by the standard.

OGC's geometry model of the simple feature specification is incorporated in the corresponding ISO norm (ISO, 2003), together with the topological operators. OGC's standard is one of several implementation specifications of OGC for making GIS interoperable. The standard is only two-dimensional and, hence, is insufficient for bridging the gap between CAD, AEC, and GI systems. However, the principles of standardization apply for all spatial information systems in the same way.

6.5.3 LIMITATIONS OF TODAY'S DATA STANDARDS FOR CAD, AEC, AND GIS INTEGRATION

Besides the commonalities shared by CAD, AEC, and GIS due to the spatial aspect of their data, there are also important differences. Several of them are discussed in detail elsewhere in this book. Differences concern which kind of spatial information is represented explicitly and which kind of spatial information is omitted or represented only implicitly. We will mention here differences in dimensionality of the data and the capability to extract information about topology. In these areas, we need to develop data standards for CAD, AEC, and GIS applications that go beyond standards that exist today.

Dimensionality. In the domains of CAD and AEC, we typically process information about spatial entities of larger-than-geographic scale. Since information about location and extension in all three spatial dimensions is required, three-dimensional semi-algebraic sets are used to model spatial properties. The language used is the language of polynomials with three free variables for x, y, and z point coordinates.

GIS are designed to process information about entities of geographic scale. For these kinds of entities, it is often sufficient to process information of location and extension with respect to the surface of the Earth. For this reason, two-dimensional semi-algebraic sets are used. The language to describe zero, one, and two-dimensional portions of the Euclidean plane is the language of (semi-algebraic) polynomials with two free variables for x and y point coordinates.

However, the surface of the Earth is not flat; it can be described in a complex mathematical language in three dimensions. Since the curvature of the Earth is relatively small, neglecting it is an acceptable simplification for areas of small geographic extent, e.g., in CAD and AEC. For areas of larger extent, curvature has to be considered. Hence, GIS represent the surface of the Earth in a cartographic projection onto a map plane, such that the third axis points (approximately) in the direction of the center of gravity.

All cartographic projections show necessarily areal or angular distortions. The type of distortion at a specific location, as well as its size, depend on the chosen projection. Consequently, transformations between different projections are complex but are necessary for integrating two data sets showing the same geographic area in different projections. Dealing with cartographic projections and transformations between them will be an essential part of standards that cover CAD, AEC, and GIS applications.

Topology. Topology is implicit in any geometric representation. Hence, in a perfect mathematical world, topology can be extracted from the information provided to specify the semi-algebraic sets. However, in computers we have to deal with finite representations of numbers, and finite precision of computations. Consider once again the relation denoted by the symbol "equal." In the perfect world of mathematics, a pair (1.000001, 1) does not belong to the relation denoted by "equal." In a computer, however, where we can only distinguish a certain number of digits, the numbers 1.000001 and 1 might be indistinguishable, since 1.000001 has been truncated to 1.

Similarly, if we extend that example to topological relations, we can easily show that often the intersection point of line a and line b computed using computer arithmetic is neither on line a nor on line b (Gueting and Schneider, 1995). This problem occurs if the coordinates of the mathematically correct intersection point of a and b cannot be represented in the language of the underlying computer arithmetic. In those cases, a nearby point with representable coordinates is chosen as a result. This point, however, often does not lie on a or b.

Geometric representations that are the result of a construction process (e.g., a mechanical tool constructed using a CAD program) are different from geometries generated from measurement and observation data. Constructed geometries fit together nicely. Independently observed and measured geometries, however, are subject to measurement and observation errors. Different methods of observation and measurement yield data of different accuracy. Consequently, the geometric representations of the same entity derived from data gained by different observation and measurement devices will be different semi-algebraic sets. Consequently, we cannot identify the different representations of the same entity using the predicate "equal," which identifies sets only if they have the same members.

Similar problems occur for other topological relations such as disjoint, touches, and overlap. Given geometric representations of two entities generated by different observation methods, it is often the case that according to the representations built from one data set, the entities are disjoint and according to representation built from another data set, the entities overlap, while in fact both objects touch.

Both errors caused by the specific character of computer arithmetic, as well as measurement and observation errors, particularly affect boundary representations used in early GI systems. For this reason, software vendors felt a need for topological data models. In those data models, topological relations are represented explicitly and not derived from the underlying geometric representation. GIS vendors started to include explicit representations of topology in their data models in the early nineties, with the first instance of TIGRIS, a system completely designed on the basis of a topological data model (Herring, 1987), based on algebraic topology. Today, all major GIS products include topology in their data model and implement the standard set of topological relations (Beddoe et al., 1999; ISO, 2003).

Topology in three-dimensional space is more complex and problematic (Baer et al., 1979; Homann, 1989). However, recent developments for three-dimensional GIS based on algebraic topology (Breunig, 1996) might form the common mathematical foundation for developing a standard converging CAD and AEC with GIS.

6.6   REFERENCE, DOMAIN, AND TOP-LEVEL ONTOLOGIES

After discussing the use of standards in facilitating interoperability of CAD, AEC, and GIS software, we now focus on how to use logic-based ontologies for this purpose.

6.6.1   DOMAIN ONTOLOGIES AS REFERENCE ONTOLOGIES

Domain ontologies are ontologies that provide the semantics for the terminology covering a discipline. Since such terminologies are often large and complex, they are potential fields of application for logic-based ontologies. Domain ontologies are prototypical candidates for serving as reference ontologies.

Disciplines in which logic-based domain ontologies are quite common include artificial intelligence, medicine, biomedicine, and microbiology. Examples of medical domain ontologies are GALEN (Rector and Rogers, 2002a,b), SNOMED(CT)

(Spackman et al., 1997), and the UMLS (Bodenreider, 2004). An example of a domain ontology for biomedicine and microbiology is the description logic-based version of the GeneOntology (The Gene Ontology Consortium, 2001). In artificial intelligence, the CYC-ontology is quite popular (Lenat and Guha, 1990).

Unfortunately, there are only preliminary attempts to provide logic-based domain ontologies within the geo-domains (i.e., in domains in which CAD, AEC, and GIS are used for information processing). Examples are in Grenon and Smith (2004) and Mark et al. (1999) for general ontologies of geographic categories, in Sorokine and Bittner (2005) and Sorokine et al. (2004) for domain ontologies for ecosystems, and in Feng et al. (2004) for a domain ontology for hydrology.

Logic-based geo-domain ontologies could provide semantic foundations for terminology systems used in the various geo-disciplines, for example for terms used to classify geo-political entities, or ecosystems, or to describe water flow. Logic-based domain ontologies for environmental planning, for example, may be used as reference ontologies for integrating the terms of specialized terminology systems, such as CORINE or ATKIS, as described above. A logic-based domain ontology for architectural design and engineering could serve as a reference ontology for specific terminologies underlying the usage of CAD systems and GI systems in this domain.

Building a domain ontology is an expensive and complex process (Rector, 2003). Recent research has shown that robust domain ontologies must be as follows (Guarino, 1998; Gangemi et al., 2002):

1. Developed rigorously using formal logic
2. Based on a well-designed *top-level ontology*

Above we have discussed some aspects of the first point; we now consider the second.

6.6.2 TOP-LEVEL ONTOLOGIES

In contrast to domain ontologies, top-level ontologies specify the semantics for very general terms (called here "top-level terms") that play important foundational roles in nearly every discipline. Top-level terms include relations like "equal," "is part of," "connected to," "dependent on," "caused by," "instance of," "subclass of," etc. (E.g., Germany is part of the European Union, Canada is connected to the United States, and South America is an instance of continent.) These relations are used to structure information and define domain-specific terminology in geo-disciplines such as hydrology and environmental science, as well as in medicine, biology, and politics. Within, for example, an environmental planning domain ontology, we need to use top-level relations to regulate the usage of terms. (E.g., in our specification of the semantics of the term "city forest" we might specify every instance of the class city forest is a part of some instance of the class city.)

Well-designed domain ontologies use top-level ontologies as their foundation. This means that the semantics of the domain vocabulary is specified using top-level terms with an already well-established semantics. One advantage of this approach is that top-level ontologies need to be developed only once, and then can be used in many different domains. Another advantage is that a top-level ontology provides semantic links between the domain ontologies that are based on it.

The potential power of the methodology of building domain ontologies based on a well-designed top-level ontology can be illustrated by considering the success of Egenhofer's formalization of the binary topological relations (a specific subcollection of top-level notions), such as "connected to," "overlaps with," "tangential part of," etc. (Egenhofer and Franzosa, 1991). Ten years after the introduction of Egenhofer's formalization, the functionality based on this formalization is part of all mainstream GIS, and the terminology provided by Egenhofer is part of the OGC standard, as discussed in Section 6.5.2. It was included in the standard because, despite the relatively abstract character of Egenhofer's formalization, the relations treated in the formalism are familiar to researchers and practitioners in many domains. Egenhofer provided one component of a top-level ontology: a formal treatment of static topological relations. The Egenhofer formalism is the basis for uniform and semantically compatible strategies for representing and reasoning about topological data in environmental science, meteorology, urban planning, and other geo-disciplines.

6.6.3 Important Components of Top-Level Ontologies

Temporal aspects. Topological relations (and any other kind of properties and relations) are treated as time independent in today's CAD, AEC, and GI systems. This means that we can say that x and y are connected or that x is a part of y, but we cannot say *when* x and y stand in these relations. *Spatio-temporal* top-level ontologies will build on atemporal formalisms by constructing time-dependent spatial relations and properties. This is important for geo-domains as well as for AEC, because spatial properties and relations among entities in these domains change over time. For example, the Czech Republic was not part of the European Union in 2001, but it is part of the European Union in 2004. The Auenwald in Leipzig was located in a singly connected region 100 years ago. Today, it consists of multiple disconnected patches. Your car may have an old engine today and a new one tomorrow. Thus, often we need to say that x was a part-of y at time t_1, but x is no longer part of y at time t_2, or that x was located in y at t_1 but is no longer located in y at t_2.

Moreover, in disciplines such as hydrology, it is insufficient to collect and represent data only about enduring things (watersheds, rivers, etc.) and their changes over time (different size at different times, different water level at different times, etc.). It is critical also to collect and to represent data about the processes that cause those changes (e.g., soil erosion, water flow, etc.). A central component of a spatio-temporal top-level ontology is a theory of the interaction between endurants (entities like watersheds that change over time) and perdurants (processes like soil erosion that unfold or develop over time).

Endurants and perdurants behave differently in time (Hawley, 2001; Gangemi et al., 2002; Masolo et al., 2004; Grenon and Smith, 2004; Bittner and Donnelly, 2004; Bittner et al., 2004a): endurants are wholly present (i.e., all their current proper parts are present) at any time at which they exist. For example, you (an endurant) are wholly present in the moment you are reading this. No current part of you is missing. Endurants can change and yet remain the same. For example, all the cells in your body are replaced over a period of 10 years, nevertheless you are the same person today you were 10 years ago.

Perdurants, on the other hand, are extended in time by virtue of possessing different temporal parts that are characterized by different temporal extents. In contrast to endurants, they are only partially present at any time at which they exist — they evolve over time. For example, at this moment only a (tiny) part of your life (a perdurant) is present. Larger parts of your life — such as your childhood — are not present at this moment.

Individuals and classes. In geo-domain ontologies a logical theory of individuals and classes needs to provide the top-level notions that are needed for specifying the semantics of classification systems (Sorokine and Bittner, 2005; Sorokine et al., 2004). Particularly in geo-classifications at small scales, the distinction between classes and individuals (I am an individual, human being is a class) is often ignored. This, in turn, leads to an inconsistent usage of relations like "part of," "instance of," and "subclass of" ("is a").

For example, in the Southeast Alaska Ecological Subsection Hierarchy (Nowaki et al., 2001), we find the following assertion: Boundary Ranges Icefield is a subclass of Icefield. An ontological analysis reveals, however, that Boundary Ranges Icefield is an individual, and Icefield is a class. Since "subclass of" is a relation between two classes, Boundary Ranges Icefield cannot be a subclass of Icefield. By contrast, "instance of" is a relation between an individual and a class. Thus, we can say that Boundary Ranges Icefield is an instance of the class Icefield. An example of the proper use of the "subclass of" relation is the statement, Icefield is a subclass of Active Glacial Terrains (the class of all active glacial terrains). (See Sorokine and Bittner, 2005, and Sorokine et al., 2004, for an extended discussion.)

Such errors in the proper use of the top-level relations "part of," "subclass of," and "instance of" make it impossible to achieve a consistent specification of the semantics underlying a classification (Guarino and Welty, 2000; Zhang et al., 2004). The resulting classification systems will be (at least partially) incompatible with other classifications. This, in turn, prevents exchanging data and interoperability at the level of software applications using those classifications. A logical theory of individuals and classes makes the distinctions between these different notions explicit and helps the domain specialist to use those notions in the appropriate manner. For a theory of this kind see, for example, Bittner et al. (2004b).

6.6.4 Top-Level Ontologies for CAD, AEC, and GIS Integration

Logic-based geo-domain ontologies are critical for integrating software used in CAD, AEC, and GI processing. Top-level ontologies facilitate the development of well-formed domain ontologies. The following top-level notions are particularly important for the development of domain ontologies for integrating software used in CAD, AEC, and GI processing.

The notions of process and change (perdurants and the endurants they change) are critical in domains in which GIS have been used traditionally, for example, in hydrology and in environmental science (Feng et al., 2004). To overcome the historical distinction between AEC and GI systems, both need to take into account the notions of process and change. Incorporating these notions into reference ontologies that provide a bridge between the two is the first step toward applications that have the strengths of both kinds of systems.

Endurants can be divided further into two major categories (Smith, 2003): independent endurants, such as cups, buildings, bridges, and highway systems, and dependent endurants, such as qualities, roles, states, or functions. Here we focus on the former. The following kinds of independent endurants can be distinguished: substances, fiat parts of substances, aggregates of substances, and boundaries of substances:

- Substances are maximally connected entities, i.e., they have connected bonafide boundaries (i.e., boundaries that correspond to discontinuities in the underlying reality).
- Neither your nose nor your arm is a substance. Both are fiat parts of you, i.e., (at least partly) bound by boundaries that do not correspond to discontinuities in the underlying reality but to a human definition on a continuum. Similarly, mountains are fiat parts of the planet Earth, or land parcels are fiat parts of the surface of the Earth.
- Aggregates of substances are not substances either. Examples of aggregates are your family, the heating facilities in a given building, the water supply facilities in a town, etc.

Historically, CAD and AEC systems have focused on modeling aggregates, while fiat subdivisions, such as land parcels, were modeled primarily in GIS. To overcome this distinction, it is important to incorporate the concepts of substance, fiat part, and aggregate into both systems. Top level ontologies give a formal account of relationships between substances, their fiat parts, and the aggregates they form. Again, incorporating these notions into reference ontologies that provide the bridge between software systems used in CAD, AEC, and GI processing is the first step toward interoperability between those software systems.

6.7 SUMMARY

In this paper we discussed how ontologies can be used to overcome the historic incompatibilities between software systems used in the domains of computer aided design, architectural engineering, and geographic information processing, and to facilitate the semantic interoperability among those systems.

We started with a discussion of the role of terminology systems in communication processes and how ontologies are used to specify the semantics of the terms in those systems. We distinguished two major kinds of ontologies: logic-based and nonlogic-based ontologies. We also distinguished two major strategies of applying ontologies in order to facilitate interoperability: the use of data standards and the use of reference ontologies. The former strategy is based on a shared nonlogic-based ontology, which is encoded into a standard, and all applications that adhere to the standard are interoperable by using the same terminology in an unambiguous fashion. In the second strategy, a logic-based reference ontology is used as an interlingua, which provides a means of transformation between the terminologies used by the different software applications.

For software used in the domains of CAD, AEC, and GI processing, we argued that the standard-based strategy is sufficiently powerful to facilitate the interoperability of the software systems for processing purely spatial data. We also argued that, to achieve interoperability at the level of processing attribute data, the more powerful and more flexible strategy of using logic-based reference ontologies is needed. In particular, we argued that, due to the heterogeneous character of the domain ontologies, which describe the attribute data in the domains of CAD, AEC, and GI processing, top-level ontologies need to be a foundational component of the reference ontologies.

Top-level ontologies describe notions that are so general that they are common to reference ontologies in any domain. For this reason, they are of particular importance for the design of reference ontologies that are used to facilitate interoperability between domains as heterogeneous as CAD, AEC, and GI processing.

Spatio-temporal top-level ontologies are critical for information processing, not only in all the geo-disciplines and in architectural design and engineering, but, more generally, in all disciplines dealing with any type of spatio-temporal phenomena. They facilitate the exchange of data and interoperability across different domains (e.g., geography, medicine, epidemiology, CAD, AEC), since they ensure that foundational spatio-temporal terms are used in a unified and semantically compatible manner.

ACKNOWLEDGMENTS

Bittner and Donnelly acknowledge, gratefully, financial support from the Wolfgang Paul Program of the Alexander von Humboldt Foundation, the EU Network of Excellence in Semantic Datamining, and the Volkswagen Foundation Project "Forms of Life." Winter acknowledges an internal grant from the University of Melbourne.

REFERENCES

Artale, A., Franconi, E., and Guarino. N., Open problems for part-whole relations, in *International Workshop on Description Logics,* Boston, MA, 1996.

Austin, J.L., *How to Do Things with Words*, Clarendon Press, Oxford, 1975.

Baader, F., Calvanese, D., McGuinness, D.L., Nardi, D., and Patel-Schneider, P.F., Eds., *The Description Logic Handbook*, Cambridge University Press, 2002.

Baer, A., Eastman, C., and Henrion, M., Geometric modelling: a survey. *Computer Aided Design*, 11 (5), 253–272, 1979.

Beddoe, D., Cotton, P., Uleman, R., Johnson, S., and Herring, J.R., OpenGISR simple features specification for SQL revision 1.1. OpenGISR Implementation Specification, OpenGIS Project Document 99-049, Open GIS Consortium, Inc., 1999.

Berners-Lee, T., Hendler, J., and Lassila, O., The semantic web, *Scientific American*, May 2001.

Bishr, Y., Overcoming the semantic and other barriers to GIS interoperability, *International Journal of Geographical Information Science*, 12 (4), 299–314, 1998.

Bittner, T. and Donnelly, M., The mereology of stages and persistent entities, in Lopez de Mantaras, R. and Saitta, L., Eds., *Proceedings of the 16th European Conference on Artificial Intelligence,* IOS Press, 283–287, 2004.

Bittner, T., Donnelly, M., and Smith, B., Endurants and perdurants in directly depicting ontologies, *AI Communications,* 14 (4), 247–258, 2004a.

Bittner, T., Donnelly, M., and Smith, B., Individuals, universals, collections: on the foundational relations of ontology, in Varzi, A.C. and Vieu, L., Eds., *Proceedings of the Third International Conference on Formal Ontology in Information Systems, FOIS04,* Volume 114 of *Frontiers in Artificial Intelligence and Applications,* IOS Press, 37–48, 2004b.

Bodenreider, O., The unified medical language system (UMLS): integrating biomedical terminology, Nucleic Acids Res, 2004.

Breunig, M., Integration of Spatial Information for Geo-Information Systems, Volume 61 of *Lecture Notes in Earth Sciences,* Springer, Berlin, 1996.

Chomicki, J. and Revesz, P.Z., Constraint-based interoperability of spatiotemporal databases, *Geoinformatica,* 3 (3), 211–243, 1999a.

Chomicki, J. and Revesz, P.Z., A geometric framework for specifying spatiotemporal objects, in *Proceedings of the Sixth International Workshop on Temporal Representation and Reasoning,* 1999b.

Ciocoiu, M., Gruninger, M., and Nau, D.S., Ontologies for integrating engineering applications. *Journal of Computing and Information Science in Engineering,* 2000.

Copi, I.M., *Symbolic Logic,* Prentice Hall, Englewood Cliffs, NJ, 1979.

Davis, E., *Representations of Commonsense Knowledge,* Morgan Kaufmann Publishers, Inc., Palo Alto, CA, 1990.

Egenhofer, M., Toward the semantic geospatial web, in *Tenth ACM International Symposium on Advances in Geographic Information Systems,* ACM Press, McLean, VA, 2002, 1–4.

Egenhofer, M.J. and Franzosa, R.D., Point-set topological spatial relations, *International Journal of Geographical Information Systems,* 5 (2) 161–174, 1991.

Feng, C-C., Bittner, T., and Flewelling, D.M., Modeling surface hydrology concepts with endurance and perdurance in *Proceedings of GI-Science 2004,* LNCS 3234, Egenhofer, M.J., Freksa, C., and Miller, H.J., Eds., 2004, 67– 80.

Gangemi, A., Guarino, N., Masolo, C., Oltramari, A., and Schneider, L., Sweetening ontologies with DOLCE, in *Proceedings of EKAW,* Siguenza, Spain, 2002.

Grenon, P. and Smith, B., SNAP and SPAN: Prolegomenon to geodynamic ontology, *Spatial Cognition and Computation,* 2004.

Gruber, T., A translation approach to portable ontology specification, *Knowledge Acquisition,* 199–220, 1993.

Guarino, N., Formal ontology and information systems, in *Formal Ontology and Information Systems, (FOIS'98),* Guarino, N., Ed., IOS Press, 1998.

Guarino, N. and Welty, C., A formal ontology of properties, in *Proceedings of EKAW-2000: The 12th International Conference on Knowledge Engineering and Knowledge Management,* LNCS, Dieng, R. and Corby, O., Eds., Springer-Verlag, 2000.

Gueting, R.H. and Schneider, M., Realm-based spatial data types: the rose algebra, *VLDB Journal,* 4, 100–143, 1995.

Hawley, K., *How Things Persist,* Clarendon Press, Oxford, 2001.

Herring, J.R., Tigris: topologically integrated geographic information system, in *Auto-Carto 8,* ACSM -ASPRS, Baltimore, 1987, 282–291.

Herring, J.R., The mathematical modeling of spatial and non-spatial information in geographic information systems, in *Cognitive and Linguistic Aspects of Geographic Space,*

Volume 63 of *Nato ASI Series D*, Mark, D.M. and Frank, A.U., Eds., Kluwer, Dordrecht, The Netherlands, 1991, 313–350.

Homann, C.M., *Geometric and Solid Modeling*, Series in Computer Graphics and Geometric Modeling, Morgan Kaufmann, San Mateo, CA, 1989.

ISO, Geographic information — spatial schema, International Standard ISO 19107, ISO, 2003.

ISO, Information technology computer graphics and image processing extensible 3d (x3d). International standard 19775:200x, ISO/IEC, 2004.

Jasper, R. and Uschold, M., A framework for understanding and classifying ontology applications, in *Proceedings of the IJCAI99 Workshop on Ontologies and Problem-Solving Methods(KRR5)*, 1999.

Kanellakis, P.C., Kuper, G.M., and Revesz, P.Z., Constraint query languages, in *9th ACM PODS*, 299–313, 1990.

Lenat, D.B. and Guha, R.V., *Building Large Knowledge-Based Systems: Representation and Inference in the CYC Project*, Addison-Wesley, Reading, MA, 1990.

Mark, D., Smith, B., and Tversky, B., Ontology and geographic objects: an empirical study of cognitive categorization, in *Spatial Information Theory. Cognitive and Computational Foundations of Geographic Information Science*, Number 1661 in Lecture Notes in Computer Science, Freksa, C. and Mark, D., Eds., Springer-Verlag, 1999, 283–298.

Masolo, M., Borgo, S., Gangemini, A., Guarino, N., Oltramari, A., and Oltramari, A., WonderWeb deliverable D18 — ontology library (final), Technical report, ISTC-CNR, 2004.

Miller, H.J. and Wentz, E.A., Representation and spatial analysis in geographic information systems, *Annals of the Association of American Geographers*, 93 (3), 574–594, 2003.

Nowaki, G., Shephard, M., Krosse, P., Pawuk, W., Fisher, G., Baichtal, J., Brew, D., Kissinger, E., and Brock, T., Ecological subsections of southeastern Alaska and neighboring areas of Canada, Technical Report R10-TP-75, USDA Forest Service, Alaska Region, October 2001.

OGC, Conformance test guidelines for OpenGIS simple features specification for SQL, revision 1.0, OpenGIS Project Document 98-046r1, Open GIS Consortium, Inc., 1998.

Rector, A.L. and Rogers, J.E., Ontological issues in using a description logic to represent medical concepts: Experience from GALEN: Part 1— principles, *Methods of Information in Medicine*, 2002a.

Rector, A.L. and Rogers, J.E., Ontological issues in using a description logic to represent medical concepts: experience from GALEN: part ii -the GALEN high level schemas, *Methods of Information in Medicine*, 2002b.

Rector, R., Modularization of domain ontologies implemented in description logics and related formalisms including OWL, In *Proceedings of the International Conference on Knowledge Capture*, 121–128, 2003.

Riedemann, C., Towards usable topological operators at GIS user inter-faces, in *7th Conference on Geographic Information Science (AGILE '04)*, Toppen, F. and Prastacos, P., Eds., Crete University Press, Crete, Greece, 2004, 669–674.

Shannon, C.E. and Weaver, W., *The Mathematical Theory of Communication*, The University of Illinois Press, Urbana, 1949.

Smith, B., Basic formal ontology, Technical report, Institute for Formal Ontology and Medical Information Science, University of Leipzig, Germany, 2003.

Sorokine, A. and Bittner, T., Understanding taxonomies of ecosystems: a case study, in *Developments in Spatial Data Handling*, Fisher, P., Ed., Springer-Verlag, Berlin, 2005, 559–572.

Sorokine, A., Bittner, T., and Renschler, C., Ontological investigation of ecosystem hierarchies and formal theory for multiscale ecosystem classifications, in *Proceedings of GI-Science 2004*, 2004.

Spackman, K.A., Campbell, K.E., and Cote, R.A., SNOMED RT: a reference terminology for health care, in *Proceedings of the AMIA Annual Fall Symposium*, 640–644, 1997.

Stuckenschmidt, H., Visser, U., Schuster, G., and Voegele. T., Ontologies for geographic information integration, in *Proceedings of the Workshop Intelligent Methods for Handling Environmental Information: Special Aspects of Processing Space and Time*, 1999.

Stuckenschmidt, H., van Harmelen, F., Bouquet, P., Giunchiglia, F., and Serafini, L., Using C-OWL for the alignment and merging of medical ontologies, in *Proceedings of KR-MED 2004: First International Workshop on Formal Biomedical Knowledge Representation*, Hahn, O., Ed., 2004.

The Gene Ontology Consortium, Creating the gene ontology resource: design and implementation, *Genome Res*, 11, 1425–1433, 2001.

Vckovski, A., Brassel, K.E., and Schek, H.-J., Eds., *Interoperating Geographic Information Systems*, Springer-Verlag, Berlin, 1999.

Visser, U., Stuckenschmidt, H., Wache, H., and Voegele, T., Using environmental information efficiently: sharing data and knowledge from heterogeneous sources, in *Environmental Information Systems in Industry and Public Administration*, Rautenstrauch, C. and Patig, S., Eds., IDEA Group, Hershey, PA, 2001, 41–74.

Winston, M.E., Chaffin, R., and Herrmann, D., A taxonomy of part-whole relations, *Cognitive Science*, 11, 417–444, 1987.

Zhang, S., Mork, P., and Bodenreider, O., Lessons learned from aligning two representations of anatomy, in *Proceedings of KR-MED 2004: First International Workshop on Formal Biomedical Knowledge Representation*, Hahn, O., Ed., 2004.

7 Data Integration and Interoperability: OGC Standards for Geo-Information

Carl Reed

CONTENTS

7.1 INTRODUCTION TO THE PROBLEM

Geospatial content is stored in a variety of systems and formats. Different projects from AEC applications are maintained in software-dependent file formats. Data exchange or data integration has always been rather problematic between CAD systems, as well as between CAD and GIS. Increasingly, however, there is a requirement to be able to seamlessly utilize both GIS and CAD data in a common application environment.

The membership of the Open Geospatial Consortium Inc. (OGC, formerly the Open GIS Consortium) is developing standards that enable open, vendor, and format-neutral geo-information discovery, access, and sharing and application deployment. While the initial focus of the work of the OGC has mostly been on traditional 2D GIS issues and less on the integration of GIS and AEC, the focus has progressed to the next stage. For example, the OGC's current abstract model for geometry incorporates many of the geometry types required in the AEC industry, and the OGC Geography Markup Language (GML) allows encoding of these geometry types and, to a certain extent, supports modeling of abstract 3D structures.

The nature of both AEC systems and geospatial technology such as GIS is changing rapidly. An increasing number of AEC systems is offering GIS functionality, and many GIS products provide for visualization and maintenance of 3D spatial objects. Furthermore, DBMS vendors are offering support for geospatial data types and for spatial operators and functions (which can be readily used by any front-end application).

Another significant development related to geospatial content is the provision of interoperable services that allow seamless combination of spatial information from multiple, distributed sources. The underlying understanding is that data should be collected only once using the most appropriate equipment, maintained at the institution where this can be done most efficiently, but open for use to a maximum number of users and applications. The interoperable services have to facilitate this process, i.e., they have to help production, publishing, discovery, retrieval, and, eventually, use and understanding of geo-information at multiple levels (e.g., local, national, and international).

A number of OGC initiatives have already been taken in this direction, resulting in a number of specifications of the Open Geospatial Consortium being adopted not only by the OGC but also by ISO as international standards. The OGC and ISO collaboration is reflected in the increasing number of joint work efforts of OGC and ISO. Several ISO standards are incorporated into the OGC Abstract Specification and various OGC specifications for Web services, are now either ISO standards or are draft ISO standards. While the OGC interoperability initiatives have advanced open standards for geospatial Web services, members understand that continued work is needed to cover a broader set of geo-information management and utilization interoperability requirements.

Topics discussed in this chapter include the following:

1. Relevant OGC work for the integration of data from AEC applications and GIS
2. Support of parametric primitives in abstract feature specifications

3. Discussion of the LandXML ← → LandGML project
4. Map presentation
5. Future work of the OGC relevant to CAD/GIS integration

7.2 DISCUSSION

True CAD/GIS integration requires the ability to properly store and communicate geospatial content containing the third dimension. This has traditionally been an area of weakness in GIS technology. In comparison to the advancements in 3D visualization, little has been accomplished in the realization of a practical 3D GIS. This is also true of interface specifications (current or planned) within the OGC. The obvious reason for the traditional focus on 2D remains: the transition to 3D means an even greater diversity of object types and spatial relationships, as well as very large data volumes. In a 2D GIS, a feature or phenomenon is represented as an area of grid cells or as an area within a polygon boundary. A 3D GIS, on the other hand, deals with volumes. Consider a cube. Instead of looking at just its faces, there must also be information about what lies inside the cube. To work, a 3D GIS requires this information to be complete and continuous. This means that in terms of CAD/GIS integration, we have the additional requirement of the ability to encode and communicate three-dimensional, structured geospatial data. The latter is the realm of standards work in the OGC.

7.3 WHAT IS THE OGC?

The OGC is a global voluntary consensus standards organization that envisions "a world in which everyone benefits from geographic information and services are made available across any network, application, or platform." Inherent in this vision is the requirement for geospatial standards and strategies to be an integral part of business process and enterprise architectures.

The OGC consists of 260+ members — geospatial technology software vendors, systems integrators, government agencies, and universities — participating in a consensus process to develop, test, and document publicly available interface specifications and encodings for the geospatial industry. Open interfaces and protocols defined by Open Geospatial Specifications are designed to support interoperable solutions that "geo-enable" the Web, wireless and location-based services, and mainstream IT, and to empower technology developers to make complex spatial information and services accessible and useful to all kinds of applications.

Thus, OGC envisions the full integration of geospatial data and geoprocessing resources into mainstream computing and the widespread use of interoperable, commercial geoprocessing software throughout the information infrastructure.

7.4 THE OGC ABSTRACT SPECIFICATION

The abstract model that provides the foundation or lingua franca of all the OGC standards work is called the OGC Abstract Specification. The OGC Abstract Specification consists of a number of topic volumes. Each topic volume addresses a specific set of abstract models, such as for meta-data or geometry, required as a foundation unit upon which to build OGC interoperability standards. Collectively, the complete set of topic volumes is termed the Open Geospatial Abstract Specification.

The purpose of the Abstract Specification is to create and document a conceptual model sufficient enough to allow for the creation of Implementation Specifications and:

- To relate software and system design to real-world situations
- To capture and precisely state requirements and domain knowledge so that all stakeholders can understand and agree on them
- To think about the design of the system
- To capture design decisions in a mutable form separate from the requirements
- To generate usable work products (such as prototypes and proof-of-concept implementations)
- To organize, find, filter, retrieve, examine, and edit information about large systems
- To explore multiple solutions economically
- To master complexity

The Abstract Specification, specifically the Abstract Model, is used in all these capacities. Additionally, it provides an implementation-neutral, but technically complete "language" to discuss issues of interoperability.

The following adopted OGC standards are grounded in the Abstract Specification. Further, the OGC standards identified below have relevance in terms of solving a number of CAD/GIS integration and interoperability issues. A key topic volume is Topic 1 — Feature Geometry. Topic 1 is identical to the ISO TC 211 19107 (Feature Geometry) standard. This document provides an abstract model for a large number of geometry types that are of high relevance to CAD/GIS interoperability. These geometry types include b-splines, Bezier curves, triangulated surfaces, cones, spheres, parametric curve surfaces, and arc-by-bulge (cul-de-sac).

7.5 HOW CURRENT OGC STANDARDS CAN BE USED FOR CAD/GIS INTEGRATION

There are a number of OGC Specifications that can be used immediately to enhance the sharing and integration of CAD/GIS content and services. How these interface standards are used and what CAD/GIS interoperability issues they will solve is dependent on the requirements of the users and the applications. For example, if the requirement is to deploy a client application that allows the user to browse and view both CAD and GIS content as if it were stored in a single system or database, then implementing the OGC Web Map Service (WMS) Interface Specification might be the ideal solution. If the requirement is to share content, such as ingest CAD data into a GIS, then perhaps a Geography Markup Language (GML) application profile is the way to go. This section discusses existing OGC standards that are of use for solving the CAD/GIS integration problem.

7.5.1 SEAMLESS VISUALIZATION: WEB MAP SERVICE INTERFACE SPECIFICATION

The OGC Web Map Service (WMS) Version 1.3 Interface Specification provides an excellent mechanism for quickly developing applications that allow a client to display CAD and GIS data without costly data conversion. The WMS utilizes an HTTP request structure that packages a request to one or more servers that understand a WMS request. These servers could provide access to a GIS database, a CAD database, a simulation database, an imagery database, a spatially enabled RDBMS, and so forth. The server processes the WMS request and sends back a geo-registered picture to the client. The picture may be a PNG, a GIF, or a JPEG image. Since the WMS allows the client to specify a coordinate reference system, all picture images are returned to the client in the same reference system, allowing the pictures to be "displayed" one on top of the other. Since transparency is supported, then, for example, road centerlines can be displayed on top of a satellite image and then cut-and-fill design data can be displayed on top of the other two layers. Figure 7.1 provides a simple example of the use of the WMS specification.

7.5.2 RETURNING CAD/GIS CONTENT TO THE CLIENT — THE WEB MAP SERVICE INTERFACE SPECIFICATION

The purpose of the OGC Web Feature Service Interface Specification is to provide a well-known structure and mechanism for query and retrieval of geographic features. The OGC WFS interface is a collection of operations (implemented as messages carried over HTTP) for retrieving and manipulating geographic features. Specifically, the WFS interface specifies five operations: (1) get the capabilities of a WFS service,

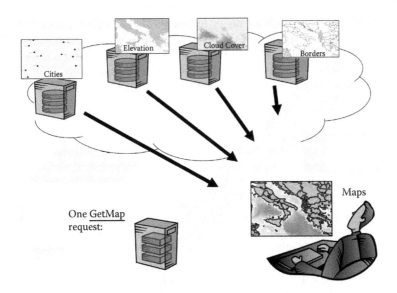

FIGURE 7.1 Example of a client accessing multiple WMS-enabled servers.

(2) retrieve feature-type descriptions (meta-data), (3) specify a query and get feature(s), (4) specify a transaction, and (5) lock one or more features in a repository.

The WFS requests are generated on the client and are posted to a WFS server using HTTP. A WFS request consists of a description of a query or data transformation operations that are to be applied to one or more features. Requests to a WFS-enabled server are restricted to features of the type(s) returned by an invocation of a WFS retrieve feature-type descriptions. This is in contrast to the OGC WMS interface, which allows a client to overlay map images (raster data) for display served from multiple WMS servers.

The default payload encoding for transferring features from the server to the client is the Geography Markup Language (GML). As the WFS service allows querying a feature repository, the features come back defined as GML. The features that are returned are selected by tests on values within the properties of a feature as specified in the query filter. (See GML description, 7.5.5.)

7.5.3 SPECIFYING PORTRAYAL RULES

The importance of the visual portrayal of geographic and CAD data cannot be overemphasized. The skill that goes into portraying data (whether it be geographic or tabular) is what transforms raw information into an explanatory or decision-support tool. From USGS's topographic map series to NOAA and the U.K.'s admiralty nautical charts to AAA's TripTik, fine-grained control of the graphical representation of data is a fundamental requirement for any GIS or CAD professional.

The OGC Style Layer Descriptor (SLD) Specification addresses the need for geospatial consumers (either humans or machines) to control the visual portrayal of the data with which they work. The current OGC WMS specification supports the ability for an information provider to specify very basic styling options by advertising a preset collection of visual portrayals for each available data set. However, while a WMS currently can provide the user with a choice of style options, the WMS can only tell the user the name of each style. It cannot tell the user what a portrayal will look like on the map. More importantly, the user has no way of defining their own styling rules. The ability for a human or machine client to define these rules requires a styling language that the client and server can both understand.

Defining this portrayal language is the main focus of the SLD specification, and it can be used to portray the output of Web Map Servers, Web Feature Servers, and Web Coverage Servers. In many cases, however, the client needs some information about the data residing on the remote server before he, she, or it can make a sensible request. This led to the definition of new operations for the OGC services in addition to the definition of the styling language.

There are three basic ways to style a data set. The simplest one is to color all features the same way. For example, one can imagine a layer advertised by a WMS as "hydrography," consisting of lines (rivers and streams) and polygons (lakes, ponds, oceans, etc.). A user might want to tell the server to color the insides of all polygons in a light blue, and color the boundaries of all polygons and all lines in a darker blue.

A more complicated requirement is to style features of the data differently depending on some attribute. For example, in a roads data set, style highways with

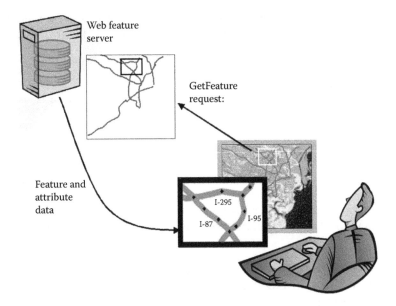

FIGURE 7.2 A transactional WFS application being used to update transportation information collected via survey techniques.

a three-pixel red line; style four-lane roads in a two-pixel black line; and style two-lane roads in a one-pixel black line.

7.5.4 THE WEB TERRAIN SERVICE INTERFACE SPECIFICATION

This document is a companion specification to the OGC Web Map Service Interface Implementation Specification Version 1.3. As previously discussed, WMS specifies how individual map servers describe and provide their map content. The present Web Terrain Service specification describes a new operation, GetView, and extended capabilities that allow a 3D terrain view image to be requested, given a map composition, a terrain model on which to drape the map, and a 3D viewpoint from which to render the terrain view. A simple attempt is also made to reconcile 2D and 3D viewpoints by allowing the requested 3D area of view to be approximated with a WMS bounding box.

Thus, a Web Terrain Service (WTS) produces views of georeferenced data. We define a "view" as a visual representation of geodata; a view is not the data itself. These views are generally rendered in a pictorial format, such as Portable Network Graphics (PNG), Graphics Interchange Format (GIF) or Joint Photographic Expert Group (JPEG) format. The WTS specification standardizes the way in which clients request views and the way that servers describe their data holdings. The current interface specification supports the following parameters:

- Point of Interest (POI): the exact location in x, y, z space of the viewer's focus
- Distance: the distance between the viewer and the POI in meters

- Pitch: the angle or inclination (in degrees) between the viewer and the POI (0° means the viewer is looking horizontally and –90° means the viewer is looking straight down on the POI)
- Yaw: azimuth, the angle representing the "head swivel" (0° faces due north, 90° faces due east, etc.)
- Angle of view (AOV): The angle representing the breadth of landscape in the viewer's scene

An SLD schema can be used to specify a limited set of portrayal rules for the terrain rendering. Supported capabilities include specifying color ranges by z-value, shaded relief mapping, opacity, and contrast enhancement. The current version of the SLD (and, hence, WTS) does not support more sophisticated visualization rules such as for texturing, multiple light sources, and anti-aliasing. Also, the capabilities accessible via a WTS interface are dependent on the capabilities of the server side 3D engine.

7.5.5 COMMUNICATING AND TRANSPORTING CAD/GIS CONTENT IN AN OPEN, INTEROPERABLE MANNER: GEOGRAPHY MARKUP LANGUAGE (GML) 3.1

Geography Markup Language (GML) is an XML grammar written in XML Schema for the modeling, transport, and storage of geographic information. The key concepts used by GML to model the world are drawn from the OGC Abstract Specification (available online at http://www.opengis.org/techno/abstract.htm) and relevant ISO TC 211 standards, especially 19107 — Feature Geometry.

GML provides a variety of objects for describing geography, including features, coordinate reference systems, geometry, topology, time, units of measure, and generalized values. A geographic feature is "an abstraction of a real world phenomenon; it is a geographic feature if it is associated with a location relative to the Earth." So a digital representation of the real world can be thought of as a set of features. The state of a feature is defined by a set of properties, where each property can be thought of as a {name, type, value} triple.

The GML specification defines the XML Schema syntax, mechanisms, and conventions that:

- Provide an open, vendor-neutral framework for the definition of geospatial application schemas and objects
- Allow profiles that support proper subsets of GML framework descriptive capabilities
- Support the description of geospatial application schemas for specialized domains and information communities
- Enable the creation and maintenance of linked geographic application schemas and data sets
- Support the storage and transport of application schemas and data sets
- Increase the ability of organizations to share geographic application schemas and the information they describe

Implementers might decide to store geographic application schemas and information in GML, or they might decide to convert from some other storage format on demand and use GML only for schema and data transport.

There are a number of functional characteristics of GML that are suited to content sharing in a CAD/GIS environment:

- A rich set of geometry types that can be used to model CAD data types, including parametric representations. These representations include but are not limited to simple and complex 2D and 3D geometry for points, line-strings, polylines, rings, circles, circularArc3Points, circularArc2PointWithBulg, circularArcCenterPointWithRadius, polynomialSpline, cubicSpline, rationalSpline, surface patches, complex surfaces, and triangulated meshes.
- The ability to represent observations. Observation models the act of observing, often with a camera, a person, or some form of instrument ("an act of recognizing and noting a fact or occurrence often involving measurement with instruments"). An observation is considered to be a GML feature with a time at which the observation took place, and with a value for the observation. A reference system provides a scale of measurement for assigning values "to a location, time, or other descriptive quantity or quality."
- The ability to represent coordinate reference systems. A coordinate reference system consists of a set of coordinate system axes that is related to the Earth through a datum that defines the size and shape of the Earth.
- A temporal reference system provides standard units for measuring time and describing temporal length or duration. Following ISO 8601, the Gregorian calendar with UTC is used in GML as the default temporal reference system.
- A units of measure (UOM) dictionary provides definitions of numerical measures of physical quantities, such as length, temperature, and pressure, and of conversions between UOMs.
- The ability to represent 3D geometry. GML 3 has introduced several new geometry types, including data types for 3D geospatial data.
- GML 3 offers a set of topology constructs.

Currently, GML 3.1 supports 2D topology. While GML 3.1 provides support for 3D geometry, there is no ability to express and encode 3D topology. There are also currently no plans to support 3D topology.

7.6 LANDGML ← → LANDXML: AN EXAMPLE OF CAD/SURVEY/GIS CONTENT SHARING THAT MAINTAINS SEMANTIC INTEGRITY

In 2004, OGC members AutoDesk, Galdos, and the U.S. Corp of Engineers completed the LandXML/LandGML Interoperability Experiment. OGC Interoperability Experiments are brief, focused, and low-overhead initiatives led and executed by

OGC members to achieve specific technical objectives that further interoperability and the OGC Technical Baseline.

The member-driven LandGML IE built and tested a GML 3.0 application schema for encoding LandXML 1.0 documents (LandGML) and provided a tool to transform LandXML 1.0 documents into LandGML documents and a tool to transform LandGML documents into LandXML 1.0 documents.

7.6.1 A Bit about LandXML

LandXML is an industry-driven, open XML data exchange standard that provides interoperability in applications serving the civil engineering, survey, and transportation industries. The LandXML.org Industry Consortium, initiated by Autodesk and now comprised of 190 companies, government agencies, and universities, developed the standard. LandXML is now broadly supported in online cadastral applications, GIS applications, survey field instruments, civil engineering desktop and CAD-based applications, instant 3D viewers, and high-end 3D visualization rendering applications. LandXML XML Schemas support the encoding of the following:

- Alignments — road centerline line, curve, and spiral geometries, vertical alignment and cross sections
- GradeModel — 3D design surface data
- Roadways — road data model
- PipeNetworks — hydraulic pipes and structures
- Project — project name and description
- Surfaces — digital terrain models
- Units — linear, angular, area, time, temperature, pressure, diameter, volume, flow, and velocity
- CgPoints — cogo point elements
- CoordinateSystem — Cartesian and other Earth-based georeferenced coordinate systems
- Monuments — survey monument data
- Parcels — parcels and legal boundary data
- Survey — survey raw data collection parameters and measurements

7.6.2 The LandXML ⬅➡ LandGML Interoperability Experiment

The goal of this OGC Interoperability Experiment was to automate the flow of civil engineering and land survey data directly into GIS applications and back again using XML-based open standards, allowing land development, transportation, and GIS professionals to exchange high precision design data throughout the entire life cycle of a project. In order to ensure the seamless, "lossless" flow of data between CAD systems and CAD/GIS environments, the GML 3.1Application Schema for LandXML needed to be defined.

In order to develop the LandGML Application Schema, the IE team incrementally modeled every type of element and attribute in LandXML. Using GML 3.1,

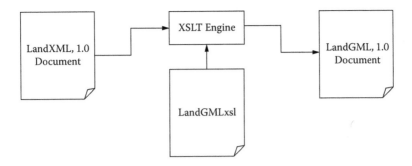

FIGURE 7.3 The process of transforming LandXML to LandGML.

they were then able to express *all* of the survey and design data model elements as geographic features with "standard" geometries — and attributes as elements where possible. This design decision will make it much easier for applications that support GML to support LandGML. Once the LandXML➔LandGML mapping was completed, the mapping was captured as an XSLT transformation tool from LandXML to LandGML and from LandGML to LandXML. Figure 7.3 captures the essence of the process.

Team member Galdos built and tested a Java/XSLT-based transformation tool for the LandXML to LandGML transformation. An online LandXML to LandGML transform demonstration was provided by Autodesk and is available at http://www.landxml.org. The LandGML to LandXML transform tool provided by Autodesk/LandXML.org is an open source C++ console application based on Xerces C SAX parser.

7.6.3 LANDXML ↔ LANDGML DEMONSTRATION

A key part of the Interoperability Experiment was a demonstration of a "roundtrip" LandXML/LandGML transformation. In the demonstration, survey data for road alignments and parcels were encoded into LandXML, transformed to LandGML, and then from LandGML back into LandXML. The final file was then ingested into AutoCAD and rendered. The roundtrip was 100% error free.

7.7 PUTTING A STANDARDS-BASED CAD/GIS WORKFLOW IN PLACE

Figure 7.5 provides an example of how multiple OGC interface standards coupled with the LandXML/LandGML transformation tools can be integrated into a CAD/GIS workflow.

In this workflow, survey information is encoded as LandXML. A client application makes a request via the WFS gateway to access the survey data and to return the survey data to the client as GML encoded using the LandGML Application Profile. Another WFS call to a GIS database is used to obtain the parcel fabric as

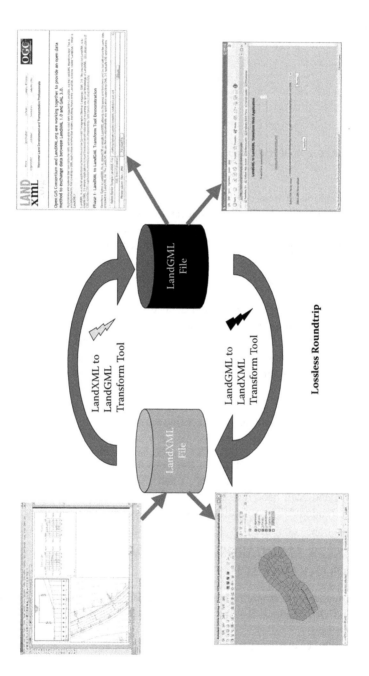

FIGURE 7.4 The LandXML ⇔ Roundtrip.

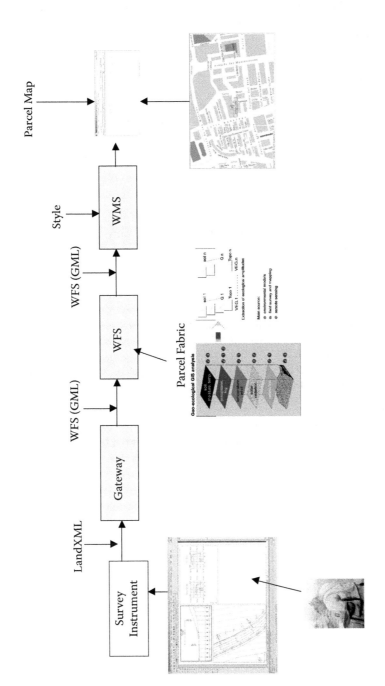

FIGURE 7.5 Multiple OGC interface standards coupled with LandXML/LandGML.

GML for the same geographic area. The client now has both the survey information and the parcel fabric. Using styling rules (Style Layer Descriptor) coupled with the WMS interface, the application can now render an integrated presentation of the survey and GIS data.

7.8 WHAT'S NEXT?

While considerable progress has been made by the OGC membership, there is still much work to be done on the standards front to enable the seamless use and integration of CADD, GIS, and 3D content and services. To provide a focused forum for the discussion of the requirements for CAD/GIS interoperability, the OGC has formed a new Working Group (WG). The mission of this new OGC WG is to address the increasingly complex issues of seamless integration of data and applications between CAD, AEX, GIS, and 3D rendering. The OGC WG would also identify and document critically important use cases that would help the OGC and other consortia, such as the Web3D, IAI, SISO, and OMG, rally together to advance standards and solutions for seamless CAD/GIS integration workflows.

REFERENCES

OpenGIS, Abstract Specification Topic 1: Feature Geometry, OGC document 01-101, 2003.
OpenGIS, Geography Markup Language (GML) 3.1, Implementation Specification, Lake, R. et al., Eds., 2004.
OpenGIS, Styled Layer Description (SLD) 1.0.0, Open Geospatial Consortium Implementation Specification, Lalonde, W. Ed., 2002.
OpenGIS, Web Map Service (WMS) 1.3 Interface Specification, de La Beaujardier, J., Ed., 2004.
OpenGIS, Web Feature Service (WFS) Interface Specification 1.1, Vretanos, P., Ed., 2005.
OpenGIS, Web Terrain Service (WTS) Interface Specification 1.0, Lieberman, J., Ed., 2005.

Part IV

Alternatives

8 3D Topological Framework for Robust Digital Spatial Models

Rodney J. Thompson

CONTENTS

8.1 INTRODUCTION

This chapter will concentrate on spatial relationships, with an emphasis on 3D topology. Topology has proved to be a useful tool in the management and analysis of digital spatial data, for the definition of spatial relationships, and for the maintenance of consistency. Although more visible in the GIS world, topology is equally important in CAD/AEC applications. Commercially available database software in the GIS field restricts topological storage to 2D only (or 2D with elevation values), while CAD/AEC operates within a more restricted form of topology, with relationships between objects being determined "on the fly."

One of the critical issues in closing the gap between the disciplines of GIS and CAD/AEC is the requirement that representations of spatial objects be shared and handled consistently by different software environments. While some progress is being made in the definition and nomenclature of spatial primitives, a major inhibitor can be found in the representations currently used to implement these primitives.

Most research to date, in the field of vector representation of spatial data, has concentrated on developing the mathematical model with the digital implementation of the mathematical model being less well understood. This chapter reviews some of the issues that this imbalance has created. The focus is on how well these approaches extend from 2D to higher dimensionality systems.

An alternate approach, known as the "regular polytope" is introduced and shown to support a rigorous and closed logic — in 2D, 3D, or higher dimensionality. This approach should enable the richness and power of the 3D representations currently available in the AEC/CAD environment to be combined with the large-scale consistency of GIS. The regular polytope approach is then further analyzed to determine its advantages and limitations, and its practicality as a spatial data storage and retrieval strategy is discussed. Finally, possible future directions for this line of research are suggested and discussed.

8.2 OUTLINE OF THIS CHAPTER

Section 8.3 to Section 8.5 provide nomenclature and background to the problem area and indicate some of the specific issues that need to be addressed.

Section 8.6 discusses some of the approaches currently applied to these issues.

Section 8.7 to 8.10 introduce the concept of the "regular polytope." The practicality of the approach as a strategy for the storage and interchange of spatial data is explored.

Finally, Section 8.11 suggests some possible future lines of research.

8.3 NOMENCLATURE

8.3.1 OPEN AND CLOSED

The terms **"open"** and **"closed"** have several different meanings in different mathematical disciplines, leading to some confusion. In this chapter, they are used in the topological sense of open or closed sets.

- **Cycle**, following the ISO 19107 (ISO-TC211, 2001) convention, has been used to describe a curve whose start and end point are the same (often called a "closed curve") or a 3D "closed" surface (see Figure 8.1).
- **Bounded**, is used to indicate an object that is fully enclosed. For example, a "volumetric parcel" defines a volume of space and is bounded. A cadastral property parcel is often not bounded above or below.

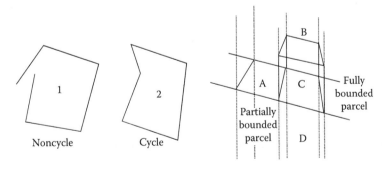

FIGURE 8.1 Nomenclature — "cycle" and "bounded." The 2D objects 1 and 2 illustrate the concept of "cycle." The 3D objects represent cadastral parcels A, B, and D being un-bounded. Parcel C is fully bounded.

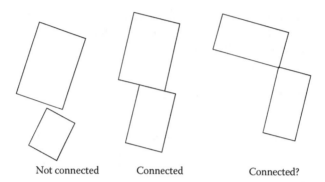

FIGURE 8.2 Connectivity of Regions. Note: the question of whether the region on the right should be considered to be connected is beyond the scope of this chapter.

8.3.2 Continuity

"Continuity" of sets can have two possible meanings. In this chapter, the following terminology is used:

- **Density** is used in the sense of a continuum. For example, an axiom of the Region-Connection Calculus (RCC) requires each region to contain a nontangential proper part, defining the regions as "dense."
- **Connectivity** means that for any two points in the region, a path can be found joining them, which remains within the region. A region with this property is known as a connected region (see Figure 8.2).

8.3.3 Accuracy and Resolution

In this chapter:

- **Accuracy** means the difference between the value recorded for a measurement, and the ideal value that would be recorded if no errors or limitations on the measurement had occurred.
- **Resolution** means the finest unit of accuracy possible in the digital representation. Usually the resolution will be significantly finer than the accuracy. The accuracy cannot be finer than the resolution.

8.3.4 Geometric Primitives

Generally speaking, the following terms are used to describe geometric primitives. It is not intended to give rigorous definitions at this time, since this is, in effect, one of the aims of this research. Loosely, the terms are:

- **Point:** The representation of an object by its position only.
- **Line segment:** A line joining two points. It is usually straight but could be a parametrically defined curve.

- **Polyline (or "linestring"):** a series of line segments connected end to end with no branching.
- **Ring:** A polyline that is joined as a cycle, i.e., the first and last points are joined together.
- **Polygon:** The area defined by a ring, possibly with exclusions defined by additional rings inside the outer ring.
- **Polyhedron:** The volume enclosed by a set of planar polygonal faces, with possible exclusions defined by other sets of planar polygonal faces.
- **Polytope:** The generalization of polygon and polyhedron to any number of dimensions.

At present, there is significant disparity in the GIS industry as to the exact definitions of these concepts, and issues such as what constitutes validity.(van Oosterom et al., 2003).

8.4 BACKGROUND

This section reviews some of the issues that are important to topology in a 3D environment. Some specific case studies are introduced to provide a background to the issues.

The functionality provided by spatial database management systems is couched in the language of topology and set theory. For example, "union," "intersection," etc., in the form of function names, are used in SQL statements such as:

```
"select union(geometry, fixed_geom) from …"
```

The behaviors assigned to these functions, generally speaking, are approximate to the usual topological or set theoretical meanings of these terms. This leads to the impression that these functions satisfy the axioms of union, intersection, etc. as defined in the discipline of topology. Unfortunately, this impression is not justified, as the following case studies indicate. Note that these are symptoms of the failure of the underlying logic and should not be interpreted as the problem itself.

8.4.1 CASE 1. ROUNDING, ACCURACY, AND RESOLUTION

Many implementations require that geometric features conform to a requirement similar to the ISO1107 definition of "isSimple()" (ISO-TC211, 2001) (See 8.4.4, Case 4, for further discussion.) The problem manifests when a test such as this is applied without regard to the accuracy of the data, and features are accepted which, while passing these validity tests, are not robust. That is to say that a feature such as that in Figure 8.3 might be accepted, but if it is moved or rounded (even by distances small relative to its accuracy), it could become invalid.

Using interchange protocols such as GML (Geography Markup Language) (OGC, 2000) the transfer of coordinate values is in decimal numbers with finite precision. This means that the consistency of the data can, and does, change as a result of the transmission. As a result, a feature that is valid before transmission might have a "self-intersecting boundary" after transmission.

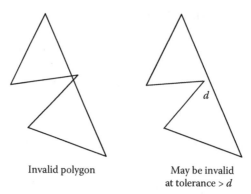

Invalid polygon

May be invalid
at tolerance > *d*

FIGURE 8.3 Self-intersection in a polygon. The polygon on the left is self-intersecting, the one on the right is not. But if the points are moved small distances, it may become so. If $d < \varepsilon$, the polygon on the right would not be valid at tolerance ε.

Milenkovic approaches this issue by defining a set of normalization rules for polygon coverages based on a parameter, ε, which is chosen so the "distance between a point and a line segment can be calculated with accuracy $\frac{1}{10}\varepsilon$" (Milenkovic, 1988). This clearly prevents interchange problems like those illustrated in Figure 8.3, provided the magnitude of the perturbation of the point positions is $< d$. On the other hand, on arrival, the data is no longer valid at a tolerance of ε, but at some smaller tolerance, $\varepsilon - \delta$.

8.4.2 Case 2. Polygon Union

The union and intersection operations in many implementations may not be associative (i.e., $A \cup (B \cup C) \neq (A \cup B) \cup C$). Particularly, the result of $\bigcup_{i=1..n} A_i$ depends on the order of execution. Each operation will typically snap the feature boundaries to the points of intersection, thus moving those boundaries. The feature that is involved in the greatest number of individual operations has the most likelihood of being moved (see Figure 8.4 to 8.7). Even the approach proposed by Milenkovic (1988), may have this failing.

8.4.3 Case 3. Geometric Equality

Since the equivalence relation axioms are referred to here and later, they are restated here. R is an equivalence relation on set X if:

- Reflexive: aRa $\forall a \in X$
- Symmetric: aRb $\Rightarrow$ bRa $\forall a, b \in X$
- Transitive: aRb, bRc $\Rightarrow$ aRc $\forall a, b, c \in X$.   (Weisstein 1999a)

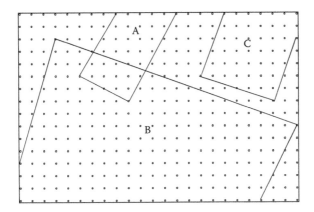

FIGURE 8.4 Forming the union of polygons A, B, and C.

Ideally, the "equal" relational operator a = b between spatial representations should determine the truth of the proposition "a is an equivalent representation of the same (or identical) real-world feature as represented by b, and is of the same accuracy."

The ISO 19107 definition of isEqual() (ISO-TC211 2001) uses the phrase "shall return true if this GM_Object is equal to another GM_Object," but qualifies this definition with: "Since an infinite set of direct positions cannot be tested, the internal implementation of equal must test for equivalence between two, possibly quite different, representations. This test may be limited to the resolution of the coordinate system or the accuracy of the data. Application schemas may define a tolerance that returns true if the two GM_Objects have the same dimension and each direct position

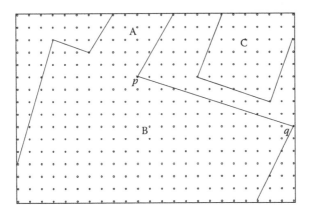

FIGURE 8.5 Forming the union as (A ∪ B) ∪ C. When A ∪ B is calculated, the snapping of the intersections of the lines causes the line *pq* to move away from polygon C, which is now not within the snap distance.

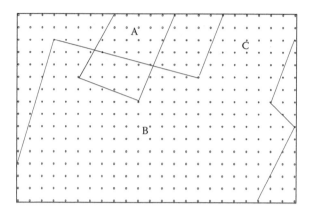

FIGURE 8.6 Forming the union B ∪ C first. With the operations applied in the other order, C would have been within the snapping distance of B as B ∪ C was formed.

in this GM_Object is within a tolerance distance of a direct position in the passed GM_Object and visa-versa" (ISO-TC211 2001 Section 6.2.2.18.3).

This definition has several weaknesses:

- The implementation is problematic since the number of possible representations that are (set-theoretically) equal to a given polygon is very large. In many implementations, the assumption will be that two objects are equal if their representations are defined by the same number of vertices in approximately the same positions. For example, a redundant point such as that introduced in Figure 8.8 is significant, contrary to the ISO definition.
- It is not definitive — the choice of a tolerance value and the technique of applying that tolerance are left to the application schema. Thus, a pair of objects might be equal in one application but not in another.

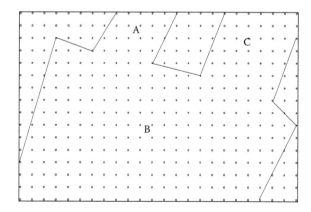

FIGURE 8.7 The Result of A ∪ (B ∪ C).

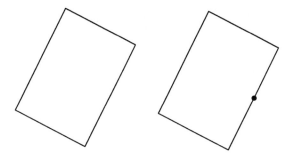

FIGURE 8.8 Polygon and "equal" polygon with redundant vertex.

- It is not transitive — it is quite possible, using this definition that a.isEqual(b), and b.isEqual(c), but not a.isEqual(c). (Note that the "ideal" definition given above is transitive.)

8.4.4 CASE 4. ISO 19107 DEFINITION OF ISSIMPLE()

In the ISO 19107 standard, this operation determines that there is "no interior point of self-intersection or self-tangency." Note that, in contrast to the definition of "isEqual()," there is no provision for any tolerance in the definition.

Also, by contrast, there is no guidance given in the standard toward the implementation of an algorithm for testing "self-intersection or self-tangency." This is particularly serious, since some implementations treat the isSimple() requirement as necessary for acceptance of a geometry. Note that in objects f and h of Figure 8.9 the overlaps could be invisibly small. It can be very difficult to locate such an error in a complex or large feature.

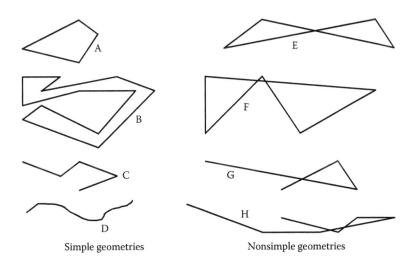

FIGURE 8.9 Simple and nonsimple geometries.

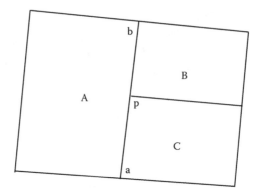

FIGURE 8.10 Subdivision of Adjoining Parcel. Point p becomes part of the definition of Parcel A

8.4.5 CASE 5. ADJOINING POLYGON POINTS

In cadastral data, a common technique to handle the subdivision of an adjacent lot is the insertion of a redundant point. For example, in Figure 8.10 point p is made a part of the definition of parcel A, which thereby becomes a five-sided polygon. This is necessary because the representation of the point p as calculated is unlikely to fall on line ab, and has several unfortunate effects.

The original line, ab, no longer exists in the database, so any attributes (e.g., measured bearing and distance) that attached to it must be managed in some other way. If a locking strategy is in use, it is necessary to lock parcel A, even though it is not really being changed in any way. This also creates an update to parcel A.

Significantly, if A is the original four-sided parcel, and A' is the parcel after the update, with point p included, by the ISO 19107 definition, A.isEqual(A'). Thus, a parcel has been replaced by an equal parcel. This highlights one of the difficulties, which can be caused by confusing equality of the digital representation with equality of the mathematical abstraction.

An equivalent problem arises in 3D cases. In practice, where volumetric parcels[1] are present, they only constitute a small percentage of all property parcels. To represent all parcels in a cadastre as 3D objects is impractical at present (and probably not particularly useful). Given current technology, hybrid approaches are most appropriate, where the vast majority of parcels are represented as 2D polygons, with the volumetric lots being represented as regions of space bounded by 3D planar polygons (Stoter and Salzmann 2003; Stoter 2004). Where volumetric parcels adjoin normal 2D parcels, a situation analogous to the above (Figure 8.10), occurs:

Figure 8.11 represents a side view of a section of the cadastre. The majority of volumetric parcels are of this form. Parcels 1 and 3 are normal 2D parcels, parcel 2 has been subdivided into strata parcels 2a, 2b, and 2c, by defining horizontal planes (p-q) and (r-s). Note that parcels 1, 2c, and 3 have no defined top, and 1, 2a, and 3 have no defined bottom.

---

[1] Normal Cadastral parcels typically are defined as 2D polygons, and are taken to be unrestricted in elevation. Volumetric parcels are defined as regions of space, bounded by (usually plane) surfaces.

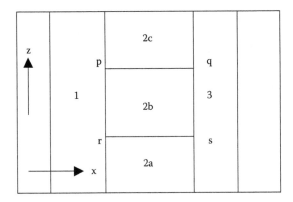

FIGURE 9.11 Volumetric parcels adjoined by normal 2D parcels. (Viewed from the side.)

Is it necessary, by analogy with Figure 8.10, to convert parcels 1 and 3 to 3D representations, so that the lines p, q, r, and s are included in their definition (making the surface (p-r) be a common boundary between parcel 1 and parcel 2b)?

8.4.6 CASE 6. DATUM CONVERSION

During the lifetime of the Digital Cadastral Data Base at the Department of Natural Resources and Mines in Queensland, it has twice been necessary to change datum. This can be expected to occur again in the future. The necessity arises for one or more reasons: the improvement of measurement technologies makes a redefinition of datum desirable; continental drift causes a movement of local features relative to distant features; or policy decisions mandate a change.

In the process of a datum change, the coordinate values of all points must be recalculated, and this calculation is necessarily of a finite accuracy. In a database of finite precision, the result is then rounded to the resolution of the database storage, introducing a pseudo-random relative movement of points.

8.5 TOPOLOGY IN 2D AND 3D

This section explores some of the current issues in 2D topology, addresses some of the attempts that have been made to extend to 3D, and discusses the ramifications of the 2D issues on the 3D approaches.

8.5.1 TOPOLOGICAL CLEANING OPERATION

The generation of "clean topology" (effectively, ensuring that the Milenkovic Normalization Rules are applied) (Milenkovic, 1988) is often a part of the acceptance of spatial data into a database. Determining appropriate parameters such as the value of ε in the Milenkovic rules for this operation is almost an art form. If this parameter is set too large, lines, points, and whole polygons can be crushed out of existence. For example, ESRI[2] recommend that "the clustering parameter you choose should be as small as possible, depending on the precision level of your data. For example,

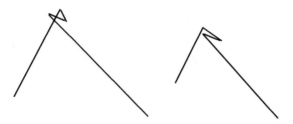

FIGURE 8.12 "Knots" in linework.

if your data is accurate within 10 metres, you would want to set your cluster tolerance no larger than 10 metres and smaller if possible." (Minami et al., 1999)

Unfortunately, this is often misinterpreted as suggesting that the smallest value that gives a clean topology be used. This is not correct, since a too small clustering parameter can cause problems later on. For example, when data is initially captured by digitizing or other methods, "knots" are sometimes formed. It is the removal of these knots that is one of the aims of topology cleaning operations.

In Figure 8.12, both of the pieces of linework are incorrect, but if the clustering distance is set too fine, the one on the right will not be detected. This discussion has been based on 2D data, however, the situation applies equally in 3D.

The calculation of topological relationships between objects is also trouble-prone. The difficulty of operations on data from different sources is discussed in Burrough and McDonnell (1998). For example: "Polygon overlay can lead to a large number of spurious small polygons that have no real meaning and must be removed." All major GIS vendors provide such "sliver removal" mechanisms, but the choice of parameters to eliminate spurious gaps and overlaps without destroying real information is not trivial. There is no agreement between implementations on (1) the set of parameters, and (2) the procedures to be followed, so it is difficult to ensure comparable results on different systems.

8.5.2 Levels of Topology in 3D

There are several variants on 2D topology, but they all have in common the concept of defining nodal points, joining those points by linestrings, and then either closing those to form a polygon coverage or utilizing the network of linestrings for graph-theory analysis (Burrough and McDonnell, 1998; Baars 2003). The network topology can be generalized into 3D by simply adding the elevation values to the point definitions, and this provides useful functionality for river tracing, etc.

The polygon coverage form of topology is more difficult to apply to a 3D equivalent. It would seem fairly obvious to continue the process started in the 2D case, defining polygonal faces as closed linestrings, and volumes as the enclosures defined by polygonal faces. The problem arises that a polygon defined by more than three points in 3D will not, in general, be planar, so it might be necessary to "triangulate" the faces as shown in Figure 8.13.

---

[2] Environmental Systems Research Institute, Inc.

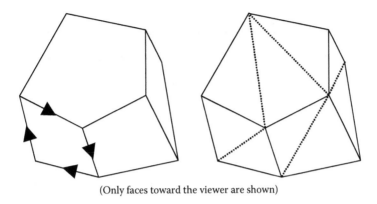

(Only faces toward the viewer are shown)

FIGURE 8.13 Left: a volume defined by planar polygonal faces, showing the orientation of one face. Right: the faces triangulated.

It is also possible to generalize triangular decomposition, breaking the volume into a "simplical complex" (Weisstein, 1999b). On the other side of this question, the real situation is that the faces of many solid representations are intended to represent planes (e.g., the boundaries of volumetric cadastral parcels, and the faces of many architectural objects), so that unnecessary triangulations should be avoided. In particular, a surface should not be triangulated if it is only the effects of rounding errors that has caused it to be detected as nonplanar.

The level of topology required in 3D will obviously depend on the type of data being recorded — and on the application to be supported by that data. There is a continuum of requirements, as described above, with the most appropriate technology dependent on the particular case. Zlatanova et al., 2002, give some guidelines in determining which of many alternatives might be appropriate.

8.6 THEORETICAL PERSPECTIVES

8.6.1 REALM-BASED GEOMETRY AND TOPOLOGY

Even the application of Milenkovic's rules (Milenkovic, 1988) does not ensure logical consistency. Correct results from the evaluation of operations are only guaranteed if the objects have been prevalidated as part of the same layer of data. Where new features are introduced, the final state of the database can still depend on the order of insertion.

In order to improve this situation Guting and Schneider (1993) introduced the concept of "Realms." In effect, all feature representations on entry to the database are compared with all existing representations in the vicinity, and the points of intersection are calculated. This can be an expensive operation, but it results in a closed and correct logic for the operations between the objects. The realms concept is further developed by Guting et al. (1995), leading to a complete, numerically robust and efficient algebra ("ROSE").

In order to prevent such problems as the nonassociativity of operations (see 8.4.2, Case 2, the realms approach is to trap lines within an envelope — introducing extra

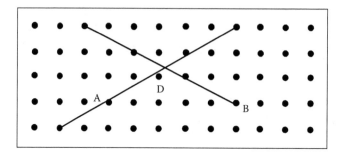

FIGURE 8.14 Calculating the intersection of two lines. (Adapted from Guting and Schneider, 1993.)

points if necessary. The technique is described thus: "Think of segment s as a rubber band and the points of the envelope as nails on a board. Now grip s at the true intersection point and pull it around P (the grid point nearest the intersection). The resultant polygonal path is the redrawing" (Guting and Schneider, 1993). The envelope of a line is the set of grid points that could be contacted by such an operation.

In the operations depicted in Figures 8.14 to 8.16, the movement of line FG has caused it to pass to the south of point A. Originally (in Figure 8.14) it passed to the north of A. This may affect the results of later operations, so extra vertices are introduced, preventing any line from crossing any grid point.

The modified solution shown in Figure 8.17 provides a solution, but at the cost of extra complexity in the final geometry. Note that the introduction of a point in a "straight" line may involve the introduction of several "envelope points." It is not clear just how many points could be required, and this is an area that has been identified as requiring further research. On the other hand, comparing Figure 8.17 with Figure 8.18, it can be seen that the wanderings of a line caused by these operations cannot exceed √2 times the grid size, thus a limit has been set on any "creeping" of the data.

Note: a datum shift could pose a difficulty for the "realms" approach (see 8.4.6, Case 6), since unless the "envelope points" in line definitions are flagged as distinct

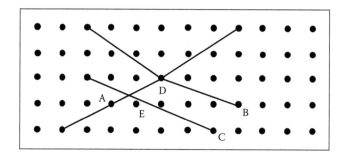

FIGURE 8.15 Movement caused by the intersection of two lines. (Adapted from Guting and Schneider 1993.)

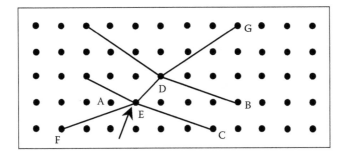

FIGURE 8.16 Movement caused by the intersection of a third line. Since point E has been inserted into line DF, point A is no longer south of the line. (Adapted from Guting and Schneider 1993.)

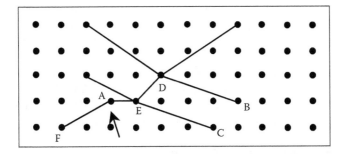

FIGURE 8.17 Modified solution — proposed by Green and Yao (1986). The line has been broken to include point A. (Adapted from Guting and Schneider 1993.)

from the "true" points, all will have to have the datum shift applied — leading to spurious complexity of the linework.

In presenting the "realms" approach, the cited papers are restricted to 2D, but there is no reason why it should be thus limited. Presumably, the same form of envelope would be defined, and any line or plane surface would be similarly constrained.

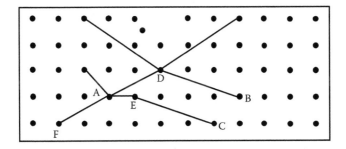

FIGURE 8.18 The result of forming intersections in a different order. Note that, in this case, the form of the final result is different, but all lines maintain the correct relationship with respect to all grid points.

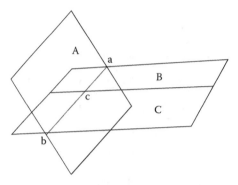

FIGURE 8.19 Intersecting plane surface A with the plane surfaces B and C.

Consider Figure 8.19, in which the plane surface A is being intersected with B and C (assumed to be coplanar). Even in this simple example, snapping of the calculated points a and b might cause envelope points to be contacted by the perimeter of A. Similarly, the calculation of c might cause generation of extra points in ac and bc. Even more, the movement of the perimeter of A will cause movement of the plane, so that envelope points can be contacted by A itself (see Figure 8.20).

This is not to say that the approach will not work in 3D, but the complexity of the resultant objects would be expected to increase dramatically.

8.6.2 CONSTRAINT DATABASE APPROACH

Jeansoulin (1998) refers to the topological encoding of data as "compiling" the topological relationships into the database. This is a useful concept, since it stresses

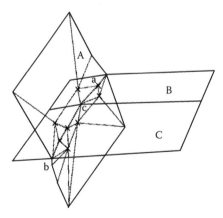

FIGURE 8.20 Additional envelope points included in lines and surfaces. The points marked × are envelope points of A contacted by the plane and now included in the surface definition. The fine lines are the "crease lines" caused by these points. (Only surface A has been used to illustrate the "creasing" effect, but the same would apply to B and C).

that the stored relationships are a redundant addition to the original information. It is an attractive proposition to retain these relationships, especially since deriving them in the first place may well have been a difficult and costly exercise. It is, however, only a limited class of topological questions that are precompiled. A default logic is assumed to cover other relationships — e.g., two objects are not adjacent if there is no adjacency relationship between them. The difficulties of default reasoning have been described in the literature vis. Ginsberg and Smith (1988).

An alternative but theoretically appealing approach is the constraint database approach (Kanellakis et al., 1995). In this approach, the geometric definition of a spatial object is a set of constraints. Using this model, a region can be recorded in terms of the mathematical constraints that define that region (e.g., "Brussels = $(y \leq 13) \wedge (x \leq 11) \wedge (y \geq 12) \wedge (x \geq 10)$").

A linear constraint model has been proposed by Gunther (1988) and by Vandeurzen et al. (2001), in which geometric objects are represented as a "polyhedral chain," defined as a finite sum of convex "cells," each of which is a finite intersection of half planes. Although, using the language of 2D, this approach has no dimensionality limitations. It can further be shown that it is topologically correct in its results.

The representation can also be made robust. If the constraints are chosen carefully, small changes in the constants will cause commensurately small movements of the positions of the boundaries. Furthermore, these movements will not in any circumstances cause the region to become invalid.

On the other hand, the complexity of representing a polygon coverage of the plane as a collection of constraint sets would be quite extreme. It might be some years before this approach bears fruit in the form of practical commercial database management systems.

8.6.3 Region Connection Calculus

An attractive approach ("RCC theory") sees the distinction between open, semi-open, and closed regions as "arguably too rich for our purposes." Randell et al. (1992) developed a logic that does not utilize this distinction. Bennett (1995) further explores and refines this logic.

RCC theory assumes a single primitive relation $C(x, y)$ between regions x and y (meaning "x is connected with y"), and the two basic axioms:

Reflexivity: $\forall x \, C(x,x)$ (any region is connected with itself)
Symmetry: $\forall xy \, C(x,y) \rightarrow C(y,x)$ (x connected with y implies y is connected with x)

From this basis, a rich series of relationships can be defined:

$DC(x, y)$ "x is disconnected from y"
$P(x, y)$ "x is part of y"
$PP(x, y)$ "x is a proper part of y"

EQ(x, y)   "x is identical with y"
O(x, y)   "x overlaps y"
DR(x, y)   "x is discrete from y"
PO(x, y)   "x partially overlaps y"
EC(x, y)   "x is externally connected to y"
TPP(x, y)   "x is a tangential proper part of y"
NTPP(x, y)   "x is a nontangential proper part of y"

For example, P(x, y) is defined as $\forall z[C(z, x) \rightarrow C(z, y)]$ (x is part of y, if any region z that connects with x must connect with y).

Further functions, sum(x, y), compl(x, y), prod(x, y), diff(x, y), and the universal set are similarly defined.

8.6.4 THE RATIONAL POLYGONAL REGION

RCC theory adds a further axiom — to ensure density of the regions:

$\forall x \exists y$ [NTPP(y, x)] (loosely, every region contains a smaller region that it completely encloses).

It is this axiom that cannot be satisfied by a finite (integer or floating point) digital representation of a region. One could satisfy this axiom using an infinite precision rational number representation.

Lemon and Pratt (1998) have developed a complete calculus for qualitative spatial reasoning based on rational polygonal regions. These rational polygons are closely related in form to the "polygonal chains" of the linear constraint databases but rely on infinite precision rational number representations for implementation. It is this concept that suggests the regular polytope as defined below.

8.7 THE REGULAR POLYTOPE

A regular polytope is defined as the union of a finite set of (possibly overlapping) "convex regular polytopes," which are, in turn, defined as the intersection of a finite set of half spaces (in 3D, half planes in 2D). These half spaces (planes) are defined by finite precision integer representations. This definition is similar to the "polygonal chain" of the linear constraint databases, and the "rational polygon" of Lemon and Pratt (1998) but is based on the computation representation itself. That is to say, the definitions of the half planes are given in terms of integers.

In the following discussion, an operator in a circle is used to represent the result of executing that operation digitally so that, for example, the symbols $\oplus \otimes \oslash$ 3 are used to indicate computation of the sum, product, quotient, and difference, while "+", ".", "/", "−", are used to indicate the actual sum, product, quotient, and difference of the real numbers or integers that the values represented. Thus the statement: A $\oplus$ B = A + B should be interpreted as an assertion that the computer addition of the variables gives the correct result. (Note that this assertion is generally true for integer arithmetic but not for floating-point operations.)

8.7.1 HALF SPACE

A half space[3] is defined as:

$H(A,B,C,D,S)=\{(X,Y,Z)|((A \otimes X \oplus B \otimes Y \oplus C \otimes Z \oplus D) 1 0) 2 S,$
$-M < X \le M, -M < Y \le M, -M < Z \le M \}$
M is the maximum range of coordinate values.
The values of the integers A, B, C, and D, and the Boolean parameter, S, define the half space. (S is chosen so that A > 0 or A = 0, B > 0, or A = B = 0, C > 0).

Note: the half space can be defined by the values A, B, C, and D only, without the need for a Boolean S, if the following definition is used:

Point (X,Y,Z) is within the region if $(A \otimes X \oplus B \otimes Y \oplus C \otimes Z \oplus D) 1 0$
Point (X,Y,Z) is within the region if $(A \otimes X \oplus B \otimes Y \oplus C \otimes Z \oplus D) 2 0$
and A 1 0
Point (X,Y,Z) is within the region if $(B \otimes Y \oplus C \otimes Z \oplus D) 2 0$ and A 2 0
and B 1 0
Point (X,Y,Z) is within the region if $(C \otimes Z \oplus D) 2 0$ and A 2 0, B 2 0 and
C 1 0

The constraints $A \ge 0$ etc., coupled with the use of the Boolean S, have been used to simplify the statement of this definition, but the actual implementation may well use the latter form.

It can be shown that for integer values of A, B, C, and D, with $-M < A, B, C < M$, and $-3M^2 < D < 3M^2$, a half space can be generated with a boundary plane within one unit of resolution of any three points within the range of coordinate values. Special cases H_0 and H_∞ can be defined as:

$H_0 = H(0,0,0,1,false)$ (i.e., the set of all points for which 1 > 0 is false)
$H_\infty = H(0,0,0,1,true)$ (i.e., the set of all points for which 1 > 0 is true)

Two half spaces, H(A,B,C,D,S), and H(A',B',C',D',S') are defined to be equal if there exists a rational number r(=I/J) such that $A = rA', B = rB', C = rC', d = rD', S = S'$. (In practice, this can be tested by verifying that $A \otimes D' 2 D \otimes A', B \otimes D' 2 D \otimes B', C \otimes D' 2 D \otimes C'$ and S 2 S'.) If $H_1 = H_2$ by this definition, for any point P = (X,Y,Z), $P \in H_1 \Leftrightarrow P \in H_2$.

8.7.2 CONVEX POLYTOPE

A convex polytope is defined as the intersection of any finite number of half spaces. See Figures 8.21 and 8.22. Convex polytope representation C is defined as:
$C = \{Hi : Hi, i = 1..n \in H\}$ where H is the set of all half spaces.

The point set definition of the representation C is:
Point $P \in C$ iff $P \in H_i, i = 1..n.$ (i.e. P is within every half space of set C).

---

[3] A half plane would equivalently be defined as:
$H(A,B,D,S)=\{(X,Y)|((A \otimes X \oplus B \otimes Y \oplus D) 1 0) 2 S, -M<X \le M, -M < Y \le M\}$
$O = \{Ci : Ci, i =1,m$ are convex polytopes$\}$

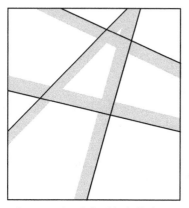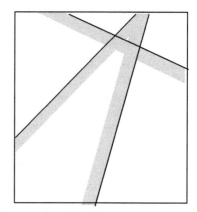

Convex region defined by half-planes   Convex region defined, not completely bounded

FIGURE 8.21 Convex polytopes defined by half planes.

The special cases are the universal convex polytope $C_\infty = \{\}$ (the empty set) and the empty convex polytope $C_0 = \{H_0\}$.

The representation C can be described by the shorthand $C = \bigcap_{i=1,n} H_i$

8.7.3   REGULAR POLYTOPE REPRESENTATION

A polytope representation O is then defined as the union of a finite set of convex polytopes. See Figure 8.23.

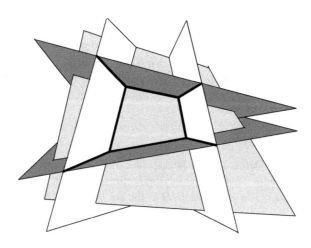

FIGURE 8.22 A convex polytope in 3D defined by half spaces. The planes, which represent the half space definitions, should extend to "infinity" but have been truncated to make the diagram clearer.

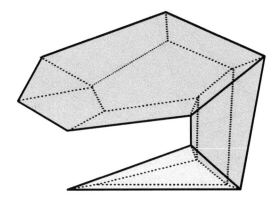

FIGURE 8.23 Definition of regular polytope from convex polytopes.

A half plane would equivalently be defined as:

$$H(A,B,D,S) = \{(X,Y)|((A \otimes X \oplus B \otimes Y \oplus D)\ 1\ 0)\ 2\ S,\ -M<X\leq M,\ -M<Y\leq M\}$$

$$O = \{Ci : Ci,\ i = 1,\ m\ \text{are convex polytopes}\}$$

The point set definition of O is:
Point $P \in O$ iff $\exists C_i \in O$: $P \in C_i$. (i.e., P is within at least one convex polygon of O)

The representation O will be described by the shorthand $P = \bigcup_{i=1,m} Ci$.
The special case definitions are:

The null polytope $O_0 = \{\}$ (the empty set)
The universal set $O_\infty = \{C_\infty\}$, where C_∞ is the universal convex polytope
   as defined above.

This can be shown to satisfy the axioms of a topological space:

(O.1) $O_0 \in O$ and $O_\infty \in O$
(O.2) if $O_1 \in O$ and $O_2 \in O$ then $O_1 \cap O_2 \in O$
(O.3) if $O_i \in O$ for all $i \in I$ then $\bigcup_{i \in I} O_i \in O$(Gaal 1964)

It can also be shown that these regions form a "regular set" as described by
Lemon and Pratt (1998). These polytope representations can form good representations of most features.

A regular polytope, by this definition, is a finite point set[4] and can be shown to
be both closed and open — and possess a true inverse. If two polytopes are separated
by an edge in common, as in Figure 8.24, there are no points that belong to both,
and no points "missing" between them. Further, a complete coverage of the universal

---

[4] Defined as the set of computationally representable points that fall within all of the half planes that
define any of the convex polytopes of the regular polytope.

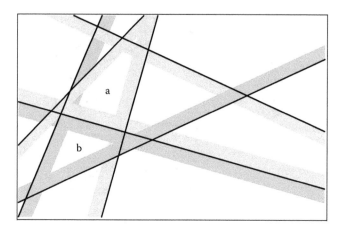

FIGURE 8.24 Common line or plane between regular polytopes. Note that, if the line that separates the two regions is defined with the same values of A, B, C, and D, then there will be no points common to the two regions and no points missed along the common boundary.

region by a set of regular polytopes can be defined with the useful property that each point in the universal region falls within one and only one polytope. (The points that would be calculated as exactly on an edge are defined to fall within one or other of the polytopes. The decision as to which polygon a point falls into is arbitrary but consistent.)

The definition of a region as a regular polytope is not unique, as can be seen in Figure 8.25, in the sense that there may be many ways to define a set of convex regions whose union consists of the points of the region. Since the convex polytopes can overlap, there are a vast number of alternative ways of defining the same region. The question of equality of regular polytope representations will be discussed later.

This representation is atomic in nature, given that the number of points that can be represented using any finite representation, such as "integer" or "floating point," is finite. Clearly, any such representation of regions cannot be dense in the sense of the RCC axiom: $\forall x \exists y \, [NTPP(y,x)]$ (loosely, every region has a smaller region that

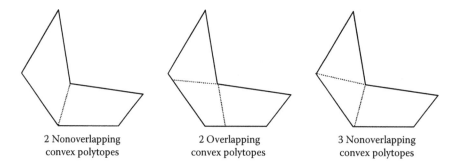

2 Nonoverlapping convex polytopes	2 Overlapping convex polytopes	3 Nonoverlapping convex polytopes

FIGURE 8.25 Some alternative ways of representing the same region. (These can be shown to be "equal" but not "identical.")

is completely contained within it). Thus, the Region-Connection Calculus[5] (RCC) in its entirety cannot be applied directly.

At least three possible modifications of the RCC have been suggested to allow for atomic regions, two by Randell et al. (1992) and, more recently, by Roy and Stell. (2002).

The regular polytope approach thus shares some advantages of the constraint database, and the rational polygon approach, including:

Rigor of operation definitions (e.g., union and intersection are associative)
Robustness — small perturbations of the definition of the half plane parameters do not cause topological failures

However, the approach also shares some of their difficulties:

Nonuniqueness of representation
Computational complexity

On the other hand, it seems that a practical implementation of this approach in a database management system is possible using current technology.

8.7.4 OPERATIONS ON REGULAR POLYTOPES

The **intersection** of two regular polytopes can be defined as follows:

For $C = \{Hi : Hi, i = 1..n\}$, $C' = \{H'j : H'j, j = 1..m\}$
Let $C \cap C' = \{Hi : Hi, i = 1..n\} \cup \{H'j : H'j, j = 1..m\}$

For $O = \{C_i: C_i, i = 1, n\}$, $O' = \{C'_j: C'_j, j = 1, m\}$
Let $O_1 \cap O_2 = \{C_i \cap C'_j, i = 1, n, j = 1, m\}$

Since, by definition, each $C_i \cap C'_j$ is itself a convex polytope, the defined $O_1 \cap O_2$ is a polytope. The **union** of a set of convex polytopes O_i, $i = 1, n$ can be defined:

For $O_i = \{C_{ji}: C_{ji}, j = 1, n_i\}$, $i = 1, n$
Let $O = \bigcup_{i=1, m} Oi = \{C_{ij} : j = 1, n_i; i = 1, n)$

i.e., O is the union of all the convex polytopes that comprise the original regular polytopes.

The **inverse** of a polytope is defined as follows:

The inverse of $H(A,B,C,D,S)$ is defined as $H(A,B,C,D,not(S))$
The inverse of a convex set $C = \bigcap_{i=1,n} H_i$, is defined as $C^- = \bigcup_{i=1,n}\{H_i^-\}$

---

[5] For a brief discussion of Region-Connection Calculus, see Section 0.

Thus C is the union of a set of convex polytopes and is, therefore, a regular polytope representation by definition.

Finally, the inverse of a polytope representation $O = \bigcup_{i=1,m} C_i$, is defined as $O^- = \bigcap_{i=1,m} C_i^-$.

This is the intersection of a number of regular polytope representations and is, therefore, a polytope representation in itself.

8.7.5 REGULAR POLYTOPE EQUALITY

The closure of the logic means that we can define an algorithm for testing for equality.

Define $P \subseteq Q$ as $P \subseteq Q$ iff $P \cap Q^- = O_0$ (i.e., P is a subset of Q if the intersection of P with the inverse of Q is empty)
Define $P = Q$ iff $P \subseteq Q$ and $Q \subseteq P$

In order to apply this test, inverses must be calculated and intersection operations applied. Both of these operations generate many convex polytopes (see definition above) and, as stated earlier, many of these will be empty. In fact, the definition states that all must be empty if regular polytope equality applies.

Thus, the equality test between regular polytopes reduces to the detection of empty convex polytopes. Two cases arise:

1. The convex polytope may have in its definition a pair of half spaces that are the inverse of each other (i.e. (A,B,C,D,S) and (A,B,C,D,notS)).
2. The convex polytope may contain one half space that excludes every point within all of the other half spaces.

Two half spaces, H(A,B,C,D,S) and H(A',B',C',D',S') are equal if there exists a rational number r (=I/J) such that A = rA', B = rB', C = rC', d = rD', S = S'. (In practice, this can be tested by verifying that A⊗D' = D⊗A', B⊗D' = D⊗B', C⊗D' = D⊗C' and S = S'.) Two half spaces are mutually inverse if one is equal to the inverse of the other (i.e., A⊗D' = D⊗A', B⊗D' = D⊗B', C⊗D' = D⊗C', and S = notS').

The second case can be determined by verifying that all points of intersection of the other half planes are outside this one. While computationally intensive, acceptable algorithms can be developed to calculate rigorous equality.

8.7.6 DUAL REPRESENTATION OF REGULAR POLYTOPE

Figure 8.26 shows, in the Unified Modeling Language (UML) (OMG, 1997), a possible implementation of the regular polytope representation (in 3D). The interpretation of the diagram is that:

• A convex polytope is a specialization of a regular polytope.
• A half space is a specialization of a convex polytope (which means it is also a regular polytope).

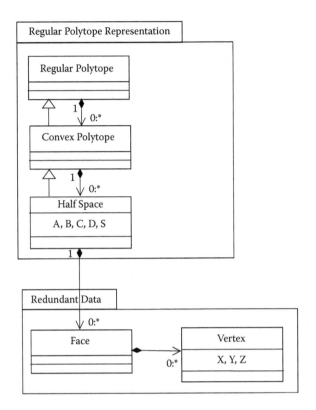

FIGURE 8.26 Storage scheme for a regular polytope (in UML).

- A regular polytope consists of zero or more convex polytopes.
- A convex polytope consists of zero or more half spaces.
- A half space has the attributes A, B, C, D, and S.
- Each half space is composed of zero or more faces (most often one). (The reasons for allowing more than one are discussed in Section 8.9.5, the review of Case 5.)
- Each face is composed of zero or more vertices.
- Each vertex carries as attributes the (approximate) X, and Z values of its coordinates.

Note: in a 2D implementation, the vertex class would not be needed, since a "face" is a line segment between two points. These point coordinate values can be stored in the face class itself.

The classes marked "face" and "vertex" are not necessary to the definition of a regular polytope, but, as discussed below, may be of use in improving the responsiveness of the implementation. Since these faces and vertices will need to be calculated in a range of operations, the calculation times may be sufficient to

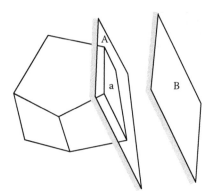

FIGURE 8.27 Calculation of polygonal faces of a regular convex polytope. Face a is calculated by intersection of half-space A with the other half spaces of this convex polytope. Note that the half space B contains all the other faces, and is redundant, so no face is generated. B can therefore be dropped from the convex polytope definition.

justify the extra storage. The algorithm for the calculation of faces and vertices is in outline:

> For each convex regular polytope in the regular polytope definition, calculate the intersections between the half planes that compose it, and form a set of conventional polygons (rounding intersection points to the nearest grid points). There will be one polygon for each original half space, unless the half-space was redundant (see Figure 8.27), or a degenerate face was produced. These polygons can be assembled to form a conventional convex polyhedron.
>
> These polyhedron are then combined by union operations to form one or more disjoint polyhedra. This operation is simply the conventional conversion of objects defined by "constructive solid geometry" to boundary representation form. For example, see Gunther, 1988.

The decision whether or not to store the face and vertex objects is an implementation issue. It would be quite possible to generate a complete topological encoding as per Lee and Lee (2001). Thus, it is possible to combine the rigor of the rational polytope with the well-known advantages of traditional topological encoding.

It must be remembered that the face-vertex information is a derived approximation to the actual definition, which is, in the classes, "regular polytope," "convex polytope," and "half space." In order to apply any topological operations, such as union, complement, or intersection, the information in these foundation classes must be used. The face-vertex data may, however, be of value in preliminary calculations in much the same way as "minimum bounding rectangles" are often used to preselect objects in spatial searches. For example, in forming the intersection between two regular polytopes, a large number of intersections of convex polytopes may be generated. A large number of these will be empty and

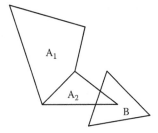

FIGURE 8.28 Calculating the intersection of two regular polytopes, A and B. A is shown split into the two convex polytopes A_1 and A_2.

can be discarded. If all the vertices of a convex polygon are outside any one of the other convex polygon's half spaces, then that intersection will be known to be empty.

In calculating the intersection of region B with region A in Figure 8.28 even though all the half planes that define A_1 intersect all the half planes that define B (since they are not parallel, it can be determined by a conventional polygon overlap test that all the vertices of A_1 are completely separated from the vertices of B. Therefore, $A_1 \cap B$ is empty. Even though the vertex positions are approximate, the accuracy is known, so this kind of logic can be used to pre-eliminate large numbers of the partial intersections. (This could be preceded by a comparison of minimum bounding rectangles to further improve the calculation speed.)

8.8 DATA STORAGE REQUIREMENTS

The "regular polytope" will require more storage than the more conventional approaches (except perhaps the "realms" approach, but this is an open question at present). In order to evaluate its practicality, an estimate of this space is required.

The actual storage requirement will vary depending on the shape of the features being stored. Features that tend to be convex in shape will require less storage than those with many points of concavity, since the regular polytope must be divided into convex parts. Every vertex at which the feature is concave creates the requirement for an additional convex polygon object.

For "reasonable" shapes of features (with not too many concavities), such as, for example, cadastral parcels, there should not be more than two convex polytopes required for each regular polytope on average. Thus, it could be expected that the regular polytope, convex polytope, and half space classes should together amount to not more than about double the storage requirement expected of a conventional polygon/polyhedron storage scheme. The redundant data classes can be expected to require about the same storage as conventional schemes.

Thus, it could be expected that about three times the storage will be required in comparison with conventional schemes. This assertion will be tested in later research efforts as will be described in Section 8.11.

8.9 REVIEW OF THE CASE STUDIES

Reconsidering the case studies from Section 8.4, the following can be stated.

8.9.1 CASE 1. ROUNDING, ACCURACY, AND RESOLUTION

While rounding, accuracy, and resolution issues still apply, they do not lead to breakdown of the underlying logic, and it is possible to predict behavior under conditions of small random perturbation. In no case will any perturbation lead to the generation of an invalid representation.

8.9.2 CASE 2. POLYGON UNION

Since the representation can be shown to define a topological space, then the associativity of union and intersection is assured.

8.9.3 CASE 3. ISO 19107 DEFINITION OF EQUALS

The closure of the logic means that a rigorous algorithm can be defined for testing for equality, as described in Section 8.7.5.

8.9.4 CASE 4. ISO 19107 DEFINITION OF isSIMPLE()

The regular polytope approach is not sensitive to self-intersection, so spatial representations can be stored at a resolution appropriate to their accuracy. There is no need for problematic concepts such as "isSimple" to be imposed as a validation requirement. It is still possible to ensure that the generation of a conventional polygon or polyhedron from a regular polytope is done in such a way that the Milenkovic rules are observed, provided that it is recognized that this involves an approximation.

8.9.5 CASE 5. ADJOINING POLYGON POINTS

Referring to Figure 8.29, the definition of parcel A would remain after subdivision as the intersection of four half planes. The point p would not be a part of the true definition of A.

There may be a case for the insertion of a point at p in the definition of A for the purpose of carrying some attributes, or to allow a full topological encoding of the adjacency. This is not precluded by the regular polytope representation, since the lines bp and pa could be recorded as "faces" of A within the same half plane. (This is the reason for the "1 to many" link between half space and face in Figure 8.26).

The 3D cadastral case is particularly well handled by the regular polytope representation. The large majority of parcels that are 2D can be represented as "prisms" defined by half spaces, which are defined by vertical planes (C = 0 in the $(Ax + By + Cz + D > 0) = S$ representation). There is no need for any "top" or "bottom" planes to be defined, and the only extra overhead above the 2D regular polytope representation is the (probably 4-byte) value of C, which is wasted. For example, in Figure 8.30, Parcels *b*, *c*, and *d* are defined as 3D parcels, with *c* being bounded by six half spaces. Parcel *a*, defined as a 2D parcel, would be delineated

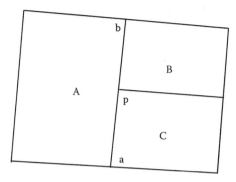

FIGURE 8.29 Subdivision of adjoining parcel (copy of Figure 8.10).

by four half planes. If this definition is changed to four half spaces, each with parameter C = 0, *a* becomes a 3D regular polytope unbounded above or below. This allows the full range of operations between regular polytopes to be extended to mixed dimensionality.

8.9.6 CASE 6. DATUM CONVERSION

This requires careful processing, since the definition of a half plane is not localized, while the datum shift may involve different displacements of points in different regions. First, it must be recognized that the current approach is only an approximation anyway, and that, in theory, straight lines are not preserved by a datum shift.

The best approach is to take the half spaces of a regular polytope individually and recalculate the parameters based on the local shift. The face-vertex values will

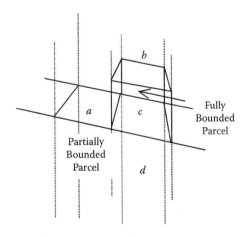

FIGURE 8.30 3D cadastral parcels adjoined by 2D parcels.

assist in calculating the local shift values. This is a simple mathematical approximation and will result in a new set of half space definitions, which then lead to a new regular polytope definition.

It may be that some changes occur in the object definition — for example, in rare cases, it could become "not connected" after the transformation, but no validation failures can be generated.

8.10 CONCLUSIONS

It has been shown that many of the logic failures that exist in current implementations of spatial database management systems could be avoided by the use of the regular polytope schema. This would be at the cost of an increase in the storage requirements, but as was argued in the "realms" approach (Guting and Schneider, 1993), this can be justified by the improved reliability.

8.11 FUTURE RESEARCH

8.11.1 IMPLEMENTATION ISSUES

A prototype database will be built based on the schema given above, implementing a sufficient amount of the functionality to determine the practicality of the approach.

8.11.2 CONTIGUITY

The definition of a regular polytope does not include any requirement for contiguity. Indeed, any such requirement is incompatible with the requirement that operations such as union and intersection are closed. On the other hand, the concept of contiguity is of practical value, this will be addressed in further research.

8.11.3 FLOATING POINT REPRESENTATIONS

In this chapter, an integer representation has been assumed, but there is no reason that this approach cannot be implemented in floating point. This would allow the 9 significant figures of the integer representation to be extended to about 12 significant figures. This equates to better than 0.001mm over a range the size of the Earth.

8.11.4 APPROXIMATED POLYTROPE REPRESENTATION

There is also a very promising line of research to be followed in the concept of an "approximated polytope." This approach takes the face-vertex objects from Figure 8.26 and omits the remaining objects to give the schema of Figure 8.31. The half space definition parameters are retained and used for rigorous calculations.

This approach can be shown to allow the operations of union and intersection to be associative, but instead of the rigorous point set containment achieved by the regular polytope approach, points fall into three categories with regard to a particular

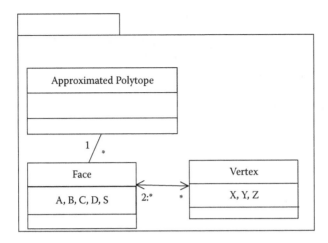

FIGURE 8.31 Approximated regular polytope schema.

polytope. The point might be definitely included, definitely excluded, or the result might be indefinite. In the case of indefinite points, the fact that the point is indefinite can be rigorously determined and, for example:

$a \in A \Rightarrow a \in A \cup B \; \forall \; B$ (where $a \in A$ means a is definitely included in A)

$a \in A, a \in B \Rightarrow a \in A \cap B$

$a\iota A, a \notin B \Rightarrow a\iota A \cup B \; \forall \; B$ (where $a\iota A$ means a is indefinite with respect to A)

A point will be indefinite with respect to a region only if it is within one unit of resolution of the boundary of that region.

This approach may give most of the advantages of the rigorous regular polytope approach, while reducing the storage requirement to no more than double the current approaches.

It is interesting to compare this approach with the "realms" approach — see Section 8.6.1. The realms approach, in effect, defines a polygon representation but constrains any movements introduced by any geometric or topological operations to within one unit of resolution of the "original position." This is achieved by defining an envelope for each line and breaking that line to prevent its straying outside that envelope.

The "approximate polytope" approach, in effect, achieves the same result by refusing to break the line at all but by retaining a parameterized form of the original line at all times. Thus, at the cost of about double the storage of an unconstrained system, it achieves the same result as the realms approach, which generates a number of interposed points, and may well result in even larger storage requirements.

In addition, the "approximated polytope" approach retains the simplicity of the original data, even better than does the Milenkovic normalization.

8.11.5 Lower Dimensionality Objects

The use of a regular polytope representation for features of a lower dimensionality than the space in which they are embedded has some issues to be addressed. This will be the subject of further research.

8.11.6 The "ROSE" Algebra

Given the fact that the regular polytope representation can achieve the same kind of rigor as the "realms" approach, it may be fruitful to investigate the implementation of the ROSE algebra (Guting et al., 1995) over regular polytope-based spatial data types.

REFERENCES

Baars, M., A comparison between ESRI geodatabase topology and Laser-Scan radius topology, Geo-Database Management Center, Delft University of Technology, http://www.gdmc.nl/publications/, 2003.

Bennett, B., Carving up space: existential axioms for a formal theory of spatial relations, *The IJCAI95 Workshop on Spatial and Temporal Reasoning,* Montreal, Canada, 1995.

Burrough, P.A. and McDonnell, R.A., *Principles of Geographical Information Systems,* Oxford University Press, Oxford, 1998.

Gaal, S.A., *Point Set Topology,* Academic Press, New York, 1964.

Ginsberg, M.L. and Smith, D.E., Reasoning about action II: the qualification problem, *Journal of Artificial Intelligence,* 35, 1988.

Green, D. and Yao, F., Finite resolution computational geometry, *27th IEEE Symposium on Foundations of Computer Science,* Los Alamitos, CA, 1986.

Gunther, O., *Efficient Structures for Geometric Data Management,* 337, Goos, G. and Hartmanis, J., Eds., Springer-Verlag, Berlin, 1988.

Guting, R.H., deRidder, T., and Schneider, M., Implementation of the ROSE algebra: efficient algorithms for realm-based spatial data types, *Advances in Spatial Databases,* 951, 216–239, 1995.

Guting, R.H. and Schneider, M., Realms: a foundation for spatial data types in database systems, *3rd International Symposium on Large Spatial Databases (SSD),* Singapore, 1993.

ISO-TC211, Geographic Information — Spatial Schema, IS19107, International Organization for Standards, Geneva, 2001.

Jeansoulin, R., Using spatial constraints as redundant information to improve geographical knowledge, in *Data Quality in Geographic Information,* Goodchild, M. and Jeansoulin, R., Eds., Editions Hermes, Paris, 1998.

Kanellakis, P.C., Kuper, G.M., and Revesz, P.Z., Constraint query languages, *Journal of Computer and System Sciences,* 51, 26–52, 1995.

Lee, S.H. and Lee, K., Partial entity structure: a compact non-manifold boundary representation based on partial topological entities, in *Proceedings of the Sixth ACM Symposium on Solid Modeling and Applications, Ann Arbor, MI,* ACM Press, New York, 2001.

Lemon, O. and Pratt, I., Complete logics for QSR [Qualitative Spatial Reasoning]: a guide to plane mereotopology, *Journal of Visual Languages and Computing,* 9, 5–21, 1998.

Milenkovic, V.J., Verifiable implementations of geometric algorithms using finite precision arithmetic, *Artificial Intelligence,* 377–401, 1988.

Minami, M., Sakala, M., and Wrightsell, J., *Using ArcMap,* Environmental Systems Research Institute, Inc (ESRI), Redlands, CA, 1999.

OGC, Geography Markup Language (GML) 1, Open GIS Consortium, http://www.opengeospatial.org, 2000.

OMG, UML 1.5, *Object Management Group,* http://www.omg.org/technology/documents/formal/uml_2.htm, 1997.

Randell, D.A., Cui, Z., and Cohn, A.G., A spatial logic based on regions and connection, *3rd International Conference on Principles of Knowledge Representation and Reasoning,* Morgan Kaufmann, Cambridge, MA, 1992.

Roy, A.J. and Stell, J.G., A qualitative account of discrete space, in *GIScience 2002,* Boulder, CO, 2002.

Stoter, J., *3D Cadastre,* Delft University of Technology, Delft, 2004.

Stoter, J. and Salzmann, M.A., Towards a 3D cadastre: where do cadastral needs and technical possibilities meet? *Computers, Environment and Urban Systems,* 27, 395–410, 2003.

van Oosterom, P., Quak, W., and Tijssen, T., Polygons: the unstable foundation of spatial modeling, *International Society of Photogrammetry and Remote Sensing,* Quebec, 2003.

Vandeurzen, L., Gyssens, M., and Van Gucht, D., On the expressiveness of linear-constraint query languages for spatial databases, *Theoretical Computer Science,* 254 (1-2), 423–463, 2001.

Weisstein, E.W., Equivalence Relation, *Math World — A Wolfram Web Resource,* http://mathworld.wolfram.com/EquivalenceRelation.html, 1999a.

Weisstein, E.W., Simplical Complex, *Math World — A Wolfram Web Resource,* http://mathworld.wolfram.com/SimplicialComplex.html, 1999b.

Zlatanova, S., Rahman, A.A., and Shi, W., Topology for 3D spatial objects, *International Symposium and Exhibition on Geoinformation,* Kuala Lumpur, 2002.

9 Virtual Geographic Environments

Hui Lin and Qing Zhu

CONTENTS

9.1 INTRODUCTION

Visualization is a natural extension of communication and functions in the "visual thinking" domain (DiBiase, 1990). Visualization emphasizes intuitive representation of data so as to enable individuals to understand the nature of phenomena represented by the data. In other words, visualization is concerned with the graphic exploration of data and information as a means of gaining understanding and insight into the data. Visualization is a fusion of a number of scientific disciplines, such as computer graphics, user-interface methodology, image processing, system design, and cognitive science.

The visualization of data is one of the central tasks in the field of architecture, engineering, construction (AEC) and geographic information systems (GIS). Data visualization makes use of the ability of the human eye to recognize structures and relationships that may be inherent within the data. First, data visualization makes communication and the presentation of graphically oriented applications more accessible. Second, it facilitates interpretation and visual analysis of data through visual data exploration, i.e., it engenders the individual to gain insight into the data, draw conclusions, and to interact directly with the data. However, the rapidly increasing amount of data precludes the presentation of all given data items. Furthermore, the complexity of many data sets surpasses the user's ability to identify the gist or the underlying concepts. It is universally recognized that natural user interfaces are a very important component of GIS/CAD (computer aided design) for all levels of data user. Advances in human-computer interaction have created completely new paradigms for exploring graphical information in a dynamic way, with flexible user control. Therefore, more intuitive and efficient interactive visualization environments become increasingly significant for the visual exploration of large amounts of complicated spatiotemporal information. As the topmost geographic information communication tool and human-computer interface, the virtual geographic environments (VGE) provide the augmentation of sensory reality, and open up new ways for us to comprehend the real world, as well as the AEC and the GIS worlds. VGEs provide multidimensional and multisensory user interfaces, intended to facilitate both browsing of the multidimensional data set and further specific exploration within the same visualization context. Therefore, the two distinct areas of AEC and GIS are seamlessly merged in the same VGEs.

9.1.1 FROM MAP TO GIS AND VGES

Geographic space is the environment around us and the greater world in which we live. We can directly experience many things in geographic space, but the scale is such that we cannot experience them all at once. From a cognitive perspective, we use "mental maps" to drive to work, to decide where to live, and, in general, to understand our surroundings (Peuquet, 2002). Geographic spatiotemporal information is the most important component of the human recognition of reality. Maps are powerful graphic tools that classify, represent, and communicate spatial relations. Therefore, cartographic maps have been used for centuries as a method to communicate the spatial information between cartographer and map users, through visualizing geographical distributions across a world that is too large and too complex to be seen directly. For both the makers and users of maps, knowledge and experience about spatial information, geography, and maps play important roles during the information communication. However, most of this knowledge can only be obtained by learning, accumulated by practicing and training, and used by relying on experience. The modern computer has fundamentally changed the predominant way maps are produced and used. Instead of the traditional paradigm of the professional cartographer designing a map product for the map user. At the end of the twentieth century, cartography has undergone two major evolutions. One change is digitalization, including the widespread use of computer systems such as CADs, which are able to store, process, manipulate, and transform spatial and attribute data. The second has been in the move away from static maps to interactive, dynamic, and animated geographic visualizations that can be designed by anyone with access to software and data (Kitchin and Dodge, 2002). The clear separation between cartographer and users is thus blurred since noncartographers are able to access data and tools to produce their own maps.

Along with the development of the digital maps, or electronic maps, more and more applications are being used to develop more comprehensive and more powerful functionalities, such as spatial database management and computerized spatial analysis. The first well-known GIS (the Canada Geographic Information System, CGIS) was initiated in 1966 to serve the needs of the Canada Land Inventory to map current land uses and the capacity of these areas for agriculture, forestry, wildlife, and recreation. It was recognized that the manual map analysis tasks necessary for such an inventory over such a large area would be prohibitively expensive and that a technological solution was necessary. After approximately four decades of evolution, GIS has proven to be a successful technology for the handling, integration, and visualization of diverse spatial data sets. But like any rapidly evolving technology, its roots and initial trajectory have resulted in certain defining standards in the way spatial data are handled and manipulated (Brimicombe, 2003). One of the primary objectives of GIS is to adapt the computer instead of the brain for spatial data management, processing, and analysis. To date, unfortunately, much of our knowledge of geography, sociology, mathematics, aesthetics, psychology, etc., cannot be accepted and processed automatically by computers. We therefore continue to use map forms for spatial information communication in GIS. As shown in Figure 9.1, the transmission of cartographic information can be illustrated by a model: sender–media–receiver. From this model, the fundamental elements of cartographic communication can be defined as: data, information, and knowledge. Data are characteristically raw observations that have been remembered or recorded in some way, whereas information is data that are ordered and contextualized in ways that give them meaning. Information is, thus, selective with regard to data, separating the important from the relatively unimportant. Knowledge is a cumulative understanding of information based upon a "world model" (i.e., an overall representative structure and a set of generalized rules that pertain to the relevant phenomena). Our understanding of the world and our ability to acquire new knowledge is due, in large part, not to the amount of information about places, people, and things we can remember, but rather to the way in which we structure that information (Peuquet, 2002).

The use of such map media, in the sense of perception of the information contained in them, depends primarily on the linguistic competence of the users. Otherwise, during the selection and arrangement of the visual elements that produce meaning, much useful information about the real world has to be omitted due to the

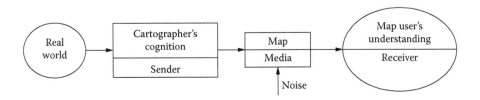

FIGURE 9.1 The transmission model of cartographic information.

limitations of the 2D map space — and the introduction of some noise. The intrinsic obscure tendency of map metaphor-based information encoding and decoding in lower dimensions of space misdirects the communication between information and humans. The innovation of information technology drives us to research and develop a further, more powerful geographic language to maximize the information bandwidth from the environment to the brain. Thus, the VGE as the new generation of geographic languages is proposed (Lin et al., 2003).

9.1.2 DEFINING VGEs

VGE is a virtual representation of the natural world that enables a person to explore and interact, in cyberspace, with the vast amounts of natural and cultural information gathered about the physical and cultural environment. In other words, VGE consists of the avatar-based human society and the surrounding objective environments, such as the hardware of computer networks and sensors, and the software of data and cultural environments. In particular, the avatar-based humans here are a combination of the humans in the real world and the 3D avatar in the virtual world. From this point of view, users become part of the data set, part of a VGE, where they can explore and interact with the virtual world. Compared with the data-centered GIS, VGE is, therefore, also defined as a human-centered environment that represents and simulates geographic environments (physical and human environments) and allows distributed multiusers to implement exploratory geospatial analysis, geocomputation, and geovisualization, and to conduct collaborative work for supporting design and decision (Lin and Gong, 2002; Lin et al., 2003).

As shown in Figure 9.2, the VGE consists of the following five types of space, the last three of which are similar to those defined by Cheesman et al. (2002) for virtual realities:

- Network spaces are made of networked computers with geographical referent such as the IP address; these spaces bridge the real world and the virtual worlds.
- Data spaces are the fundamental support spaces of VGE, which enable the virtual worlds to possess their own coordinates and territories through a set of organized 3D geometric spatial data. Based on these spaces, the data and actions in the virtual worlds have consequences in real life, and the virtual worlds are thus related to the natural physical world.
- Image/graphical spaces use spatial metaphors to add understanding; these metaphors are the visual presentation (externalization) of the data spaces. There are multidimensional views for choice, including the 3D perspective views and stereoscopic views, as well as the 2D planar views.
- Sensory/perceptual spaces provide augmentation to such spaces to provide a qualitatively enriched experience of a geographic space. In these spaces, users could have multimodal experiences — information is gathered through visual, auditory, haptic, and other means.
- Social spaces are spaces in which multiusers can interact or geocollaborate through some form of communication.

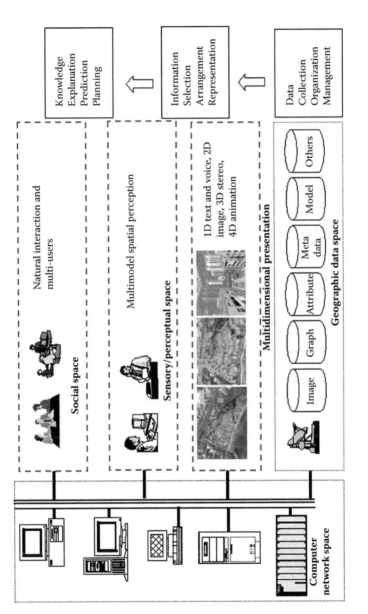

FIGURE 9.2 The five distinctive spaces of VGEs.

These spaces make VGE quite different from the traditional virtual reality space associated with unrealistic expectations. VGE is equated with reality by making the spaces continuous and coextensive. Even though the concept of VGE bears many expectations for scientists, computer-generated simulations do not need to follow the ordinary rules of physical reality with which they are familiar. Compared with traditional geographic languages, especially GIS, the VGE has its own distinguishable characteristics, such as the multidimensional representation of geographic information, multisensory perceptual features, and multimodal natural interaction, which concentrate on its smart interfaces.

9.1.3 INTERFACES OF VGEs

VGE is well known as the topmost human-computer interface for geographic information communication and is definitely related to certain adopted devices or intermedia. With reference to the devices for VGE, the computing and storage devices are the most fundamental, from the Silicon high-end graphics supercomputer, to the popular low-end desktop or laptop PC with a high performance graphics card and portable computing devices, such as PDAs (personal digital assistants). There are a large number of platform choices for different applications. However, in this chapter, only the interface technologies will be introduced, which are quite different from the keyboard, mouse, and trackball interfaces used in traditional GIS/CAD. The interface technologies include visual, auditory, tracking, primary user input, and haptic interfaces, which offer a more intuitive metaphor for human-computer interaction and are widely used in virtual environments. In theory, all the interface technologies have similar applications in VGE (MacEachren et al., 2003; Stoter and Zlatanova, 2003).

Visual interfaces: currently available stereoscopic displays for immersive VGEs typically require the user to wear a head-mounted display (HMD) or special glasses, such as active (shutter) and passive (red-green) glasses. But the use of this specialized equipment introduces a range of new issues, such as ergonomics and health concerns. For multiple users, sharing the same purpose at the same time, a large-screen display known as the CAVE (CAVE Automatic Virtual Environment) or Barco's large-screen projection solutions (workbench, panorama) are necessary. Of course, the more ideal devices are those that directly provide autostereoscopic displays. Since full immersion is not necessary for most applications in the AEC and GIS domains, in this case, the perspective display shown directly through a computer monitor or some other display medium (e.g., a projector) is enough.

Auditory interfaces: a wide continuum of commercial product is available for the development of 3D sound. These begin at low-cost, PC-based, plug-in technologies. In fact, most powerful functions of auditory devices depend on digital signal processing software, such as microphones with automatic speech recognition, which are intended as input devices to command or control applications.

Tracking interfaces: provide wire or wireless devices for tracking the position and orientation of users. Trackers are used to measure the motion of the user's body, head, or hands, and sometimes the eyes. This information is then used to correlate visual and auditory inputs to the user's position. For example, the global positioning system (GPS) is generally used for long distance body position tracking, and gyros are used for head orientation tracking. In particular, the computer vision (CV)-based hand gesture interface (the 3D position and orientation of the user's hand are detected automatically by a CV system) is considered an important natural input device for VGEs.

Sketch-based interfaces: provide sketches (graphics and handwriting) drawn by a stylus directly on a screen or tablet as input.

Primary user input interfaces: provide direct input to the VGE system. There are two categories of devices: (1) gloves and exoskeleton devices; the more popular devices are the gloves with flexible sensors that accurately and repeatedly measure the position and movement of the fingers and wrist, such as the 18- or 22-sensor CyberGlove (*Virtual Technologies, Inc.*). (2) 3D pointing devices; 3D input via a mouselike joystick or trackball device is a principal form of user input in both immersive and nonimmersive VGEs.

Generally speaking, there are several critical problems to be solved for creating VGEs: (1) the unified data structure that integrates the 2D/3D, CAD/GIS data and facilitates both the manipulation and multidimensional visualization, (2) the multiscale database management, as well as the temporal database management, (3) the collaborative visualization of multiple users at the same time and in different places, (4) natural interactions, as well as the multisensory representation rather than the visual presentation, (5) the applications for mobile computing and display devices. The critical issues of VGEs are considered as two aspects, the multidimensional representations and natural interactions. Therefore, Section 9.2 discusses the multidimensional representations with multiviewpoint and multiple levels of detail (LOD), Section 9.3 discusses the multimodal natural interactions and geocollaboration across time, space, and scale. Finally, several concluding remarks are presented.

9.2 THE MULTIDIMENSIONAL REPRESENTATIONS

Geospatial information is quite different from other kinds of information for its unique properties of territorial, multidimensional structural, and dynamic change (Goodchild, 2002). Therefore, the multidimensional and dynamic analysis methods become the fundamental approaches for exploring spatial problems from all dimensions. From a philosophical viewpoint, dimension is one type of methodology and epistemology that humans use to represent spatiotemporal architectures. The multidimensional communication of spatial information is the method and process of human spatial cognition. For instance, 1D stands for linear methods, 2D is planar, 3D is stereoscopic of 1D plus 2D, 4D is dynamic and stereoscopic of 3D plus the time dimension, and 5D is 4D plus psychological methods. The evolution of geographic languages from verbal language through text, map, and GIS to VGE is simply the continuously improving process of spatial information communication. Since VGE possesses full multidimensional space, almost all kinds of information may be embedded, without channel limitations or loss of information. Herein, the dimensions related to VGE mean not only the traditional (X,Y,Z) orthogonal spatial dimensions, but also other nonspatial dimensions, i.e., the thematic and temporal dimensions, such as shadow, color, material, force, and sound (Usery, 2000). Whatever we are discussing, 1D speech or text, 2D map, 2.5D DTM (digital terrain model), 3D GIS, 4D animation, or xD thematic attributes, each has its own relative advantages and disadvantages in spatial expression and conception; each dimension is suitable to a specific representation of reality. According to spatial analysis methodology and data cube theory, each attribute can be treated as a dimension of N-space. Due to media limitations, N-dimensional space is always represented in lower dimensional space such as 2D-3D through the dimensionality reduction and typical aggregation of information. Unusual knowledge, therefore, can be easily discovered.

Another important concept related to the multidimensional concept is the multiscale. Ordinarily, scale and resolution of spatial data are consistent, because the resolution we human beings use to observe and express things is limited. We can also say that, ordinarily, the resolution in geographic space is an indicator of the scale, because "degree of abstraction" and "levels of detail" work in inverse proportion to each other, i.e., the higher the detail degree, the lower the abstraction degree and vice versa. But resolution is not equal to scale. Resolution refers to LOD, while scale has not only the meaning of "levels of abstraction," but also the meaning of "interested relative size." As opposed to the traditional 2D map and GIS, there are no ground rules concerning scale consistency in a VGE. Furthermore, the scale of the environment, relative to the user or viewer, may be altered at will. We say that the multiscale representation in VGE obeys the natural principle, that is, *"for a given scale of interest, all details about the spatial variations of geographic objects beyond certain limitations are unable to be presented and can thus be neglected"* (Li and Openshaw, 1993).

While VGE space is three-dimensional, the representation is not limited to three dimensions. If the spatial information were limited in one or two kinds of representations, it would be inaccurate or misleading as a tool to understand the environment, making simple phenomena become more complex. The best example is the full immersive display of a virtual reality system; when we try hard to be immersed in the realistic virtual world we also suffer from the feelings of disorientation, motion sickness, and eye fatigue. It is clear that user-centered VGE offer a more ergonomic platform for humans to manage basic and high-level cognitive tasks in everyday life. When moving from 2D to 3D, even though only one dimension is extended, there are many more possible choices for the representation of spatial information. It facilitates further exploratory analysis and helps us gain real insight into the problem at hand.

Even though the visual presentation is of primary importance, the spatial representations extend beyond the visual, e.g., the spatial representations are also communicated through the spoken and written word. It appears that auditory representations provide the best options for constructing an augmented virtual environment (Jacobson et al., 2002). The sound we perceive in the environment contains information about the source of sound, and its distance and possible direction. Vision gathers a large amount of information but only from one direction at a time. In contrast, auditory perception is omnidirectional. Other benefits of auditory display include: (1) an auditory display's presence is generally an augmentation and a noninterfering enhancement to a visual display; (2) the auditory display creates user interest and engagement by decreasing learning time, reducing fatigue, and increasing enthusiasm; (3) it provides strong intermodal correlations, reinforcing experiences gained through visual or other senses; (4) superior temporal resolution. Speech provides a viable alternative for many applications in which spatial data must be presented nonvisually, particularly those requiring mobility (for example, a car driving guide accepts voice commands from the driver and provides directional assistance through synthesized speech).

9.2.1 The Multiview Interface

Vision is the most useful of the senses for understanding space; humans are therefore strongly oriented to their visual sense. VGEs also rely heavily on visual display and are designed to serve not only the presentation but also the geospatial exploration and understanding based on the databases and various interactive operations with geocomputation models. However, within the traditional immersive environment, there is no satisfactory 3D alternative for direct modeling interaction or for alphanumeric input to formulate a GIS query. A multiview interface, which includes plan view, model view, and world view, is therefore proposed (Germs et al., 1999; Kraak, 2002). As shown in Figure 9.3, the plan view presents the data as a conventional map, usually using a combination of remote sensed imagery and line map. Model view provides a 3D bird's eye view on a partly symbolic and simplified 3D representation. World view gives a photorealistic 3D display. In a world view, the visible natural attributes of the object surface, such as the geometric detail and color texture, and can be directly rendered in perspective or stereoscopic ways. Multiview interface is not new in AEC, and the traditional plan view, profile view, and bird's eye view are fundamental to design. But most of these views are independently created and manipulated, without any other information related to them.

Based on the VGEs' multiview interface and integrated database, Figure 9.4 shows the informative visualized design of road engineering. Each view provides a specific understanding of the real world, with different abstraction. These views can be used simultaneously or intermittently; each provides a repertoire of interaction possibilities, and all the views can share the same display context (e.g., data range, zoom in and out, roaming). For example, in a world view, the most popular way to let the user gain a larger context of the environment is by using a plan view of

(a) Plan-view   (b) Model-view   (c) World-view

FIGURE 9.3 (See color insert after page 86.) Multiview representation of spatial information.

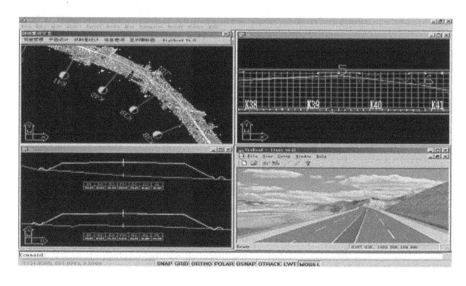

FIGURE 9.4 (See color insert after page 86.) Multiview based informative road design.

miniature metaphors simultaneously, which usually serves the purpose of path selection and tracing, locating and orienting the user, searching for other users, and moving directly to a point on the map. The user can switch between views as required, but the most suitable view depends on the type of user, the task at hand, and the medium. A spatial phenomenon is represented in multiview within multiviewpoint and multiple levels of detail. The bird's eye view, fly through, and walk through all are available to obtain a useful simplification of a complex real situation and to achieve comprehensive understanding and insight into that situation.

9.2.2 Visualization of Abstract and Thematic Information

VGE provides us with both a similar representation of the natural world as we perceive it to be in our usual life and the simulation and presentation of more interesting spatiotemporal phenomena perceived impossibly by means of our senses. We call this "the experience beyond the reality" (Faisstnauer, 1998; Lin et al., 2003). Examples include land contamination, sunlight impact, air pollution, and noise dispersion. Figure 9.5 illustrates the sunlight conical surface, from which the abstract sunlight impact at an arbitrary location in one day can be perceived directly. In the same manner, the thematic information, especially the cultural attributes of the object, referred to as nontangible data (Kraak, 2002), can also be mapped into the multiple view approach. For example, the typical thematic map is in a plan view, and a good example of model view is the 2.5 perspective view of the "prism" map. To display the prism map, each region is colored and "raised" above "sea level" to a height representing the range in which the value of the thematic analysis column for that region falls. Prism maps offer a dramatic new visual effect. In addition, the prism maps provide a new way to show more than one thematic variable on a map at one time. This type of prism map display is not new and is widely used in computer

FIGURE 9.5 The modeling of sunlight conical surface.

software applications such as Excel and Access. This power and utility of VGE enables the abstract phenomena to be more actual and intuitive, and then facilitate the spatial decision-making support. Based on the database of behavior models and physical models, and information systems, a number of progressive levels of analysis beyond straightforward retrieval and manipulation can be performed with ease, such as exploration, explanation, prediction, and planning (Peuquet, 2002).

9.2.3 Time-Dependent Data Visualization

Time and temporality, motion and change, are essential to many GIS/AEC applications. There are four kinds of changes, i.e., geometrical changes, positional changes, attribute changes, and any combination of these changes. The changes of geographic phenomena in time can be characterized by data elements being a function of time. This type of data is then called time-dependent data. Visual representation of time-dependent data is classified into two types: (1) static representation — the visual representation does not automatically change over time, but is based on the user interaction only; (2) dynamic representation — the visual representation changes dynamically over time and is a function of time (Muller and Schumann, 2003).

It is possible to produce 2- and 3D dynamic representations for time-dependent data through animation. The animation is a typical dynamic representation, where the data elements' representation changes over time (e.g., size, shape, color, texture, transformation), and the continuous images move smoothly frame by frame (e.g., from 15 to 30 frames per second). The dynamic variables are related to animation, including duration, rate of change, and order (Li et al., 2004).

1. Duration (time units for a scene, e.g., 0.01 second per scene): Normally, the frame duration of 1/30 second (i.e., 30 frames/second) will produce smooth sequence animation. Slow motion could be produced if much

more than 30 frames are displayed in one second. On the other hand, fast motion can be produced if less than 30 frames are displayed in a second.

2. Rate of change, i.e., pace of animation or the differences between two successive scenes: If the rate is too great, then the difference is too much, leading to discontinuous actions.

3. Order: The sequence of the frames. Frames can be arranged according to time, position or attributes.

Today's technology places an attractive intermediate within striking distance: real-time user-directed cruising through a virtual landscape with continuous real-time production of TV-cartoon-quality shaded, colored, stereo views. In GIS visualization, the "fly through" and "walk through" are the most commonly used methods. Walking at ground level and looking straight ahead is what people are used to, however, it is argued that due to the lack of sufficient detail at ground level, the "structure" of the environmental image is much "stronger" from a fly-through mode, when more distant cues are visible. In these methods, the animated image sequence is usually produced in an order of space, i.e., by moving the viewpoint along a certain route. The frames in Figure 9.6 are arranged according to the viewpoint at street level. Most of the AEC applications work with small areas, with a high level of geometric detail. On the other hand, GIS applications also work with large areas of highly multivariate data sets. Then, both the 3D animation of GIS and AEC applications need elaborate solutions, since there are large amounts of data involved to be retrieved from the database and rendered in real time. Techniques such as culling and dynamic data loading and progressive rendering of LOD models are proven to be the most useful for more efficient perspective rendering of complex scenes (Gruber, 1999). This theme will be presented in the next section. However, the best

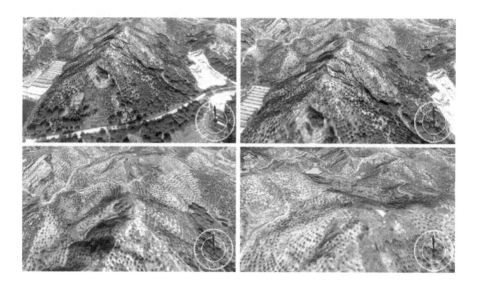

FIGURE 9.6 Four frames of fly-through animation.

representation of temporal information might be the augmented reality systems, which deal with live images of the real world through sensors or transparent display devices.

9.2.4 LOD and View-Dependent LOD Models

Even though the same phenomena can be represented in varying detail from different viewpoints through the multiview interface according to natural principle as mentioned above, in a perspective world view there will be differing levels of detail for different objects, based on their distance from the viewpoint. To meet the needs of real-time display, generating as many LOD models as possible in advance and storing them in the database is the best choice. However, due to the redundancy of data and the limitations of the storage capability of a database, generally only discrete LOD models of limited hierarchies, such as the image pyramid, e.g., 3-5 levels of detail are stored, while other continuous LOD models are generated in real time by specified surface simplifications. The continuous LOD departs from the traditional discrete approach; rather than creating individual LODs during the preprocessing stage, the simplification system creates a data structure encoding a continuous spectrum of detail. The desired LOD is then extracted from this structure at run time (Luebke et al., 2003). View-dependent LOD extends continuous LOD, using view-dependent simplification criteria to dynamically select the most appropriate level of detail for the current view. Most AEC applications, such as architecture and civil engineering, are, in fact, related to the discrete LOD concept based on certain levels of detail (1:200, 1:500, 1:1000, etc.) rather than the visualization of varying LODs at the same time in GIS.

In a world view, the user can walk through the virtual environment. When the viewpoint is moving from a distant point, closer to the object, the object can be viewed in detail, changing from coarser to finer, or vice versa. For AEC applications, most objects have detailed 3D CAD models and textures; the real-time loaded and rendered data volume can, thus, become very large. (Despite the tremendous strides made in graphics hardware, the tension between fidelity and speed continues to haunt us.) The complexity of our 3D models — measured most commonly by the number of polygons — seems to grow faster than the ability of our hardware to render them (Luebke et al., 2003). In order to bridge complexity and performance of VGE, there is the fundamental concept of LOD, i.e., when rendering, use a less detailed representation for small, distant, or unimportant portions of the scene. As shown in Figure 9.7, the object-oriented data model can directly support LOD to provide multirepresentation within different details. In this case, only the most detailed CAD model is stored in the database; the generation of LOD models, then, is just simple data selection and arrangement operation. For example, the block model can be obtained by selecting only the wall surfaces and planar roof without texture. Even though this kind of LOD is not really a continuous LOD, it is acceptable for most AEC and GIS applications. Of course, the CAD models must first be transformed into GIS models to minimize the differences between the geometric data models and data structures. In fact, almost all of the automatic surface simplification methods are suitable for smooth or linear surfaces, such as the terrain surface, especially in

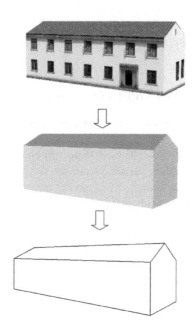

FIGURE 9.7 LODs derived from one model.

a gridded or triangulated network manner. Unfortunately, most of the surface simplification approaches do not consider the specific properties of an object type such as the right angles of urban objects; in particular, there has hardly been any work recorded on 3D building data (Forberg and Mayer, 2002). Related to the geometric simplification, the corresponding surface attribute or texture simplification is another thorny issue.

The terrain landscape represented by using digital elevation model (DEM) and digital orthoimage (DOM) is the most essential component of VGE, with respect to the georeferencing purpose, since all the natural and man-made objects will be grounded in it according to their arrangement in the natural world. In addition, a vast amount of remote sensed data within the improved spatial, temporal, and spectral resolution is increasingly available. The multiresolution virtual landscape as a visualization front end to GIS and as a fundamental carrier for virtual environment has recently been the focus of increasing attention (Brown et al., 2002; Luebke et al., 2003). Even though the terrain geometry is more constrained, normally consisting of uniform grids of height values, this allows for more specialized and potentially simpler algorithms than dealing with arbitrary 3D models. However, the large scale change of terrain also brings with it some added complications. For example, the growth in remote sensing means that it has become possible to develop terrain models in a continuum from the continental scale down to a very local level, and it is possible to have a large amount of terrain visible at any point. Through proper hierarchical data organization such as the DEM/DOM pyramid, it is possible to interactively "zoom in" from a large area to smaller areas of interest that have higher-resolution data, as well as to "fly" over the landscape at the chosen resolution, searching for anomalies or other features of interest (Brown et al., 2002). For this purpose, there are many algorithms for real-time generation of continuous LOD. For example, the simple method used for NPSNET is based on the multiple resolution Quadtree, used to perform the multiresolution rendering (Falby et al., 1993). This allows the nearby portions of terrain to be shown at a higher resolution than more distant regions. A new, easily implemented, memory efficient terrain LOD approach is based on the *longest edge bisection* scheme and data paging techniques (Lindstrom and Pascucci, 2001). The subdivided meshes (called right-triangulated irregular networks) can be refined locally without having to maintain the entire mesh at the same resolution. This also benefits the view frustum culling and triangle stripping for large-scale terrain visualization from coarse to fine.

9.2.5 IMAGE-BASED MODELING AND RENDERING

In VGE, most of the photorealistic visualizations are based on an underlying geometric description and corresponding textures, such as the DEM and DOM for landscape. However, creating accurate and photorealistic 3D models is time-consuming and creates a bottleneck for many practical applications. It is both difficult to model complex shapes and to recreate complex object appearances using standard parametric reflectance models (Matusik et al., 2002). In order to improve the visual realism of images synthesized by geometry-based rendering systems, a number of techniques have been developed. The basic mechanism to enhance the geometry-based approach is to add image-based information to the rendering primitives. The most common of those techniques is texture mapping, which greatly enhances the visual richness of raster scan images while entailing only a relatively small increase in computation. Texture mapping is simply defined as the mapping of a function onto a surface in 3D. Therefore, a texture is a one-, two-, or three-dimensional function that can be represented by discrete values in an array or a mathematical expression. A more complicated image-based modeling and rendering (IBMR) method provides us with a natural choice. IBMR refers loosely to techniques that generate new images from other images, rather than from geometric primitives. IBMRs are independent of the complexity of the scene to be rendered, making real-time realistic interactions with complex scenes possible. In addition, these methods can make use of the images of actual physical environments through CCD or TV sensors. As we know, the origin of photogrammetry is based on a stereopair of images used to reconstruct a stereoscopic model, and then accomplish the measurement and mapping from this model. Based on this principle, by means of the DOM stereopairs database, measurable stereoscopic models for large areas can be created with ease. In VGE, both image-based and geometry-based representations are used simultaneously to an increasing degree. As shown in Figure 9.8, the terrain and buildings are reconstructed using the geometry-based method, which provides accurate position and shape information. But the tree and the flower are reconstructed using the image-based method, which provides the most realistic visual impact and closest facsimile of the real thing.

FIGURE 9.8 (See color insert after page 86.) Blended scene of image-based and geometry-based representations.

9.3 THE NATURAL INTERACTIONS

The design of current windows-icons-mouse-pointing (WIMP)-based human-computer interfaces includes key limitations on both the user and the location where these interfaces can be used. In order to successfully operate the WIMO computer interfaces, users must be fully sighted, have sufficient manual dexterity to operate a mouse and keyboard, and be both generally and computer literate. In addition to the human limitations, WIMP interfaces also require a fixed location and are generally limited to a single user. However, human beings communicate with each other using a broader array of natural skills, such as speech, gestures, eye contact, and physical presence. Research in natural interaction is aimed at the creation of systems that understand these human activities and that provide appropriate feedback, while allowing people to interact naturally with each other and the environment. Users thus experience context awareness, exploiting dialogue modalities and behaviors that are commonly used in ordinary activities in everyday life (http://naturalinteraction. org/workshop/). VGE is therefore designed to provide the interaction with a virtual environment in the same way that interaction takes place in the natural world. No single modality is key to our spatial understanding. All sensory modalities work together from birth as a unitary system to provide a suite of interrelated and cross-reinforcing information. It is therefore important to increase the bandwidth of user-computer interaction of traditional GIS by means of multimodal interaction (Blaser et al., 2000). The current primary GIS interface is the WIMP; even though this kind of interface will be used for a long time, the use of keyboard and mouse is obviously decreased, and there is also no need to relate the interface to the screen. In order to alleviate the dependency on WIMP interface technology, other technologies have been introduced, i.e., speech recognition-based and computer vision-based input interfaces, such as the speaking, gesturing, writing, and sketching. These are most useful to the VGE, enabling it to be used by different users of varying physical and intellectual capacities and in a wider range of situations, such as mobile and hands-free usage through speech. With virtual environments, we have the opportunity to optimize reality to suit our perceptual systems. Because of the multisensory perceptual capability, the human-computer communication channel is broadened, and we can take advantage of unused "bandwidth" for more flexible spatial information communication.

9.3.1 SPEECH INTERFACE

Standard approaches to natural language interfaces focus on a linguistic analysis of the input data. A speech interface framework is defined by the Voice Browser Working Group (http://www.w3.org/TR/2000/WD-voice-intro-20001204). The basic components of this framework include the automatic speech recognizer (ASR), language understanding component, language generator, and text-to-speech synthesizer (TTS). Regardless of the potential advantages of speech interfaces, widespread use of this technology will require the resolution of many human factors issues, including the information requirements of the task, the limitations and capabilities of the voice technology, and the expectations, expertise, and preferences of the user (Kamm, 1995). While speech provides an effective and direct way of expressing actions, pronouns, and abstract relations, it fails when spatial relations or locations have to be specified. Speech is not self-sufficient and, therefore, needs an effective second modality such as gesture for expressing spatial relations (Rauschert et al., 2002).

9.3.2 HAND GESTURE INTERFACE

Integration of speech and gesture has tangible advantages in the context of human-GIS interaction, especially when coping with the complexities of spatial representations. Aiming at multiuser geocollaboration and its applications in crisis management, the natural spoken language and free-hand gestures-based interface provides relatively more effortless and speedier interactions than can be achieved through the use of traditional WIMP interfaces using keyboard and mouse (MacEachren et al., 2003). Untethered gesture recognition (not requiring a data glove or other device) allows group members to use natural forms of communication to share ideas (such as pointing to indicate emphasis). The recognized gesture and speech components from all active users (clients) derive the meaningful commands intended by individual users. The hand gesture-based interface is usually implemented by tracking the position of the fingertip in which the user points the map directly into the 2D cursor movement on the screen. Special devices such as an active camera and large screen are necessary to capture the natural gestures as direct input that drives the system's response on the map display.

9.3.3 SKETCH INTERFACE

Today's methods for interacting with GISs and geographic databases are primarily aspatial, as they require users to deal with geographic data primarily through alphanumeric command languages. Spatial querying by typing a command in some spatial query language or by selecting the same syntax from pull-down menus is a tedious process, because it often requires extensive training in the use of the particular query language, and forces users to translate a spatial image they might have in their mind into a nonspatial language (Egenhofer, 1996). To overcome this conceptual gap, the intuitive method is to directly specify the spatial relations by drawing them based on a sketch interface. Using sketches to deliver information is not a new idea. Sketching with a pen is a mode of informal, perceptual interaction that has been shown to be especially valuable for creative design tasks. For designers, the ability to rapidly sketch objects of uncertain types, sizes, shapes, and positions is important to the creative process. Sketch-based user interfaces allow a user to sketch a spatial query directly on an electronic sketching device (screen or tablet), from where the sketch is translated into a query statement and processed against a spatial database (Blaser et al., 2000). During the interactive process of sketching, users sketch directly to express their provisional ideas; the system continuously provides similar candidates for confirmation. When the sketching is completed, the semantic network is translated into a spatial query statement or graphics object with proper parameters that can be processed against a spatial database. This kind of query style supports human spatial thinking more directly, which is critical, because users frequently have an image-like representation in their minds when they query spatial configurations. Handwriting is very close to sketching, since the same data acquisition device (PDA or digitizer) is used. In a sense, handwriting is also graphics, as it can be represented by 2D binary arrays. However, the characters in handwriting are fixed, predefined, and well-known graphics objects, among writers and readers, that have strict definitions for strokes and stroke sequence. Online handwriting recognition is simpler than graphics recognition, so that even for complicated cursive handwriting recognition, there are various commercial hardware and software programs available. Therefore, along with the speech and gesture interfaces, the sketching interface is a useful addition to VGE for group users' interaction.

9.3.4   GEOCOLLABORATION

One of the most important characteristics of VGE is the distribution and interlinkage of systems. A key aspect of the distributed VGE is its accessibility in various ways, such as the wire/wireless connection, and client/server or browser/server architecture. In this way, multiusers can share the same environment that mediates distributed thinking and decision-making and allows them to not only interact with the environment but also with each other at same-or-different time and same-or-different place, i.e., geocollaboration (MacEachren et al., 2003). One important area of Web-based VGE and geocollaboration applications is the mobile augmented reality, in which 3D displays are used to overlay a synthesized world on top of the real world, and mobile computing, in which increasingly small and inexpensive computing devices, linked by wireless networks, allow us to use computing facilities while roaming the real world.

As a subset of the systems used for computer-supported cooperative work (CSCW), computer-supported geocollaboration involves a committed effort on the part of two or more people to use geospatial information technologies to collectively frame and address a task involving geospatial information. A human-centered conceptual framework to support visually enabled geocollaboration is developed, which includes six dimensions, i.e., the problem context, collaboration tasks, perspective commonality, spatial and temporal context, interaction characteristics, and tools to mediate group work. Collaboration can involve participants sharing work at the same or different place and at the same or different time (MacEachren & Brewer, 2004). MacEachren et al. (2003) introduced two geocollaborative systems emphasizing the role of large screen maps as a primary interface component in each, i.e., the HI-SPACE of a horizontal display and the DAVE_G of a vertical display. Both use the hand gestures interaction. Especially, the DAVE_G is a dialogue-assisted visual environment with speech and gesture recognition for geoinformation and, therefore, is useful in supporting the group decision making of crisis management (MacEachren et al., 2004). Aiming at the application of urban planning development control, Web-based development control aid is developed to support the geocollaboration of planner, applicant, architect, engineer, developer, and members of the public (Manoharan, 2003). For different-place collaboration, the multiple users can adjust their site's viewpoint independently by zooming, panning, and rotating. In addition, each user can also control his or her view, which is visible locally as well as globally, and can pass the actions performed on one machine to other connected machines. This working context sharing provides multiple views to show the exact views of others. At the same time, the guarantee of spatiotemporal consistency is also very important for multiusers' collaborative exploration.

9.4 CONCLUSION

As multidimensional visualization forms an efficient medium for both GIS and AEC applications, more and more front-end user interfaces of GIS/AEC systems are based on multidimensional visualization. Despite the static 3D data visualization of the "before" and "after" work of AEC, for the dynamic linkage between multiview interfaces during the AEC work grounded in a large geographic environment, it is important to develop fast 3D modeling and rendering approaches based on the 3D parametric design or 2D sectioning tools. Thus, the seamless dynamic visualisation and simulation of changes in time can be achieved. In particular, photorealism, by means of the imaging technology, including remote sensed imagery, has emerged to replace the traditional 3D wireframe representations of design products. Based on such kinds of realistic representation, the design results can be evaluated and optimized online.

Traditional virtual environment (virtual reality) technologies are useful in the visualization of both GIS and AEC. However, the immersive display is not necessary in most cases, but the desktop 3D perspective views may be more suited to the public. VGE is based on a geospatial database to support the vast amount of geometric and thematic data management, data retrieval, and manipulation. Thus, multidimentional visualization can be used not only for the "before and after" work of AEC but also during the whole design procedure of multiusers' geocollaborative works. The VGE is to become an integrated ideographic system that conveys the entire multidimensional representation, provides multimodal natural interaction, and supports multisensory perception in cyberspace across software and hardware platforms. Therefore, the information bandwidth from the real world to the human brain is maximized, and VGE provides us the opportunity to explore and cognize the intriguing world more efficiently.

REFERENCES

Batty, M., Dodge, M., Jiang, B., and Smith, A., GIS and urban design, ISSN:1467-1298 CASA, http://www.casa.ucl.ac.uk/urbandesifinal.pdf, 1998.

Batty, M., Dodge, M., Jiang, B., and Smith, A., For urban designers: the VENUE Project, ISSN:1467-1298, CASA, http://www.casa.ucl.ac.uk/venue.pdf, 2000.

Blaser, A.D., Sester, M., and Egenhofer, M.J., Visualization in an early stage of the problem-solving process in GIS, *Computers & Geosciences,* 26, 57–66, 2000.

Brimicombe, A., *GIS, Environmental Modelling and Engineering,* Taylor & Francis, London, 2003.

Brown, I.M., Kidner, D.B., and Ware, J.M., Multi-resolution virtual environments as a visualization front-end to GIS, in *Virtual Reality in Geography,* Fisher, P. and Unwin, D., Eds., Taylor & Francis, London, 2002, 144–162.

Cheesman, J., Dodge, M., Harvey, F., Jacobson, R.D., and Kitchin, R., "Other" worlds, augmented, comprehensible, non-material spaces, in *Virtual Reality in Geography,* Fisher, P. and Unwin, D., Eds., Taylor & Francis, London, 2002, 295–304.

DiBiase, D., Visualization in earth sciences, *Earth and Mineral Sciences, Bulletin of the College of Earth and Mineral Sciences, PSU,* 56 (2), 13–18, 1990.

Egenhofer, M., Spatial-query-by-sketch, in *VL'96: IEEEE Symposium on Visual Languages,* Boulder, CO, 1996.

Faisstnauer, C., Navigation and Interaction in Virtual Environments, Master's Thesis, Vienna University of Technology, Austria, 1998.

Falby, J.S., Zyda, M.J., Pratt, D.R., and Mackey, R.L., NPSNET: hierarchical data structure for real-time three-dimensional visual simulation, *Computer & Graphics,* 17 (1), 65–69, 1993.

Forberg, A. and Mayer, H., Generalization of 3D building data based on scale-spaces, Symposium on Geospatial Theory, Processing and Applications, Ottawa, Canada, 2002.

Germs, R., Maren, G.V., Verbree, E., and Jansen, F.W., A multi-view VR interface for 3D GIS, *Computers & Graphics,* 23, 497–506, 1999.

Goodchild, M.F., Thinking Spatially in the Social Sciences, http://www.geog.ucsb.edu/~good/#papers, 2002.

Gruber, M., *Managing Large 3D Urban Databases, 47th Photogrammetric Week,* Fritsch, D. and Spiller, R, Eds., Wichmann Verlag, Germany, 1999, 341–349.

Jacobson, R.D., Kitchin, R., and Golledge, R., Multi-modal virtual reality for presenting geographic information, in *Virtual Reality in Geography,* Fisher, P. and Unwin, D., Eds., Taylor & Francis, London, 2002, 382–400.

Kamm, C., User interfaces for voice applications, *Proc. Natl. Acad. Sci. USA,* 92, 10031–10037, 1995.

Kitchin, R. and Dodge, M., There's no there there: virtual reality, space and geographic visualization, in *Virtual Reality in Geography,* Fisher, P. and Unwin, D., Eds., Taylor & Francis, London, 2002, 341–361.

Kraak, M.J., Visual exploration of virtual environments, in *Virtual Reality in Geography,* Fisher, P. and Unwin, D., Eds., Taylor & Francis, London, 2002, 58–67.

Li, Z. and Openshaw, S., A natural principle for objective generalisation of digital map data, *Cartography and Geographic Information Systems,* 20 (1), 19–29, 1993.

Li, Z., Zhu, Q., and Gold, C., *Digital Terrain Modeling: Principles and Methodology,* CRC Press, Boca Raton, FL, 247–266, 2004.

Lin, H., and Gong, J.H., Distributed virtual environments for managing country parks in Hong Kong — a case study of the Shing Mun Country Park, *Photogrammetric Engineering & Remote Sensing,* 68 (4), 369–377, 2002.

Lin, H., Gong, J.H., and Shi, J.J.., From maps to GIS and VGE: a discussion on the evolution of the geographic language, (in Chinese), *Geography and Geo-Information Science,* 19 (4),18–23, 2003.

Lindstrom, P. and Pascucci, V., Visualization of large terrains made easy, *IEEE Visualization 2001,* 363–370, 2001.

Luebke, D. et al., *Level of Detail for 3D Graphics,* Morgan Kaufmann Publishers, San Francisco, 2003.

MacEachren, A.M., Brewer, I., Cai, G., and Chen, J., Visually-enabled geocollaboration to support data exploration and decision-making, *International Cartographic Conference*, Durban, South Africa, 394-401, 2003.

MacEachren, A.M. and Brewer, I., Developing a conceptual framework for visually-enabled geocollaboration, *International Journal of Geographical Information Science,* 18 (1), 1–34, 2004.

MacEachren, A.M., Gahegan, M., Pike, W., Brewer, I., Cai, G., Lengerich, E., and Hardisty, F., Geovisualization for knowledge construction and decision-support, *Computer Graphics & Applications,* 24 (1), 13–17, 2004.

Manoharan, T., *Collaborative virtual environments for planning development control in cities,* Ph.D. dissertation, Heriot Watt University, Edinburgh, UK, 2003.

Matusik, W., Pfister, H., Ngan, A., Beardsley, P., Ziegler, R., and McMillan, L., Image-based 3D photography using opacity hulls, http://graphics.lcs.mit.edu/~mcmillan/pubs.html, 2002.

Muller, W. and Schumann, H., Visualization methods for time-dependent data — an overview, www.informs-cs.org/wsc03papers/090.pdf, 2003.

Peuquet, D.J., *Representations of Space and Time*, Guilford Press, New York, 2002.

Rauschert, I., Agrawal, P., Fuhrmann, S., Brewer, I., Wang, H., Sharma, R., Cai, G., and MacEachren, A., Designing a human-centered, multimodal GIS interface to support emergency management, *ACM GIS'02, 10th ACM Symposium on Advances in Geographic Information Systems*, Washington, D.C., 2002.

Rhyne, T.M., A commentary on GeoVRML: a tool for 3D representation of georeferenced data on the web, http://www.siggraph.org/~rhyne/carto/3D/3D-geovrml.html, 1999.

Stoter, J. and Zlatanova, S., 3D GIS, where are we standing, www.gdmc.nl/zlatanova/thesis/html/refer/ps/st_zl_03.pdf, 2003.

Usery, E.L., Multidimensional representation of geographic features, http://mcmcweb.er.usgs.gov/carto_research/multi-dimension/usery.996.pdf, 2000.

Whyte, J., Bouchlaghem, N., Thorpe, A., and McCaffer, R., From CAD to virtual reality: modelling approaches, data exchange and interactive 3D building design tools, *Automation in Construction,* 10, 43–55, 2000.

Index

Milton Keynes UK
Ingram Content Group UK Ltd.
UKHW040105071024
449327UK00019B/834